Teaching the Arts to Engage English Language Learners

D1737963

Written for prospective and practicing visual arts, music, drama, and dance educators committed to the arts and education, *Teaching the Arts to Engage English Language Learners* offers guidance for engaging ELLs, alongside all learners, through artistic thinking. By paying equal attention to visual art, music, drama, and dance education, this book articulates how arts classrooms can create rich and supportive contexts for ELLs to grow socially, academically, and personally. The making and relating, perceiving and responding, and connecting and understanding processes of artistic thinking, create the terrain for rich curricular experiences. These processes also create the much-needed spaces for ELLs to gain communicative practice, skill, and confidence. This book offers ideas and suggestions for ways in which teachers may create the classroom conditions for this learning and growth to take place. The practical, teacher-friendly strategies and techniques included in the book will prove effective, not only with ELLs, but with all students.

Special Features:

- Generative texts such as films, poems, and performances function as springboards for arts educators to adapt according to the specifics of their ELL students, other student needs, and given contexts
- "Teaching Tips", formative assessment practices, and related instructional tables and resources enable arts teachers to offer the necessary critical guidance for artistic thinking
- An annotated list of internet sites, reader-friendly research articles and texts offering practical findings and advice on related topics, instructional materials, and particularly helpful resources for students are identified for quick reference
- A glossary at the conclusion of the text serves as another useful feature for readers' reference

Margaret Macintyre Latta is an Associate Professor in the Department of Teaching, Learning, and Teacher Education in the College of Education and Human Sciences at the University of Nebraska-Lincoln.

Elaine Chan is Assistant Professor in the Department of Teaching, Learning, and Teacher Education in the College of Education and Human Sciences at the University of Nebraska-Lincoln.

Teaching English Language Learners Across the Curriculum

Series Editors: Bárbara C. Cruz, Stephen J. Thornton, and Tony Erben

Teaching the Arts to Engage English Language Learners

MARGARET MACINTYRE LATTA AND ELAINE CHAN

Routledge
Taylor & Francis Group

NEW YORK AND LONDON

First published 2011
by Routledge
270 Madison Avenue, New York, NY 10016

Simultaneously published in the UK
by Routledge
2 Park Square, Milton Park, Abingdon, Oxon OX14 4RN

Routledge is an imprint of the Taylor & Francis Group, an informa business

© 2011 Taylor & Francis

The right of Margaret Macintyre Latta and Elaine Chan to be identified as authors of this work has been asserted by them in accordance with sections 77 and 78 of the Copyright, Designs and Patents Act 1988.

Typeset in Minion by Prepress Projects Ltd, Perth, UK
Printed and bound in the United States of America on acid-free paper by Edwards Brothers. Inc.

Library of Congress Cataloging in Publication Data
A catalog record has been requested for this book

ISBN 13: 978-0-415-87385-7 (hbk)
ISBN 13: 978-0-415-87386-4 (pbk)
ISBN 13: 978-0-203-83723-8 (ebk)

We dedicate this book to educators around the world interested in exploring and addressing the multiple opportunities of working with an increasingly diverse student population in the arts.

We are deeply indebted to our partners Bill Latta and Morris Ham for their love, support, patience, and willingness to carry on with family life as we sat huddled at our computers late into many a night.

Finally, we are grateful for the insights and unique perspectives each of our children provides into the nature of learners and learning. Anna Latta, Will Latta, Scott Hottovy, and Alexandra Ham greatly informed our efforts throughout.

Contents

Figures

Tables

Series
Introduction

No educational issue has proven more controversial than how to teach linguistically diverse students. Intertwined issues of ethnic and cultural differences are often compounded. What is more, at the time of writing, December 2007, how immigrants and their heritages *ought* to fit with the dominant culture is the subject of rancorous debate in the United States and a number of other nations.

However thorny these issues may be to some, both legally and ethically, schools need to accommodate the millions of English language learners (ELLs) who need to be educated. Although the number of ELLs in the United States has burgeoned in recent decades, school programs generally remain organized via traditional subjects, which are delivered in English. Many ELLs are insufficiently fluent in academic English, however, to succeed in these programs. Since policymakers have increasingly insisted that ELLs, regardless of their fluency in English, be mainstreamed into standard courses with all other students, both classroom enactment of the curriculum and teacher education need considerable rethinking.

Language scholars have generally taken the lead in this rethinking. As is evident in Part 1 of the volumes in this series, language scholars have developed a substantial body of research to inform the mainstreaming of ELLs. The primary interest of these language scholars, however, is almost by definition the processes and principles of second language acquisition. Until recently, subject matter has typically been a secondary consideration, used to illustrate language concerns. Perhaps not surprisingly, content-area teachers sometimes have seen this as reducing their subjects to little more than isolated bits of information, such as a list of explorers and dates in history or sundry geological formations in science.

In contrast, secondary school teachers see their charge as effectively conveying a principled understanding of, and interest in, a subject. They look for relationships, seek to develop concepts, search for powerful examples and analogies, and try to explicate principles. By the same token, they strive to make meaningful connections among the subject matter, students' experience, and life outside of school. In our observations, teacher education programs bifurcate courses on content-area methods and (if there are any) courses designed to instill principles of teaching ELLs. One result of this bifurcation seems to be that prospective and in-service teachers are daunted by the challenge of using language principles to inform their teaching of subject matter.

For example, Gloria Ladson-Billings (2001) has experimented with how to prepare new teachers for diverse classrooms through a teacher education program focused on "diversity, equity, and social justice" (p. xiii). Teachers in her program are expected, for instance, to confront rather than become resigned to low academic expectations for children in urban schools. From Ladson-Billings's perspective, "no matter what else the schools find themselves doing, promoting students' academic achievement is among their primary functions" (p. 56).

The authors in this series extend this perspective to teaching ELLs in the content areas. For example, how might ELLs be included in a literature lesson on Hardy's use of landscape imagery in *The Mayor of Casterbridge*, or an economics lesson on the principle of comparative advantage, or a biology lesson on the ecosystem of a pond? Such topics, experienced educators quickly recognize, are often difficult for native speakers of English. How can teachers break down these subjects into topics in a way that is educationally significant for ELLs?

The purpose of this series is to assist current and prospective educators to plan and implement lessons that do justice to the goals of the curriculum and make sense to and interest ELLs. If the needs of diverse learners are to be met, Ladson-Billings (2001) underscores that innovation is demanded, not that teachers merely pine for how things once were. The most obvious innovation in this series is to bring language scholars and specialists in the methods of teaching particular school subjects together. Although this approach is scarcely unique, it remains relatively uncommon. Combining the two groups brings more to addressing the problems of instruction than could be obtained by the two groups working separately. Even so, these volumes hardly tell the reader "everything there is to know" about the problems addressed. But we do know that our teacher education students report that even modest training to teach ELLs can make a significant difference in the classroom. We hope this series extends those successes to all the content areas of the curriculum.

Acknowledgements

The authors deeply appreciate the support of the development of this book by the Research Council at the University of Nebraska-Lincoln.

The authors would also like to acknowledge the efforts and contributions of the following individuals who helped bring this project to fruition:

- Stephanie Baer and Orville Friesen, whose research assistance enabled the development of Part 3;
- Cindy DeRyke, whose formatting skills greatly enabled our efforts in the final stages;
- Dan Hartig of the Instructional Design Center at the University of Nebraska-Lincoln, whose technological assistance, design skills, and artistry greatly enabled our efforts;
- Soon Ye Hwang, whose research assistance enabled the development of the supplementary resource section;
- Jennifer Nelson, whose research assistance enabled the development of Part 2; and
- Routledge Series Editors, Publishers, and Reviewers who greatly enabled the development of the book.

The authors are also very much indebted to participating educators and students who enthusiastically shared and invested in generating arts experiences for all learners to adapt, change, and make meaning:

- Sylvia Bailey, musician and music educator, Lincoln Public Schools, Lincoln, NE;
- Stephanie Baer, artist, doctoral student, and arts methods instructor, University of Nebraska-Lincoln;

- Lorraine Cockle, artist and community arts educator, Calgary, Alberta, Canada;
- Jen Deets, artist and visual arts educator, Lincoln Public Schools, Lincoln, NE;
- Jean Detlefsun, artist and arts educator, University of Nebraska-Lincoln;
- Jodi Heiser, artist and visual arts educator, Ralston School District, Ralston, NE;
- Amy Rauch Himes, artist and visual arts and Spanish educator, Papillion-La Vista Public Schools, Papillion, NE;
- Lucas Hines, slam poet and high school student, Lincoln Public Schools, Lincoln, NE;
- Di Kitterer, doctoral student and social science methods instructor, University of Nebraska-Lincoln;
- Chris Maly, playwright and dramatic and communication arts educator, Lincoln Public Schools, Lincoln, NE;
- Anna Spare, musician and music education student, University of Nebraska-Lincoln;
- Sarah Thomas, writer and English and creative arts teacher, Lincoln Public Schools, Lincoln, NE; and
- Ann Watt, creative arts and early childhood program development coordinator, Dimensions, First Plymouth Early Education Program, Lincoln, NE.

Introduction

There is art in education and education in art (Dewey, 1926). This declaration voices our commitment throughout this book, and represents the underlying philosophy to teaching and learning that connects all activities and arts learning experiences included here. Written for prospective and practicing visual arts, music, drama, and dance educators who also share this commitment, our book offers guidance for engaging English Language Learners (ELLs), alongside all learners, through artistic thinking. We are convinced that arts classrooms, so engaged, create rich and supportive contexts for ELLs to grow socially, academically, and personally. This book is also written for educators interested in the integration of artistic thinking into all forms of learning, across disciplines and extending into multiple contexts. Artistic thinking attends to relational processes such as making, composing, performing, and choreographing, demanding practices that involve participants in adapting, building, and making meaning. Visual arts, music, drama, and dance all give expression to the development of such self–other relational negotiations, valuing *diversity, individuality, and surprise*. Elliot Eisner (2002) identifies these inherent qualities as being at the forefront of the contribution of arts education within schools. In this way, arts education offers experiences for individuals to grow as learners who value diverse ways of knowing, living, and belonging in the local and global communities, and who recognize the significances of learning from and alongside others. There are plenty of reasons ELL students may flourish in arts classrooms. And, there are plenty of reasons for artistic thinking to permeate all learning. This book articulates these reasons, and is invested in enabling teachers and their students to act and live in classrooms in ways that reflect these values and philosophies.

Teachers and English Language Learners

Schools, community agencies, and other educational settings are charged with the challenging task of educating an increasingly diverse student population. Educators recognize that teaching and learning are complex activities that cannot be divorced from the social and cultural contexts that frame individuals and classrooms. Research shows, however, that many educators feel inadequate when it comes to addressing the diversity they encounter in today's classrooms (e.g., Banks, 2008; Chan, 2009; Cochran-Smith, 2004; Ladson-Billings, 2001; Nieto, Bode, Kang, & Raible, 2007). Educators acknowledge this inadequacy particularly as it concerns ELLs.

According to the *United States Census 2000 Supplementary Survey* (U.S. Census, 2002), a language other than English is spoken in approximately 18 percent of U.S. households. Between 1990 and 2000, the number of children aged 5 to 17 in English-speaking families increased by 11 percent. In contrast, during the same decade, there was a startling 55 percent increase in children of the same age living in households where languages other than English are spoken (U.S. Census, 2002). This increased diversity is reflected in school settings. The National Center for Education Statistics (2002) affirms that one out of seven students in our nation's classrooms speak a language other than English at home. The National Clearinghouse for English Language Acquisition (NCELA) estimated that 3,908,095 limited-English-proficient students attended American public schools as of October of 2002, with 1,146,154 of these students enrolled in grades 7–12 in American public schools (Kindler, 2002). These students represent a total of 10.5 percent of all elementary students and 5.6 percent of all public secondary students enrolled. Yet, as the number of ELL students continues to grow—both in terms of total numbers as well as a percentage of the total student population—only 30 percent of teachers with ELLs in their classroom have received training to meet their special needs (Menken & Antunez, 2001).

While many of these students are heritage language learners and are proficient in English, many are recent immigrants with barely a working knowledge of the language, let alone a command of academic English. Meeting the needs of such students can be challenging for all educators. Arts classrooms hold much potential in this regard. Artistic processes and thinking can be vehicles enabling translation and fostering understandings of abstract and complex concepts. The arts embrace the creation and communication of ideas, feelings, and events, often transcending oral communication. Art forms can speak to others across cultures and time. Arts education, in turn, can provide arts experiences that promote self-understanding, as well as an appreciation of self within the world's social and cultural contexts. In arts classrooms, ELL students can find room to grow their English language capacities alongside their artistic thinking and capabilities, and their personal identities.

Artistic Thinking, ELLs, and Curricular Enactment

Thornton (2005) emphasizes that it is a teacher's actual "enactment of curriculum that matters" (p. 104). He explains that it is educators' purposes and the ways they act on them that really matter for learners and learning. We are reminded of the significances of this statement as we attend to an arts educator, Chris Maly[1], as he remembers the voice and experience of an ELL in one of his drama classes at Lincoln High School in Lincoln, Nebraska. Chris recollects:

> The assignment was to recount a moment of great discovery. Students were asked to verbally describe an occurrence that uncovered a moment of insight, and describe the revelation. A young woman in the class described arriving to America from her home in Africa. She spoke about the mysteries that lurked around every corner at her new school. She spoke of the new language she was attempting to learn, and how hard it was for her to learn new words at the age of seven. "Then," she said, "one day it

began to snow." She had never witnessed a snowfall before. Her eyes grew wide as she described the memory of walking into a soft snowfall for the first time and watching with amazement as snowflakes fell on her face and on her arms. All the students smiled, knowing the feeling, including myself as her teacher. I began to realize that the moment she was describing was transformational: we were ten years removed from the snowfall and she described it perfectly in the language that once scared her. She said that was the day her new home became a place of possibility... . This was the first step of what would become an incredible monologue. I often remember this monologue when I consider the undiscovered voices of my students. The arts allow revelations to be pushed, connecting with what is global—the human experience. By nature, it is intended for a wider audience. On stage, this young woman transported us down the stairs of her porch and into a moment of catharsis. Metaphors emerged. Embodied understandings were evoked. Language was revised and perfected. She awakened the performing artist/writer within herself, and within others.

Chris not only recognized the potential within this learning experience, but also acted on it to further students' learning in his drama class. This capacity to see with potential in the subject matter, the context, and each student, cultivating learning relationships across them, is the task of enacting curriculum that matters. The traditions and ideas of theorists, philosophers, and practitioners we turn to for insights into the nature of such curriculum matters and the artistic thinking involved for teachers and their students include John Dewey and Elliot Eisner, among many other contemporary thinkers that extend their ideas. Collectively, these ideas and the traditions they draw upon inform the productive learning opportunities we envision across the arts for ELLs (and all learners). We wholeheartedly concur with Chris. We see much learning potential in the active embrace of the artistic processes of making and relating, perceiving and responding, and connecting and understanding in arts classrooms for engaging all students in powerful meaning making opportunities. As teachers purposefully negotiate opportunities to do so, and sustain and nurture these efforts, the needed room for ELLs to significantly grow their English language capacities opens and can be strengthened. This book aims to support teachers in their work as they do this.

There is a deliberate interdependence across all parts of the book as the theoretical framework discussed in Parts 1 and 2 infuses the concrete examples of visual arts, music, drama, and dance experiences offered in Part 3 and the associated supporting resources of Part 4. Doll (2009) relays how curriculum ought to be *rich, related, rigorous,* and *recursive.* Doll's *four Rs* permeate our efforts in Parts 3 and 4. Richness is deliberately sought through arts experiences with breadth and depth, inviting participatory thinking. Recursion is encouraged through arts experiences that evoke re-consideration and re-visiting of previous understandings. Relations are continually fostered and become modes of interaction and deliberation for students and teachers. Rigor entails the continuous and careful search throughout for curricular coherence and continuity, embracing the generative ground encountered. The making and relating, perceiving and responding, and connecting and understanding processes of artistic thinking, create the terrain for rich, recursive, related, and rigorous arts curricular experiences. These processes also create the much-needed spaces for ELLs to gain communicative practice, skill, and confidence. It is, of course, essential that teachers understand how to create these conditions, and to further their lived consequences. This book offers ideas and suggestions for ways in which teachers may create the classroom conditions for this learning and growth to take place.

Specifically, Part 1 is written by a language scholar, Tony Erben, who maps out fundamental information every teacher who works with ELLs, regardless of content area, needs to know. We intersect Erben's thinking in Part 1 with our perspectives as an arts/curricular theorist and a diversity/curricular theorist in Parts 2 and 3. Collectively, we are invested in teacher education such that the intersections manifest the ways in which the theory and research on English Speakers of Other Languages (ESOL) and teaching and learning, alongside the nature of artistic thinking grounded in creativity and relational pedagogy, can inform each other. Purposeful connections teachers might foster for ELLs in arts classrooms are at the nexus of these discussions.

Parts 2–4 of this book are oriented toward prospective and practicing visual arts, music, drama, and dance educators, as well as educators generally interested in the arts as mediums for teaching and learning of all kinds. Part 2 is more content area specific as it summarizes and synthesizes recent research on the teaching of the visual arts, music, drama, and dance, and the intersections of this research with existing research on the teaching of ELLs mainstreamed into arts classrooms. Part 3 chronicles learning experiences that arts teachers can readily adapt to engage ELLs in artistic learning and to grow their writing, speaking, listening, and viewing English skills through meaningful processes and accommodations. These perspectives are articulated and embedded in the arts experiences offered, as images of practice for readers to engage and to re-imagine in their own practices. Uhrmacher and Matthews (2005) term this process, "working the ideas"—it was with a similar participatory spirit that ten teachers gathered from across the arts to work the ideas for Part 3, to both affirm and to generate artistic thinking in themselves and in prospective and practicing educators reading this text. The cross-arts disciplinary conversations that ensued were invigorating, and prompted unforeseen curricular connections for all involved. These are the worked ideas extended to the reader in this book, so that "curriculum, in other words, is not merely a product developed by distal experts as a script for teachers, but a classroom enactment, properly differing from one classroom to the next" (Thornton, 2005, p. 6). This book intends for educators to bring their expertise and the particulars of their students and contexts to bear on their planning and enacting efforts, investing in arts experiences that act as catalysts for all students' artistic thinking and creating the necessary room for ELLs to navigate such thinking alongside language acquisition and communication. Finally, Part 4 presents a list of annotated resources of websites, articles, texts, and instructional materials that arts teachers and their students may utilize to further enhance the work of teaching and learning English.

Equal attention to visual art, music, drama, and dance education is given throughout the book. This acknowledges "*The Arts*" as an umbrella term that has been useful for articulating the shared significances for learners and learning regarding policy and curricular documents in recent years. It also acknowledges that the arts cross boundaries by nature, and in doing so, create new art forms and perspectives that challenge predetermined disciplinary boundaries. There is every reason to anticipate that the visual art, music, drama, and dance experiences serving as examples in this book will inspire "cross-fertilization" (Bresler, 2007, p. xvii), and inform and generate unique arts experiences fitting particular contexts. The potential for such cross-fertilization is highlighted throughout this volume as distinct arts experiences for visual arts, music, dance, and drama are intentionally designed to be rich and complex in nature and concomitantly suggest cross-disciplinary connections and possibilities (Seidel, Tishman, Winner, Hetland, & Palmer, 2009).

Who Can Benefit from this Book?

This book is aimed at pre-service and practicing teachers and teacher educators who need straightforward advice on how to teach (a) English to ELLs through the subject areas of arts education, and (b) arts content to ELLs who are at different levels of English language proficiency, as well as (c) providing important access to what is possible through concrete descriptions of ways these efforts might unfold in teaching/learning practices across each of the arts. We are not suggesting this book as a generic ELL course—there are appropriate ELL-specific books for that purpose.

Primarily, this book is written for arts teachers at the middle and secondary education levels. Teachers generally report feeling woefully unprepared to adequately teach their ELL students. As Clair (1995) puts it, teachers are, by and large, "learning to educate these students on the job" (p. 194). Although general ESOL books exist, they are typically more appropriate for ESOL teachers, rather than for arts teachers who have ELLs in their classrooms. This book provides guidance for teaching ELLs that specifically focuses on the instructional issues inherent to the arts, particularly those focusing on arts in the middle and secondary school mainstream classrooms. This book is designed for:

- pre-service teachers enrolled in content-specific method courses (including visual arts, music, drama, and dance);
- teacher educators engaged in pre-service teacher education; and
- practicing teachers.

Additionally, given that the concrete arts experiences in this book offer practical strategies, techniques, and resources that are effective not only with ELLs, but with all students, we see much potential in this book for interest from other educational sectors. Such interest may include teacher educators and curriculum supervisors in public school districts conducting ESOL training, and arts curriculum leaders and arts advocates in higher education, school, and community settings.

How to Use this Book

The central purpose of this book is to provide guidance for visual arts, music, drama, and dance teachers, by informing and generating ways arts educators can engage ELL students (alongside other students) in arts learning experiences. We acknowledge the importance of language acquisition in the academic success of ELLs, and explore visual arts, music, drama, and dance education as mediums for supporting English acquisition through their capacity to engage students in the production of language, and to enhance the motivation of students to communicate with their peers in English.

This book can be read in parts, depending on the interests and needs of the reader. In Part 1, readers will learn about what to expect in the language abilities of ELLs as their proficiency in English develops over time from Tony Erben, a language scholar. He refers to research describing this process, called interlanguage, as highly systematic and regularized. More specifically, this research reveals that all second language learners, regardless of first language background, go through very specific and predefined stages of language acquisition. Language learners move from Preproduction to Early Production to Speech Emergence and finally to Intermediate Fluency. Part 1 begins with an outline of what these stages of interlanguage look like, what teachers can linguistically expect from an ELL at any given stage and how teachers can best facilitate the language development of ELLs as they move through each stage. Beyond this, Part 1 includes: (a) a discussion about pedagogical pros and cons of an array of ESOL programs, clarifying terminology used in the field, and descriptions of ways in which school systems differ across America in how they address curriculum for ELL populations; (b) an overview of first language acquisition processes and how they relate to and affect second language acquisition processes, and descriptions of the diverse backgrounds of ELLs found in U.S. classrooms due to differences in reasons for emigration, immigration status, and home languages and cultures; (c) descriptions of ways in which teachers can move towards more culturally responsive curriculum and teaching pedagogy through the use of inclusive language, carefully selected images, critical and reflexive teaching, and respect for the history and culture of ELLs in the classroom; (d) an outline of the steps schools and teachers can take to enhance home-school communication that fosters ELL parental involvement; and (e) an outline of the errors commonly made in identifying ELLs with special needs.

In Part 2, the reader will find research that maps out and supports the teaching of visual arts, music, drama, and dance as fundamental to the education of all students and as offering unique educational significances for learners and learning. Research included in this part will assist teachers and their students to navigate artistic thinking with greater confidence through: (a) articulating the principles for arts instruction grounded in creativity as fundamental to the nature of being human; (b) establishing the necessity of teachers promoting caring relationships between students and subject matter; (c) identifying the role of the arts educator in creating learning opportunities for ELL students to participate in interactions with peers as essential to their progress towards English fluency and integration with peers in school; and (d) taking a representative look at existing research in the visual arts, music, drama, and dance education fields. This literature review encourages and supports the partnering of English language acquisition with arts-based curriculum, suggesting ways of enhancing learner identity, the development of English language proficiency, cultural sensitivity, and expression and the development of skills and knowledge across each of the arts. Part 2 concludes with an invitation to readers to embrace curriculum as an artistic medium in their teaching/learning practices, and to ensure formative assessments are embedded within, forming and informing the shapes, directions, and substance of arts curricular experiences in classrooms.

Part 3 provides access for readers to a varied range of arts learning experiences with individual attention given to visual arts, music, drama, and dance. These concrete arts experiences reveal how teachers can use their full repertoire of pedagogical practices to wholly engage and support ELLs through artistic thinking. The artistic processes of making and relating, perceiving and responding, connecting and understanding undergird the arts experiences in Part 3, forming the curricular ground for: (a) engaging and developing teachers' and students' thinking in specific arts' learning situations; and (b) creating the time and space for ELLs to negotiate and translate understandings requiring speculation and conjecturing about possibilities, enlarging their understandings and communication capacities in the process. Readers can select to read specific arts content experiences, but are very much encouraged to read across multiple arts content experiences to envision the inherent potential for the cross-fertilization of artistic ideas and for the generation of language learning opportunities, and to maximize their usefulness to the reader. Concrete examples of these arts processes in action are depicted through visual arts, music, drama, and dance classrooms, offering insights and directions for arts learning by ELLs as well as other learners. These insights and directions are intended to inform specific arts forms, and to transcend arts forms extending beyond to cross-disciplinary connections. Generative texts such as films, poems, and performances are included throughout Part 3 as points of departure and/ or catalytic material intended to serve as springboards for arts educators to adapt and to change, fitting the specifics of their ELL students, other student needs, and given contexts. Additionally, to enable arts teachers to offer the necessary critical guidance for artistic thinking, teaching tips, formative assessment practices incorporating the use of student arts journals, and related instructional tables and resources are included throughout Part 3.

Part 4 is intended as a supplementary resource for readers who would like more specific information on given subjects/topics. An annotated list is provided that details Internet sites, reader-friendly research articles and texts offering practical findings and advice on related topics, instructional materials, and particularly helpful resources for students. A glossary is also included at the conclusion of the text. Finally, the index can be used to locate particular information.

Collectively, the organizational parts-to-whole relationship used for this book models the complex mediation at the heart of artistic thinking that insists on interaction and deliberation by all who take part. The book as a whole is invested in promoting a bold artistic spirit that positions teachers to enjoy guiding and building an arts curriculum that matters for all students.

Part 1
Your English Language Learner

Tony Erben
University of Tampa

1.1
Orientation

English language learners (ELLs) represent the fastest growing group throughout all levels of schooling in the United States. For example, between the 1990–1991 school year and the 2000–2001 school year, the ELL population grew approximately 105 percent nationally, while the general school population grew only 12 percent (Kindler, 2002). In several states (including Texas, California, New Mexico, Florida, Arizona, North Carolina, and New York), the percentage of ELLs within school districts ranges anywhere between 10 and 50 percent of the school population. In sum, there are over 10 million ELLs in U.S. schools today. According to the U.S. Department of Education, one out of seven students in our nation's classrooms speaks a language other than English at home. Although many of these students are heritage language learners and are proficient in English, many others are recent immigrants with barely a working knowledge of the language let alone a command of academic English. Meeting the needs of such students can be particularly challenging for all teachers given the often text-dependent nature of content areas. The language of the curriculum is often abstract and includes complex concepts calling for higher-order thinking skills. Additionally, many ELLs do not have a working knowledge of American culture that can serve as a schema for new learning.

But let's now look at these English language learners. Who are they and how do they come to be in our classrooms?

ELL is the term used for any student in an American school setting whose native language is not English. Their English ability lies anywhere on a continuum from knowing only a few words to being able to get by using everyday English, but still in need of acquiring more English so that they can succeed educationally at school. All students enrolled in an American school, including ELLs, have the right to an equitable and quality education. Traditionally, many ELLs are placed in stand-alone English for speakers of other languages (ESOL) classes and learn English until they are deemed capable of following the regular curriculum in English. However, with the introduction of federal and state legislation such as *No Child Left Behind* (2002), Proposition 227 in California, and other English-only legislation in other states, many school systems now require ELLs to receive their English instruction not through stand-alone ESOL classes, but directly through their curriculum content classes.[1] Today "mainstreaming" is the most frequently used method of language instruction for ELL students in U.S. schools. Mainstreaming involves placing ELLs in content-area classrooms where the curriculum is delivered through English; curricula and instruction are typically not modified in these classrooms for non-native English speakers (Carrasquillo & Rodriguez, 2002). According to Meltzer and Hamann (2005), placement of ELLs in mainstream classes occurs for a number of reasons including assumptions by non-educators about what ELLs need, the scarcity of ESOL-trained teachers relative to demand, the growth of ELL populations, the dispersal of ELLs into more districts across the country, and restrictions in a growing number of states regarding the time ELLs can stay in ESOL programs. They predict that, unless these conditions change, ELLs will spend their time in school (1) with teachers not adequately trained to work with ELLs, (2) with teachers who do not see it as a priority to meet the needs of their ELLs, and (3) with curricula and classroom practices that are not designed to target ELL needs (Coady et al., 2003). As we shall later see, of all possible instructional options to help ELLs learn English, placing an ELL in a mainstreamed English-medium classroom where no accommodations are made by the teacher is the least effective approach. It may even be detrimental to the educational progress of ELLs.

This then raises the question of whether or not the thousands of curriculum content teachers across the United States, who now have the collective lion's share of responsibility in providing English language instruction to ELLs, have had preservice or in-service education to modify, adapt, and make the appropriate pedagogical accommodations within their lessons for this special group of students. This is important: ELLs should remain included in the cycle of everyday learning and make academic progress commensurate with grade-level expectations. It is also important that teachers feel competent and effective in their professional duties.

The aim of Part 1 of this book is to provide you the reader with an overview of the linguistic mechanics of second language development. Specifically, as teachers you will learn what to expect in the language abilities of ELLs as their proficiency in English develops over time. Although the rate of language development among ELLs depends on the particular instructional and social circumstances of each ELL, general patterns and expectations will be discussed. We will also outline for teachers the learning outcomes that ELLs typically accomplish in differing ESOL programs and the importance of the maintenance of first language development. School systems differ across the United States in the ways in which they try to deal with ELL populations. Therefore, we describe the pedagogical pros and cons of an array of ESOL programs as well as clarify terminology used in the field. Part 1 will also profile various ELL populations that enter U.S. schools (e.g., refugees vs. migrants, special needs) and share how teachers can make their pedagogy more culturally responsive. Finally, we will also survey what teachers can expect from the cultural practices that ELLs may engage in in the classroom as well as present a myriad of ways in which both school systems and teachers can better foster home–school communication links.

1.2
The Process of English Language Learning and What to Expect

It is generally accepted that anybody who endeavors to learn a second language will go through specific stages of language development. According to some second language acquisition theorists (e.g., Pienemann, 2007), the way in which language is produced under natural time constraints is very regular and systematic. For example, just as a baby needs to learn how to crawl before it can walk, so too a second language learner will produce language structures only in a predetermined psychological order of complexity. What this means is that an ELL will utter "homework do" before being able to utter "tonight I homework do" before ultimately being able to produce a target-like structure such as "I will do my homework tonight." Of course, with regard to being communicatively effective, the first example is as successful as the last example. The main difference is that one is less English-like than the other. Pienemann's work has centered on one subsystem of language, namely morphosyntactic structures. It gives us an interesting glimpse into how an ELL's language may progress (see Table 1.1).

Researchers such as Pienemann (1989; 2007) and Krashen (1981) assert that there is an immutable language acquisition order and, regardless of what the teacher tries to teach to the ELL in terms of English skills, the learner will acquire new language structures only when (s)he is cognitively and psychologically ready to do so.

What can a teacher do if an ELL will only learn English in a set path? Much research has been conducted over the past 20 years on this very question and the upshot is that, although teachers cannot change the route of development for ELLs, they *can* very much affect the rate of development. The way in which teachers can stimulate the language development of ELLs is by providing what is known as an acquisition-rich classroom. Ellis (2005), among others, provides useful research generalizations that constitute a broad basis for "evidence-based practice." Rather

TABLE 1.1. Generalized patterns of ESOL development stages

Stage	Main features	Example
1	Single words; formulas	My name is_____. How are you
2	Subject–verb object word order; plural marking	I see school I buy books
3	"Do"-fronting; adverb preposing; negation + verb	Do you understand me? Yesterday I go to school. She no coming today.
4	Pseudo-inversion; yes/no inversion; verb + to + verb	Where is my purse? Have you a car? I want to go.
5	3rd person –s; do-2nd position	He works in a factory. He did not understand.
6	Question-tag; adverb–verb phrase	He's Polish, isn't he? I can always go.

Source: Pienemann (1988).

than repeat them verbatim here, we have synthesized them into *five principles for creating effective second language learning environments.* They are presented and summarized below.

Principle 1: Give ELLs Many Opportunities to Read, to Write, to Listen to, and to Discuss Oral and Written English Texts Expressed in a Variety of Ways

Camilla had only recently arrived at the school. She was a good student and was making steady progress. She had learned some English in Argentina and used every opportunity to learn new words at school. Just before Thanksgiving her science teacher commenced a new unit of work on the periodic table and elements. During the introductory lesson, the teacher projected a periodic table on the whiteboard. She began asking the students some probing questions about the table. One of her first questions was directed to Camilla. The teacher asked, "Camilla, tell me what you see on the right hand side of the table." Camilla answered, "I see books, Bunsen burner, also pencils."

Of course the teacher was referring not to the table standing in front of the whiteboard, but to the table projected onto the whiteboard. Though a simple mistake, the example above is illustrative of the fact that Camilla has yet to develop academic literacy.

In 2001, Meltzer defined academic literacy as the ability of a person to "use reading, writing, speaking, listening and thinking to learn what they want/need to learn AND [to] communicate/ demonstrate that learning to others who need/want to know" (p. 16). The definition is useful in that it rejects literacy as something static and implies agency on the part of a learner who develops an ability to successfully put her/his knowledge and skills to use in new situations. Being proficient in academic literacy requires knowledge of a type of language used predominantly in classrooms and tied very much to learning. However, even though it is extremely important for ELLs to master, not many content teachers take the time to provide explicit instruction in it. Moreover, many content teachers do not necessarily know the discipline-specific discourse features or text structures of their own subject areas.

Currently, there is much research to suggest that both the discussion of texts and the production of texts are important practices in the development of content-area literacy and learning. For ELLs this means that opportunities to create, discuss, share, revise, and edit a variety of texts will help them develop content-area understanding and also recognition and familiarity with the types of texts found in particular content areas (Boscolo & Mason, 2001). Classroom practices that are found to improve academic literacy development include teachers improving reading comprehension through modeling, explicit strategy instruction in context, spending more time giving reading and writing instruction as well as having students spend more time with reading and writing assignments, providing more time for ELLs to talk explicitly about texts as they are trying to process and/or create them, and helping to develop critical thinking skills as well as being responsive to individual learner needs (Meltzer & Hamann, 2005).

The importance of classroom talk in conjunction with learning from and creating texts cannot be underestimated in the development of academic literacy in ELLs. In the case above, rather than smiling at the error and moving on with the lesson, the teacher could have further developed Camilla's vocabulary knowledge by easily taking a two-minute digression from the lesson to brainstorm with the class all the ways the word *table* can be used at school—in math, social studies, language arts, etc.

Principle 2: Draw Attention to Patterns of English Language Structure

In order to ride a bike well, a child needs to actually practice riding the bike. Sometimes, training wheels are fitted to the back of the bike to help the younger child maintain his/her balance. In time, the training wheels are taken away as the child gains more confidence. As this process unfolds, parents also teach kids the rules of the road: how to read road signs, to be attentive to cars, to ride defensively, etc. Although knowing the rules of the road won't help a child learn to ride the bike better in a physical sense, it will help the child avoid being involved in a road accident. Knowing the rules of the road—when and where to ride a bike, etc.—will make the child a more accomplished bike rider. Why use this example? Well, it is a good metaphor to explain that language learning needs to unfold in the same way. An ELL, without much formal schooling, will develop the means to communicate in English. However, it will most likely be only very basic English. Unfortunately, tens of thousands of adult ELLs across this country never progress past this stage. School-age ELLs have an opportunity to move beyond a basic command of English—to become accomplished communicators in English. However, this won't happen on its own. To do so requires the ELL to get actively involved in classroom activities, ones in which an ELL is required to practice speaking.

As mentioned above, early research into naturalistic second language acquisition has evidenced that learners follow a "natural" order and sequence of acquisition. What this means is that grammatical structures emerge in the communicative utterances of second language learners in a relatively fixed, regular, systematic, and universal order. The ways in which teachers can take advantage of this "built-in syllabus" are to implement an activity-centered approach that sets out to provide ELLs with language-rich instructional opportunities and offer ELLs explicit exposure and instruction related to language structures that they are trying to utter but with which they still have trouble.

Principle 3: Give ELLs Classroom Time to Use their English Productively

A theoretical approach within the field of second language acquisition (SLA) called the interaction hypothesis and developed primarily by Long (1996; 2006) posits that acquisition is facilitated through interaction when second language learners are engaged in negotiating for meaning. What this means is that, when ELLs are engaged in talk, they make communication modifications that help language become more comprehensible, they more readily solicit corrective feedback, and they adjust their own use of English.

The discrepancy in the rate of acquisition shown by ELLs can be attributed to the amount and the quality of input they receive as well as the opportunities they have for output. Output means having opportunities to use language. Second language acquisition researchers agree that the opportunity for output plays an important part in facilitating second language development. Skehan (1998) drawing on Swain (1995) summarizes the contributions that output can make: (1) by using language with others, ELLs will obtain a richer language contribution from those around them; (2) ELLs will be forced to pay attention to the structure of language they listen to; (3) ELLs will be able to test out their language assumptions and confirm them through the types of language input they receive; (4) ELLs can better internalize their current language knowledge; (5) by engaging in interaction, ELLs can work towards better discourse fluency; and (6) ELLs will be able to find space to develop their own linguistic style and voice.

It behooves teachers to plan for and incorporate ELLs in all language activities in the classroom. Of course an ELL will engage with an activity based on the level of proficiency (s)he has at any given time and the teacher should take this into account when planning for instruction. Under no circumstances should ELLs be left at the "back of the classroom" to linguistically or pedagogically fend for themselves.

Principle 4: Give ELLs Opportunities to Notice their Errors and to Correct their English

Throughout the day, teachers prepare activities for students that have the sole intent of getting them to learn subject matter. Less often do teachers think about the language learning potential that the same activity may generate. This can be applied to ELLs: Teachers encourage them to notice their errors, to reflect on how they use English, and to think about how English works, which plays a very important role in their language development. In a series of seminal studies, Lyster and his colleagues (Lyster, 1998; 2001; 2004; 2007; Lyster & Mori, 2006; Lyster & Ranta, 1997) outline six feedback moves that teachers can use to direct ELLs' attention to their language output and in doing so help them correct their English.

Example 1

Student: "The heart hits blood to se body. . ."
Teacher: "The heart pumps blood to the body."

In the above example, an ELL's utterance is incorrect, and the teacher provides the correct form. Often teachers gloss over explicitly correcting an ELL's language for fear of singling out the student in class. However, *explicit correction* is a very easy way to help ELLs notice the way they use language.

Example 2

Student: "I can experimenting with Bunsen burner."
Teacher: "What? Can you say that again?"

By using phrases such as "Excuse me?", "I don't understand," or "Can you repeat that?", the teacher shows that the communication has not been understood or that the ELL's utterance contained some kind of error. *Requesting clarification* indicates to the ELL that a repetition or reformulation of the utterance is required.

Example 3

Student: "After today I go to sport."
Teacher: "So, tomorrow you are going to play sports?"
Student: "Yes, tomorrow I am going to play sport."

Without directly showing that the student's utterance was incorrect, the teacher implicitly *recasts* the ELL's error, or provides the correction.

Example 4

Teacher: "Is that how it is said?" or "Is that English?" or "Does that sound right to you?"

Without providing the correct form, the teacher provides a *metalinguistic clue*. This may take the form of asking a question or making a comment related to the formation of the ELL's utterance.

Example 5

Teacher: "So, then it will be a . . ." (with long stress on "a")

The teacher directly gets the correct form from the ELL by pausing to allow the student to complete the teacher's utterance. *Elicitation* questions differ from questions that are defined as metalinguistic clues in that they require more than a yes/no response.

Example 6

Student: "The two boy go to town tomorrow."
Teacher: "The two boys go to town tomorrow." (with teacher making a prolonged stress on "boys")

Repetitions are probably one of the most frequent forms of error correction carried out by teachers. Here a teacher repeats the ELL's error and adjusts intonation to draw an ELL's attention to it.

Using these corrective feedback strategies helps to raise an ELL's awareness and understanding of language conventions used in and across content areas.

Principle 5: Construct Activities that Maximize Opportunities for ELLs to Interact with Others in English

One day, when we had visitors from up north, our daughter came home very excited and said that the teacher had announced that the class would be learning Spanish from the beginning of the month. Our friend, ever the pessimist, said, "I learned Spanish for four years at high school, and look at me now, I can't even string a sentence together in Spanish." What comes to mind is the old saying, "use it or lose it." Of course, my friend and I remember our foreign language learning days being spent listening to the teacher, usually in English. We were lucky if we even got the chance to say anything in Spanish. Since we never used Spanish in class, our hopes of retaining any Spanish diminished with each passing year since graduation. My daughter's 20-year-old brother, on the other hand, had the same Spanish teacher that my daughter will have. He remembers a lot of his Spanish, but also that his Spanish classes were very engaging. A lesson would never pass in which he didn't speak, listen to, read, and write in Spanish. He was always involved in some learning activity and he always expressed how great it was to converse during the class with his friends in Spanish by way of the activities that the teacher had planned.

I use this analogy as it applies to ELLs as well. In order for ELLs to progress with their English language development, a teacher needs to vary the types of instructional tasks that the ELL will engage in. Student involvement during instruction is the key to academic success whereas constant passive learning, mostly through lecture-driven lessons, will greatly impede any language learning efforts by an ELL.

Our five principles provide a framework with which to construct a curriculum that is sensitive to the language developmental needs of ELLs. However, to further solidify our understanding of an ELL's language progress, it is necessary to have a clear picture of what ELLs can do with their language at different levels of proficiency and what implications this has for instruction. Although many taxonomies exist that seek to categorize the developmental stages of second language learners, many education systems throughout the United States have adopted a four-tier description.

The four stages are called Preproduction, Early Production, Speech Emergence, and Intermediate Fluency (Krashen & Terrell, 1983).

The **preproduction stage** applies to ELLs who are unfamiliar with English. They may have had anything from one day to three months of exposure to English. ELLs at this level are trying to absorb the language, and they can find this process overwhelming. In a school context, they are often linguistically overloaded, and get tired quickly because of the need for constant and intense concentration. An ELL's language skills are at the receptive level, and they enter a "silent period" of listening. ELLs at this stage are able to comprehend more English than they can produce. Their attention is focused on developing everyday social English. At the preproduction stage, an ELL can engage in nonverbal responses; follow simple commands; point and respond with movement; and utter simple formulaic structures in English such as "yes," "no," "thank you," or use names. ELLs may develop a receptive vocabulary of up to 500 words.

By the time an ELL enters the **early production stage**, (s)he will have had many opportunities to encounter meaningful and comprehensible English. They will begin to respond with one- or two-word answers or short utterances. ELLs may now have internalized up to 1,000 words in their receptive vocabulary and anything from 100 to 500 words in their active vocabulary. In order for ELLs to begin to speak, teachers should create a low-anxiety environment in their classrooms. At this stage, ELLs are experimenting and taking risks with English. Errors in grammar and pronunciation are to be expected. Pragmatic errors are also common. Teachers need to model/demonstrate with correct language responses in context. Redundancies, repetitions, circumlocutions, and language enhancement strategies are important for teachers to use when interacting with ELLs at this level.

At the **speech emergence stage**, an ELL will begin to use the language to interact more freely. At this stage, ELLs have a 7,000-word receptive vocabulary. They may have an active vocabulary of up to 2,000 words. By this time, ELLs may have had between one and three years' exposure to English. It is possible that they have a receptive understanding of academic English; however, in order to make content-area subject matter comprehensible, teachers are advised to make great use of advance organizers. Teachers should make explicit attempts to modify the delivery of subject matter, to model language use, and to teach metacognitive strategies in order to help ELLs predict, describe, demonstrate, and problem solve. Because awareness of English is growing, it is also important for teachers to provide ELLs at this stage with opportunities to work in structured small groups so that they can reflect and experiment with their language output.

At the stage of **intermediate fluency**, ELLs may demonstrate near-native or native-like fluency in everyday social English, but not in academic English. Often teachers become acutely aware that, even though an ELL can speak English fluently in social settings (the playground, at sport functions, etc.), they will experience difficulties in understanding and verbalizing cognitively demanding, abstract concepts taught and discussed in the classroom. At this stage ELLs may have developed up to a 12,000-word receptive vocabulary and a 4,000-word active vocabulary. Teachers of ELLs at the intermediate fluency level need to proactively provide relevant content-based literacy experiences such as brainstorming, clustering, synthesizing, categorizing, charting, evaluating, journaling, or log writing, including essay writing and peer critiquing, in order to foster academic proficiency in English.

At the University of South Florida, we have developed online ELL databases that have been created to provide pre- and in-service teachers with annotated audio and video samples of language use by ELLs who are at each of the four different levels of language proficiency. The video and audio files act as instructional tools that allow teachers to familiarize themselves with the language ability (speaking, reading, writing) of ELLs who are at different stages of development. For example, teachers may have ELLs in classes and not be sure of their level of English language development, nor be sure what to expect the ELL to be able to do with English in terms of production and comprehension. This naturally impacts how a teacher may plan for instruction. By looking through the databases, a teacher can listen to and watch representations of ELL language production abilities at all four levels (preproduction, early production, speech emergence, and intermediate fluency). In addition, the databases feature interviews with expert ESOL teachers, examples of tests used to evaluate the proficiency levels of ELLs, and selected readings and lesson

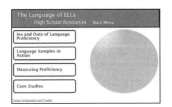

plans written for ELLs at different levels of proficiency. Lastly, they provide case studies that troubleshoot pedagogical problem areas when teaching ELLs.

There are three databases: one that features ELLs at the elementary school level, one featuring ELLs at the middle school level, and one featuring ELLs at high school.

The three ELL databases can be found at:

- http://esol.coedu.usf.edu/elementary/index.htm (elementary school language samples);
- http://esol.coedu.usf.edu/middleschool/index.htm (middle school language samples); and
- http://esol.coedu.usf.edu/highschool/index.htm (high school language samples).

It is important to remember that a lack of language ability does not mean a lack of concept development or a lack of ability to learn. Teachers should continue to ask inferential and higher-order questions (questions requiring reasoning ability, hypothesizing, inferring, analyzing, justifying, and predicting) that challenge an ELL to think.

Teaching Help

For two good websites that outline ways to enhance questioning using Bloom's taxonomy see www.teachers.ash.org.au/researchskills/dalton.htm (Dalton & Smith, 1986) and www.nwlink.com/~donclark/hrd/bloom.html (Clark, 1999). The latter gives a further detailed breakdown of Bloom's Learning Domains in terms of cognitive, affective, and psychomotor key words and how these can be used to foster an ELL's language learning.

Zehler (1994) provides a list of further strategies that teachers can use to engage ELLs at every stage. These include:

- asking questions that require new or extended responses;
- creating opportunities for sustained dialogue and substantive language use;
- providing opportunities for language use in multiple settings;
- restating complex sentences as a sequence of simple sentences;
- avoiding or explaining use of idiomatic expressions;
- restating at a slower rate when needed, but making sure that the pace is not so slow that normal intonation and stress patterns become distorted;
- pausing often to allow students to process what they hear;
- providing specific explanations of key words and special or technical vocabulary, using examples and non-linguistic props when possible;
- using everyday language; and
- providing explanations for the indirect use of language (for example, an ELL student may understand the statement, "I like the way Mary is sitting" merely as a simple statement rather than as a reference to an example of good behavior).

1.3
Deciding on the Best ESOL Program

This section outlines the learning outcomes that ELLs typically accomplish in differing ESOL programs and the importance of the maintenance of first language development. Although school systems differ across America in the ways in which they try to deal with ELL populations, this section describes the pedagogical pros and cons of an array of ESOL programs and clarifies terminology used in the field.

There are several factors that influence the design of an effective ELL program. These include considerations regarding the nature of the ELL student demographics to be served, district resources, and individual student characteristics. The MLA Language Map at www.mla.org/map_main provides an interactive look into the distribution of languages spoken in the United States. The online maps are able to show numbers as well as percentages by state, district, and zip code. Over 30 languages may be geographically represented and compared. The MLA Language Map shows graphically that not all districts are the same. ELL populations differ across the country. Some areas may have an overwhelming majority of Spanish speaking ELLs whereas other districts may have an equally large number of ELL students but speaking 50–100 different languages. On the other hand, some districts may have very few ELLs while other districts experience an influx of ELLs of whose language and culture the area's schools have little knowledge (for example, Hmong in Marathon County in Wisconsin, Haitian Creole in Palm Beach, Broward, and Dade counties in Florida, and Somali/Ethiopian in Hennepin and Ramsey counties in Minnesota). Cultural and linguistic differences, as well as factors such as size, age, and mobility of community members, very much influence the types of ESOL instructional programs that school districts choose to develop. Refer to *English Language Learner Programs at the Secondary Level in Relation to Student Performance* (www.nwrel.org/re-eng/products/ELLSynthesis.pdf) for a wonderful research-based yet easy-to-read outline of how the implementation of different ELL programs in schools affects the language learning gains of ELLs.

As mentioned above, not all ELLs are the same. ELLs may enter a school with vastly different educational backgrounds. Some enter U.S. schools with a strong foundational knowledge in their first language. This means that they may have had schooling in their first language, have literacy skills in their first language, and/or have developed social everyday language competency as well as academic proficiency in their first language. Other ELLs may have had less or even no academic schooling in their first language. Many ELLs, especially refugees, may have attended school in their homeland only for it to have been interrupted by famine or war, or for other socioeconomic or political reasons. Some ELLs arrive in the United States with their families at a very young age and, although they speak their first language at home, they may have never developed reading or writing proficiency in it. As will be discussed in the next chapter, it is of great importance to uncover the nature of an ELL's first language development since this has a profound bearing on how an ELL manages to acquire English.

A third factor, according to the Center for Applied Linguistics (CAL, 1987, at www.cal.org), is the resources that a district has at its disposal. Some districts may have a cadre of qualified ESOL specialists working in schools, whereas other districts may only be able to use paraprofessionals and yet others draw on the surrounding community for help. Based on these constraints, one can classify different ESOL programs into what Baker (2001) terms strong and weak forms of bilingual education. Table 1.2 provides an overview of the merits of the many types of ESOL programs operating across the United States.

According to a report submitted to the San Diego County Office of Education (Gold, 2006), "there is no widely accepted definition of a bilingual school in published research in this country" (p. 37). As a rule of thumb, they are widely understood to be schools that promote bilingualism and literacy in two or more languages as goals for students (Baker, 2001; Crawford, 2004).

TABLE 1.2. Types of ESOL programs in the United States

Type of program	Target ELLs and expectations	Program description	What research says
Submersion	All ELLs regardless of proficiency level or length of time since arrival. No accommodations are made. The goal is to reach full English proficiency and assimilation	ELLs remain in their home classroom and learn with native speakers of English. The teacher makes no modifications or accommodations for the ELL in terms of the curriculum content or in teaching English	States such as Florida have in the past faced potential litigation because of not training teachers to work with ELLs or modifying curriculum and/or establishing ELL programs. In order to avoid submersion models, Florida has established specific ELL instructional guidelines (Consent Decree, 1990)
ESL class period	As above, though usually in school districts with higher concentrations of ELLs	Groups ELLs together, to teach English skills and instruct them in a manner similar to that used in foreign language classes. The focus is primarily linguistic and ELLs visit these classes typically 2 or 3 times per week	This model does not necessarily help ELLs with academic content. The effect is that these programs can tend to create "ESL ghettos." Being placed in such programs can preclude ELLs from gaining college-entrance applicable credits (Diaz-Rico & Weed, 2006)
ESL-plus (sometimes called submersion with primary language)	ELLs who are usually at speech emergence and/or intermediate fluency stage. The aim is to hasten ELLs' ability to integrate and follow content classroom instruction	Includes instruction in English (similar to ESL class period and pull-out) but generally goes beyond the language to focus on content-area instruction. This may be given in the ELL's native language or in English. Often these programs may incorporate the ELL for the majority or all of the school day	According to Ovando and Collier (1998) the most effective ESL-plus and content-based ESL instruction is where the ESL teacher collaborates closely with the content teacher
Content-based ESL	As above	ELLs are still separated from mainstream content classes, but content is organized around an academic curriculum with grade-level objectives. There is no explicit English instruction	See above

continued overleaf

TABLE 1.2. *(continued)* Types of ESOL programs in the United States

Type of program	Target ELLs and expectations	Program description	What research says
Pull-out ESL	Early arrival ELLs. Usually in school districts with limited resources. Achieving proficiency in English fast is a priority so that the ELL can follow the regular curriculum	ELLs leave their home room for specific instruction in English: grammar, vocabulary, spelling, oral communication, etc. ELLs are not taught the curriculum when they are removed from their classrooms, which may be anything from 30 minutes to 1 hour every day	This model has been the most implemented though the least effective program for the instruction of ELLs (Collier & Thomas, 1997)
Sheltered instruction or SDAIE (specifically designed academic instruction in English). Sometimes called structured immersion	Targets all ELLs regardless of proficiency level or age. ELLs remain in their classrooms	This is an approach used in multilinguistic classrooms to provide principled language support to ELLs while they are learning content. Has same curriculum objectives as mainstream classroom in addition to specific language and learning strategy objectives	ELLs are able to improve their English language skills while learning content. Exposure to higher-level language through content materials and explicit focus on language fosters successful language acquisition (Brinton, 2003)
Transitional bilingual	Usually present in communities with a single large ELL population. Geared towards grades K–3. Initial instruction in home language and then switching to English by grade 2 or 3	ELLs enter school in kindergarten and the medium of instruction is in the home language. The reasoning behind this is to allow the ELL to develop full proficiency in the home language so that the benefits of this solid linguistic foundation may transfer over to and aid in the acquisition of English. Intended to move ELL students along relatively quickly (2–3 years)	Of all forms of traditional bilingual programs, the transitional model entails the least benefit to the ELL in terms of maintaining and building cognitive academic language proficiency (CALP) in their home language

TABLE 1.2. *(continued)* Types of ESOL programs in the United States

Type of program	Target ELLs and expectations	Program description	What research says
Maintenance bilingual	As above, but the ELL continues to receive language and content instruction in the home language along with English	As above, but are geared to the more gradual mastering of English and native language skills (5–7 years)	ELLs compare favorably on state standardized tests when measured against achievement grades of ELLs in transitional bilingual programs or ESL pull-out, ESL class period and ESL-plus programs (Hakuta, Butler, & Witt, 2000)
Dual language/ Two-way immersion	This model targets native speakers of English as well as native speakers of other languages, depending on which group predominates in the community	The aim of this program is for both English native speakers and ELLs to maintain their home language as well as acquire another language. Curriculum is delivered in English as well as in the ELL's language. Instructional time is usually split between the two languages, depending on the subject area and the expertise of the teachers	Dual language programs have shown the most promise in terms of first and second language proficiency attainment. Research results from standardized assessments across the United States indicated that ELLs can outperform monolingual English children in English literacy, mathematics, and other content curriculum areas. Has also many positive social and individual affective benefits for the ELL (Genesee, 1999)
Heritage language	Targets communities with high native population numbers, e.g., Hawai'i, Native Americans in New Mexico. Community heritage language maintenance is the goal	In heritage language programs, the aim can be to help revitalize the language of a community. Sometimes English is offered as the medium of instruction in only a few courses. Usually the majority of the curriculum is delivered in the home language	Language diversity can be seen as a problem, as a right, or as a resource. Heritage language programs are operationalized through local, state, and federal language policies as emancipatory (Cummins, 2001)

1.4
Teaching for English Language Development

This section explains the very practical implications of research in the phenomenon of bilingualism for classroom teachers as it relates to a context where many ELLs are learning English as their second, third, or even fourth language. One very important objective of this section is to help teachers understand how they can positively and purposefully mediate an ELL's language development in English.

A very prevalent concept of academic English that has been advanced and refined over the years is based on the work of Jim Cummins (1979; 1980; 1986; 1992; 2001). Cummins analyzed the characteristics of children growing up in two language environments. He found that the level of language proficiency attained in both languages, regardless of what they may be, has an enormous influence on and implications for an ELL's educational success. One situation that teachers often discover about their ELLs is that they arrived in the United States at an early age or were born in the United States but did not learn English until commencing school. Once they begin attending school, their chances for developing their home language are limited, and this home language is eventually superseded by English. This phenomenon is often referred to as limited bilingualism or subtractive bilingualism. Very often ELLs in this situation do not develop high levels of proficiency in either language. Cummins has found that ELLs with limited bilingual ability are overwhelmingly disadvantaged cognitively and academically from this linguistic condition. However, ELLs who develop language proficiency in at least one of the two languages derive neither benefit nor detriment. Only in ELLs who are able to develop high levels of proficiency in both languages did Cummins find positive cognitive outcomes.

The upshot of this line of research in bilingualism seems counterintuitive for the lay person, but it does conclusively show that, rather than providing ELLs with more English instruction, it is important to provide ELLs with instruction in their home language. By reaching higher levels of proficiency in their first language, an ELL will be able to transfer the cognitive benefits to learn English more effectively.

Of course, we don't live in a perfect world, and it is not always feasible to provide instruction in an ELL's home language, so it behooves all teachers to be cognizant of the types of language development processes that ELLs undergo. Cummins (1981) also posited two different types of English language skills. These he called BICS and CALP. The former, basic interpersonal communication skills (BICS), correspond to the social, everyday language and skills that an ELL develops. BICS is very much context-embedded in that it is always used in real-life situations that have real-world connections for the ELL, for example in the playground, at home, shopping, playing sports, and interacting with friends. Cognitive academic language proficiency (CALP), by contrast, is very different from BICS in that it is abstract, decontextualized, and scholarly in nature. This is the type of language required to succeed at school or in a professional setting. CALP, however, is the type of language that most ELLs have the hardest time mastering exactly because it is not everyday language.

Even after being in the United States for years, an ELL may appear fluent in English but still have significant gaps in their CALP. Teachers can be easily fooled by this phenomenon. What is needed is for teachers in all content areas to pay particular attention to an ELL's development in the subject-specific language of a school discipline. Many researchers (Hakuta et al., 2000) agree that an ELL may easily achieve native-like conversational proficiency within two years, but it may take anywhere between five and ten years for an ELL to reach native-like proficiency in CALP.

Since Cummins's groundbreaking research, there has been a lot of work carried out in the area of academic literacy. An alternative view of what constitutes literacy is provided by Valdéz (2000), who supports the notion of *multiple literacies*. Scholars holding this perspective suggest that efforts to teach academic language to ELLs are counterproductive since it comprises multiple dynamic and ever-evolving literacies. In their view, school systems should accept multiple ways of communicating and not marginalize students when they use a variety of English that is not accepted in academic contexts (Zamel & Spack, 1998).

However, one very important fact remains. As it stands now, in order to be successful in a school, all students need to become proficient in academic literacy.

A third view is one that sees academic literacy as a dynamic interrelated process (Scarcella, 2003), one in which cultural, social, and psychological factors play an equally important role. Scarcella provides a description of academic English that includes a phonological, lexical (vocabulary), grammatical (syntax, morphology), sociolinguistic, and discourse (rhetorical) component.

Regardless of how one defines academic literacy, many have criticized teacher education programs for failing to train content-area teachers to recognize the language specificity of their own discipline and thus being unable to help their students recognize it and adequately acquire proficiency in it (Bailey, Butler, Borrego, LaFramenta, & Ong, 2002; Kern, 2000).

Ragan (2005) provides a simple framework to help teachers better understand the academic language of their content area. He proposes that teachers ask themselves three questions:

- What do you expect ELLs to know after reading a text?
- What language in the text may be difficult for ELLs to understand?
- What specific academic language should be taught?

Another very useful instructional heuristic to consider when creating materials to help ELLs acquire academic literacy was developed by Cummins and is called Cummins' Quadrants. In the Quadrants, Cummins (2001) successfully aligns the pedagogical imperative with an ELL's linguistic requirements. The four quadrants represent a sequence of instructional choices that teachers can make based on the degree of contextual support given to an ELL and the degree of cognitive demand placed on an ELL during any given instructional activity. The resulting quadrants are illustrated in Table 1.3.

TABLE 1.3. Cummins' Quadrants

Quadrant I: High context embeddedness, and Low cognitive demand (easiest)	Quadrant III: High context embeddedness, and High cognitive demand
Quadrant II: Low context embeddedness, and Low cognitive demand	Quadrant IV: Low context embeddedness, and High cognitive demand (most difficult)

Quadrant I corresponds to pedagogic activities that require an ELL to use language that is easy to acquire. This may involve everyday social English and strategies that have a high degree of contextual support (i.e., lots of scaffolding, visual clues and manipulatives to aid understanding, language redundancies, repetitions, and reinforcements) or this may include experiential learning techniques, task-based learning, and already familiarized computer programs. Activities in this quadrant also have a low degree of cognitive demand (i.e., are context embedded). In other words, they are centered on topics that are familiar to the ELL or that the ELL has already mastered and do not require abstract thought in and of themselves.

Quadrant IV corresponds to pedagogic activities that require the ELL to use language that is highly decontextualized, abstract, subject-specific, and/or technical/specialized. Examples of these include lectures, subject-specific texts, and how-to manuals. The topics within this quadrant may be unfamiliar to the ELL and impose a greater cognitive demand on the ELL. Academic language associated with Quadrant IV is difficult for ELLs to internalize because it is usually supported by a very low ratio of context-embedded clues to meaning (low contextual support). At the same time, it is often centered on difficult topics that require abstract thought (high cognitive demand). It is important for the teacher to (1) elaborate language, as well as (2) provide opportunities for the ELL to reflect on, talk through, discuss, and engage with decontextualized oral or written texts. By doing this the teacher provides linguistic scaffolds for the ELL to grasp academically.

Quadrants II and III are pedagogic "go-between" categories. In Quadrant II, the amount of context embeddedness is lessened, and so related development increases the complexity of the language while maintaining a focus on topics that are easy and familiar for the ELL. In Quadrant III, language is again made easier through the escalation of the level of context embeddedness to support and facilitate comprehension. However, Quadrant III instruction allows the teacher to introduce more difficult content-area topics.

When a teacher develops lesson plans and activities that are situated within the framework of Quadrant I and II, the ELL engages in work that is not usually overwhelming. In low-anxiety classrooms, ELLs feel more comfortable to experiment with their language to learn more content. As an ELL moves from level 1 of English language development (preproduction) to level 3 (speech emergence), a teacher may feel that the time is right to progress to creating lesson plans and activities that fit pedagogically into Quadrants III and IV. A gradual progression to Quadrant III reinforces language learning and promotes comprehension of academic content. According to Collier (1995):

> A major problem arising from the failure of educators to understand the implications of these continuums is that ELLs are frequently moved from ESOL classrooms and activities represented by Quadrant I to classrooms represented by Quadrant IV, with little opportunity for transitional language experiences characterized by Quadrants II and III.

Such a move may well set the stage for school failure. By attending to both language dimensions (level of contextual support and degree of cognitive demand) and planning accordingly, schools and teachers can provide more effective instruction and sounder assistance to second-language learners. (p. 35)

The degree of cognitive demand for any given activity will differ for each ELL, depending on the ELL's prior knowledge of the topic.

1.5
Not All ELLs are the Same

The United States continues to be enriched by immigrants from countries the world over. Many cities have ethnic enclaves of language minority and immigrant groups and these populations are reflected in school classrooms. This section outlines the background characteristics of ELLs that teachers need to be aware of when planning or delivering instruction. Certainly, ELLs bring their own strengths to the task of learning but they also face many challenges. Equally, these diverse backgrounds impact classroom practices culturally in terms of how ELLs behave in classrooms, how they come to understand curriculum content, and how their interactions with others are affected (Zehler, 1994). The following affords a glimpse of their diversity:

María is seven years old and is a well-adjusted girl in second grade. She was born in Colombia, but came to the United States when she was four. Spanish is the medium of communication at home. When she entered kindergarten, she knew only a smattering of English. By grade 2 she had developed good basic interpersonal communication skills (BICS). These are the language skills needed to get by in social situations. María sounded proficient in English; she had the day-to-day communication skills to interact socially with other people on the playground, in the lunchroom, and on the school bus. Of course, all these situations are very much context-embedded and not cognitively demanding. In the classroom, however, María had problems with her cognitive academic language proficiency (CALP). This included speaking, reading, and writing about subject-area content material. It was obvious to her teacher that Maria needed extra time and support to become proficient in academic areas but, because she had come to the United States as a four-year-old and had already been three years in the school, she was not eligible for direct ESOL support. Collier and Thomas (1997) have shown that, if young ELLs have no prior schooling or have no support in native language development, it may take seven to ten years for them to catch up to their peers.

Ismael Abudullahi Adan is from Somalia. He is 13 and was resettled in Florida as a refugee through the Office of the United Nations High Commissioner for Refugees (UNHCR; see www.unhcr.org/home.html). As is the case with all refugees in the USA, Ismael's family was matched with an American resettlement organization (see www.refugees.org/). No one in his family knew any English. They were subsistence farmers in Somalia and, because of the civil war in Somalia, Ismael had never attended school. The resettlement organization helped the family find a place to live, but financial aid was forthcoming for only six months. While all members of the family were suffering degrees of war-related trauma, culture shock, and emotional upheaval, as well as the stress and anxiety of forced migration, Ismael had to attend the local school. Everything was foreign to him. He had no idea how to act as a student and all the rules of the school made no sense to him. All Ismael wanted to do was work and help his family financially; he knew that at the end of six months financial aid from the government would stop and he worried about how his family was going to feed itself. He is currently placed in a sheltered English instruction class at school.

José came to the United States from Honduras with his parents two years ago. He is now 14. His parents work as farm laborers and throughout the year move interstate depending where crops are being harvested. This usually involves spending the beginning of the calendar year in Florida for strawberry picking, late spring in Georgia for the peach harvest, early fall in North Carolina for the cotton harvest, and then late fall in Illinois for the pumpkin harvest. When the family first came to the United States from Honduras as undocumented immigrants, José followed his parents around the country. His itinerancy did not afford him any consistency with schooling. Last year, his parents decided to leave José with his uncle and aunt in North Carolina so that he would have more chances at school. Now he doesn't see his parents for eight months out of the year. He misses them very much. At school José has low grades and has been retained in grade 8 because he did not pass the North Carolina High School Comprehensive Test. He goes to an ESOL pull-out class once a day at his school.

Andrzej is 17 years old. He arrived with his father, mother, and 12-year-old sister from Poland. They live in Baltimore where his father is a civil engineer. The family immigrated the year before so that Andrzej's mother could be closer to her sister (who had married an American and had been living in the United States for the past 10 years). Andrzej always wanted to be an engineer like his father, but now he isn't sure what he wants to do. His grades at school have slipped since leaving Poland. He suspects that this is because of his English. Even though he studied English at school in Poland, he never became proficient at writing. Because he has been in the United States for more than a year, he no longer receives ESOL support at school. His parents, however, pay for an English tutor to come to his house once a week.

The above cases reflect the very wide differences in the ELL population in schools today. One cannot assume that every ELL speaks Spanish or that all ELLs entered the country illegally. The ELL population in a school may include permanent residents, naturalized citizens, legal immigrants, undocumented immigrants, refugees, and asylees. Of this foreign-born population, 4.8 million originate from Europe, 9.5 million from Asia, 19 million from Latin America, 1.2 million from Africa, and 1 million from other areas including Oceania and the Caribbean (U.S. Census Bureau, 2005).

Stages of Cultural Adjustment

What the above cases of María, Ismael, José, and Andrzej also identify is that since the nation's founding immigrants have come to the United States for a wide variety of reasons. These may include one or any combination of economic, political, religious, and family reunification reasons. Depending on the reason for coming to the United States, an ELL might be very eager to learn English since they might see having English proficiency as the single best means to "get ahead" economically in their new life, or they might resist learning English because they see this as an erosion of their cultural and linguistic identity. A teacher may find an ELL swaying between these two extremes simply because they are displaying the characteristics and stages of *cultural adjustment*.

The notion of cultural adjustment or, as it is sometimes called, "culture shock" was first introduced by anthropologist Kalvero Oberg in 1954. The emotional and behavioral symptoms of each stage of this process can manifest themselves constantly or only appear at disparate times.

Honeymoon Stage

The first stage is called the "honeymoon" stage and is marked by enthusiasm and excitement by the ELL. At this stage, ELLs may be very positive about the culture and express being overwhelmed with their impressions particularly because they find American culture exotic and are fascinated by it. Conversely, an ELL may be largely passive and not confront the culture even though (s)he finds everything in the new culture wonderful, exciting, and novel. After a few days, weeks, or months, ELLs typically enter the second stage.

Hostility Stage

At this stage, differences between the ELL's old and new cultures become aggravatingly stark. An ELL may begin to find anything and everything in the new culture annoying and/or tiresome. An ELL will most likely find the behavior of those around him/her unusual and unpredictable and thus begin to dislike American culture as well as Americans. They may begin to stereotype Americans and idealize their own culture. They may experience cultural confusion and communication difficulties. At this stage, feelings of boredom, lethargy, restlessness, irritation, antagonism, depression, and feelings of ineptitude are very common. This occurs when an ELL is trying to acclimatize to the new culture, which may be very dissimilar to the culture of origin. Shifting between former cultural discourse practices and those of the new country is a problematic process and can take a very long time to overcome. If it is prolonged, an ELL may withdraw because of feelings of loneliness and anxiety.

Home Stage

The third stage is typified by the ELL achieving a sense of understanding of the new culture. The ELL may feel more comfortable living in the new country and experiencing the new culture. They may regain their sense of humor. In psychological terms, an ELL may start to feel a certain emotional balance. Although feelings of isolation may persist, the ELL may stop feeling lost and even begin to have a feeling of direction. The ELL re-emerges more culturally stable, being more familiar with the environment and wanting to belong. For the ELL, this period of new adjustment could initiate an evaluation of old cultural practices versus new ones.

Assimilation Stage

In the fourth stage, the ELL realizes that the new culture has positives as well as negatives to offer. Integration patterns and practices displayed by the ELL become apparent. It is accompanied by a more solid feeling of belonging. The ELL enjoys being in the new culture, functions easily in the new environment (even though they might already have been in the new culture for a few years) and may even adopt cultural practices of the new culture. This stage may be seen as one of amalgamation and assimilation.

Re-Entry Shock Stage

This happens when an ELL returns to the old culture for a visit and notices how many things have changed in the country as well as how they themselves have changed. Upon returning from the home country, an ELL will have developed a new sense of appreciation and of belonging to the new culture.

Worthy of note is the fact that the length of time an ELL spends in each of these stages varies considerably. The stages are neither discrete nor sequential and some ELLs may completely skip stages. They may even exhibit affective behaviors characteristic of more than one stage.

Cultural Practices at School

Whenever an ELL steps into a new school environment, the ELL will be sure to go through a process of cultural adjustment. For an ELL, the countless arrays of unspoken rules acquired in his/her culture of origin may not be suitable in the new school and a new set of practices needs to be discovered and internalized. These include, but are of course not limited to, school rules, what it means to be a "good" student, how to interact with fellow students and teachers, eating practices, bathroom practices, and even ways of learning. It would be fairly easy to learn new rules for living if such were made explicit and one were provided with lists of things to learn. However, most cultural rules operate at a level below conscious awareness and are not easily relayed to students.

Often ELLs find themselves in the position of having to discover these rules on their own. Shared cultural discourse practices can be seen as the oil that lubricates social interaction; however, what a community's cultural practices are, as well as the meanings that group members attach to their shared repertoire of cultural practices, are not always made explicit. Unfamiliarity with these cultural rules on the part of an ELL can cause a great deal of stress.

Many definitions regarding what culture is or is not abound. Diaz-Rico and Weed (2006) provide a very nice overview of the characteristics of culture. For them, culture is an adaptive mechanism, culture is learned, cultures change, culture is universal, culture provides a set of rules for living and a range of permissible behavior patterns, culture is a process of deep conditioning, culture is demonstrated in values, people usually are not aware of their culture, people do not know all of their own culture, culture is expressed verbally and nonverbally, culture no longer exists in isolation, and, last but very poignantly, culture affects people's attitudes toward schooling and it governs the way they learn. It can affect how they come to understand curriculum content and how they interact with fellow students.

Diaz-Rico and Weed (2006) offer a number of strategies to promote cultural pluralism and assuage potential exclusionary practices such as stereotyping, prejudice, and racism in the classroom. Ways to acknowledge different values, beliefs, and practices include accommodating different concepts of time and work rhythms, as well as different concepts of work space. Being open to culturally sensitive dress codes and inclusive of culture in school rituals are effective ways of promoting cultural pluralism. Considering different notions about work and play and maintaining an inclusive understanding of different health and hygiene practices as well as being tolerant of different religious practices and food and eating practices are critical in teaching acceptance. Most important to remember in relation to your ELL students are culturally based educational expectations (roles, status, gender), different discourse patterns, and your need to foster cultural pride and home–school communication.

One way to ease your ELL's cultural adjustment while demonstrating inclusiveness is to get to know where your ELLs come from and then incorporate aspects of their culture into your lessons. You could overtly ask your ELL about their home country, but this tactic may not provide you with the type of information you want since your ELL may not have the language proficiency in English to express abstract cultural concepts. Therefore, you should observe your ELL and how they behave, interview people from the same country, conduct a home visit, or visit the community in which the ELL lives. Of course, teachers are often constrained by time, so an alternative is to conduct internet research or buy appropriate books.

1.6
Culturally Responsive Pedagogy

As more and more students from diverse backgrounds populate 21st century class-rooms, and efforts mount to identify effective methods to teach these students, the need for pedagogical approaches that are culturally responsive intensifies. Today's classrooms require teachers to educate students varying in culture, language, abilities, and many other characteristics.

(Gollnick & Chinn, 2002: 21)

The question is: How does a teacher adequately respond to the multicultural classroom?

In 2000 Gay wrote that culturally responsive pedagogy is validating, comprehensive, multidimensional, empowering, transformative, and emancipatory. In other words, culturally responsive pedagogy necessitates that teachers tread outside their comfort circles. It is only natural for humans to see, understand, judge, make sense of, and canonize the world around them through their own discursive norms of practice. What this means in the context of education is that teachers make choices every day about what they will and will not teach. More importantly, teachers make choices as to how they will present and frame their curriculum choices. Of course this sends a subtle message to students: What curriculum matter is taught and how it is framed tends to legitimatize, validate, and endorse it over other potential curricular perspectives, which by default are marginalized.

Thus, teachers instruct in ways and about things that are familiar to them. They usually adopt and transmit the dominant voice in society, namely that of white middle-class America. The problem is, if a student is an ELL, (s)he is usually not white, middle-class, or American. This is where the practice of culturally responsive pedagogy can help. Look at the reflection vignette below. It shows how the media can tend to reinforce dominant societal perspectives, perspectives that are reinforced and repeated in school curricula and textbooks across the country.

Reflection Vignette

I was driving my 12-year-old son to school in the fall of 2003 when over the radio we heard a commercial for the movie *Alamo*. Coincidently, the previous day we had been to the movies and one of the trailers was for the same movie. Kevin Costner was one of the Texan heroes in the movie, and every time the movie trailer showed the Texans the screen was bright and full of smiling people. The music was light and they were obviously the "good guys." However, when the screen shot showed the Mexican antagonists, the screen was dark, with hues of blue and red, the background images were full of cannon sounds, and the faces were "mean-looking."

Back in the car, I asked my son, who at the time was focused on playing his Gameboy, "You're doing American history now in your social studies class, right?"

My son, recognizing that another of dad's teachable moments was upon him, just rolled his eyes and disgruntledly put down his Gameboy.

"Yes, why?" he said.

"What aspect of U.S. history are you learning about now?" I asked.

"We're learning about the westward colonization of North America."

"Did you hear that ad?" I asked.

"Sure."

"Let me ask you something. What do you think would happen if a bunch of Cubans came into the middle of Florida, bought up a cluster of farms, and then told the government they were not going to pay taxes?"

"I suppose the government would fine them," he said.

"Well, what would happen if those same Cubans then told the government that they were going to create their own country?"

"The government would send in the army and kick 'em all out and probably send them back to Cuba."

At that point, I could see a flash of realization cross my son's face. "Oh, I get it," he said, "the Cubans are the Texans."

In the United States the Alamo is usually constructed as part of a righteous war of independence against an autocratic foreign government, namely Mexico. Yet in Mexican schools the war surrounding the Alamo is constructed as an aggressive grab for land by non-Spanish speaking settlers. Who is right? Perhaps the question should be: Am I teaching curriculum matter in a way that alienates and inadvertently marginalizes my students? How would a Mexican ELL feel in your classroom if you taught a unit on the Alamo, or on the westward European settlement of North America, and Mexico and the Mexicans were portrayed as the baddies? At the very least it marginalizes an ELL's voice in the classroom and indirectly discredits his/her potential contribution of another perspective for the class to think about.

Using Gay's (2000) principles of culturally responsive pedagogy, how does a teacher make the curriculum more validating, comprehensive, multidimensional, empowering, transformative, and emancipatory?

The first step is to be conscious of our choice of language. Language is never neutral. What and how we say things in the classroom affects the way our students perceive curriculum matter. The second step is to be conscious of the images we present to the students. The third step is to engage in critical and reflexive thinking and writing tasks. By getting teachers to reflect critically on the language, images, and content of their teaching, we begin to open the door on *other* ways to think about teaching that are less ethnocentric. The fourth step is to learn the history and culture of the ELL groups in your classroom. The fifth step is to try and visit teachers who are successful at implementing culturally responsive pedagogy and, last, become an advocate in your own educational institution to reform ethnocentric discursive practices so that it becomes more inclusive. Richards, Brown, and Forde (2004) suggest the following activities to become more culturally responsive:

1. acknowledge students' differences as well as their commonalities;
2. validate students' cultural identity in classroom practices and instructional materials;
3. educate students about the diversity of the world around them;
4. promote equity and mutual respect among students;
5. assess students' ability and achievement validly;
6. foster a positive interrelationship among students, their families, the community, and school;
7. motivate students to become active participants in their learning;
8. encourage students to think critically;
9. challenge students to strive for excellence as defined by their potential; and
10. assist students in becoming socially and politically conscious.

1.7
Not All Parents are the Same
Home–School Communication

Any school administrator and teacher will readily admit that the key to a school's success and indeed the key to a child's learning success is the active involvement of parents in the learning process. In the case of ELLs, parents are often at a loss because of barriers that prevent them from fully participating in the school community. Parents' hesitancy to involve themselves in their child's school arises from barriers such as the frustration they feel because of their own limited knowledge of English, their own possible lack of schooling, perceptions about power and status roles, or the anxiety they have because of different cultural norms such that they do not readily understand American school cultures or the cultural expectations, rights, roles, and responsibilities of teachers, parents, and students.

Schools can greatly enhance the effectiveness of ELL home–school communication and involvement by taking active steps to reduce these barriers. Careful planning is required to meet these challenges, though it can be done.

1. *Knowledge is King!* Get as much background information as is possible. Information useful to schools and teachers includes home language, home cultural/ethnic values, parental attitudes towards education, work schedules of parents, English proficiency, and the circumstances under which they have come to be in the United States (e.g., are they refugees, itinerant migrants, political asylees, second or third generation heritage speakers?). Depending on the information a school receives, a classroom teacher may make informed decisions about bilingual aide support, translation support, and changing school cultural practices that raise rather than bring down barriers to ELL home–school communication and parental involvement.

2. *Communicate as if it is going out of style!* The importance of fostering ELL parental involvement centers foremost on fostering and maintaining good lines of communication between the

school/teacher and the home/parents. An important facet that frames parents' participation in schools is their perceptions of school personnel. Is the school inviting and welcoming? Are teachers and the administration approachable? Are teachers empathetic to ELL parental concerns, wishes, contributions, values, and cultural practices? How often are they invited to attend school functions? Do teachers follow through on their communications? Do teachers make an effort to talk directly and in person with parents? Are parents allowed to visit often and learn what goes on in the classroom? Do teachers take the time to explain the whats, whys, and hows of their teaching and the ELL child's learning?

3. *It's not just about educating the ELL!* If schools want to enlist the support and help of ELL parents, then both the administration of a school and its teachers need to be prepared to extend their instruction beyond the ELL student to the ELL parent—beyond the classroom and into the ELL home. In other words, in order to break down the types of barriers that inhibit ELL parents from school involvement, steps need to be taken to educate the parents in matters concerning English language, as well as U.S. school customs. What would such steps look like? In an article published in *Essential Teacher* (2004), Bassoff says it centers solely on *access, approachability,* and *follow-through.*

Ideas: On Fostering Access

- Create, endorse, and implement an ELL parent–school participation program/policy.
- Have an ELL parent representative on school committees.
- Make the school a place to foster ELL community events.
- Provide access to the school library to aid ELL parents' learning of English.
- Translate all school communications into the home language.
- Make sure all written communication reaches the ELL parent.
- Foster in-school support groups for ELL parents.
- Advocate that your school district establish an "Intake Center" for new arrivals that will help ELL newcomers with school registrations, placement, testing, and information services.
- Allow ELL parents to come to school professional development opportunities.
- Provide ELL parent education workshops and orientation opportunities.
- Advertise the contact information of bilingual school staff.

Ideas: On Fostering Approachability

- Use ELL parents as sources of information.
- Invite ELL parents to school.
- Use parents to raise multicultural awareness in the school and classroom; multiculturalism is a two-way street—foster inclusion through the provision of multicultural workshops, presentations, and events to mainstream monolingual school personnel and students.
- Multicultural appreciation events could include ethnic music and dance performances, art displays, drama shows, science fairs, and festival evenings, all accompanied by talks from ELL parents or ELL community leaders.
- Be amenable and open to different ways about thinking about education—show this through inclusive classroom practices, activities, realia, and visuals.
- Embed multicultural routines in everything and all the time.
- Foster ELL literacy family evenings.
- Establish native language parent groups.

Ideas: On Achieving Good Follow-Through

- Give mainstream students service-learning opportunities to help ELL parents/families adjust to U.S. life.
- Foster ELL parent network circles.
- Provide classes that help ELL parents to meet their children's education needs.
- Have the school library purchase a wide range of fiction and non-fiction bilingual books.
- Take the time to learn about the culture, language, and education system of the ELLs' home countries and apply what you learn in your classroom.
- Create virtual spaces to post ongoing information for ELL parents as well as WWW links to useful websites.[1]

1.8
English Language Learners with Special Needs

We want to highlight an important subset of the ELL population that is often disadvantaged because its members fall simultaneously into two underrepresented groups: special needs and ELL. They are underprivileged because many teachers within these separate discipline areas have not been trained to work with this population of students—ESOL teachers with special needs students, or special needs teachers with ELLs.

In 1984 the National Office for Educational Statistics reported that 500,000 students in the United States were English language learners with exceptionalities. Today, more than 20 years later, it is projected that there are more than 1 million ELLs with special needs in the United States (Baca & Cervantes, 2004).

Despite an abundance of legislative initiatives (*Civil Rights Act—Title VI* in 1963, *Title VII of the Elementary and Secondary Education Act* (ESEA) reauthorized in 1974, 1978, 1984, and 1998, *Lau v. Nichols* in 1974, and the *Equal Educational Opportunity Act*, extending the Lau decision to all schools, *President's Committee on Mental Retardation* in 1970, the *Education for All Handicapped Children Act* in 1975, the *Bilingual Education Act* in 1984, reauthorization of the ESEA in 1994 coupled with a Presidential Executive Order in 2000, the *Individuals with Disability Education Act* (IDEA) of 1997 and *Title II* of the *No Child Left Behind* (NCLB) *Act* 2002), inappropriate referrals, assessments, and the institutionalization of inappropriate instructional processes remain crucial issues in the education of ELL special needs children.

A colleague of ours once told the story of when he first came to the United States. His son was seven years old and at the end of the summer in 2005 was ready to be placed in grade 2. In Florida, the parents of every newly enrolled student are obliged to fill out a home language survey form. Our colleague was raising his children bilingually and both his children were equally fluent in English and German. When asked on the form what languages were spoken at home, he wrote German and English. A week later, his son innocuously said at the dinner table that he enjoyed being pulled out of the classroom, whereupon both parents asked the son what he meant. "Why I love being in the ESOL class with all the kids who speak other languages." Little did my colleague know that, because he had written German on the home language survey, the school was legally bound to place his son in ESOL classes. The upshot of the story was that our colleague went to the school and explained to the administration that his son was a balanced bilingual speaker and having him in ESOL classes was unnecessary. The administration told him that there was nothing they could do because the home survey was filled out as it was. Ultimately, my colleague had to disenroll his son, re-enroll him in the same school, and fill out the home survey again (this time just putting English as the home language) to finally have him pulled from the ESOL classes. The reason this story is related is because parents and teachers are all too familiar with the fact that, within education environments, rule-driven practices, acronyms, and terminologies abound that more often than not pigeon-hole students into predetermined roles and assign these students to inevitable and predictable expectations. Unfortunately, ELLs with special needs have fallen prey to this stereotyping. There is, however, an ever-increasing but incomplete body of research that spotlights instructional strategies for ELLs with special needs that teachers may draw upon to help them in their efforts to identify, instruct, and assess. The following section summarizes some of the more important aspects of this research. The following two points may act as instructional guides:

- Students with mild to severe disability levels benefit from native language instruction (de Valenzuela & Niccolai, 2004).
- Instruction needs to be enriching and not remedial, empower language learners, recognize the learners' culture and background, provide learners with authentic and meaningful activities, connect students to real-life experiences, begin with context-embedded material that leads to the use of context-reduced material, and provide a literacy/language-rich environment (Echeverria and McDonough, 1993).

But how can we translate the above into effective classroom practice?

There are various pedagogic models that have been developed based on theoretical frameworks, research findings, and recommended practices appropriate for ELLs with special needs (Ruiz, 1995a, 1995b). Ortiz (1984) describes four basic types of pedagogic models that offer structured institutional support for ELLs with special needs to achieve more accomplished social and academic skill levels. These models are:

1. *Coordinated services model*—assists the ELL with special needs with a monolingual English speaking special education teacher and a bilingual educator.
2. *Bilingual support model*—bilingual paraprofessionals are teamed with monolingual English speaking special educators and assist with the individualized education plans of ELLs with special needs. Wherever noted on the individualized education program (IEP), the bilingual paraprofessional provides home language instruction concurrently with the teacher providing content expertise.
3. *Integrated bilingual special education model*—consists of one teacher who is certified in both bilingual education and special education, where the teacher is able to assist with level-appropriate English language instruction as the learner develops in proficiency.
4. *Bilingual special education model*—in this model all professionals interacting with the ELL special needs student have received bilingual special education training and are qualified to provide services that meet the goals outlined in any IEP.

Another model, the Optimal Learning Environment (OLE) Project (Ruiz, 1989), is based on a constructivist philosophy and works within a holistic–constructivist paradigm, focusing on the extensive use of interactive journals, writers' workshops, shared reading practices, literature conversations, response journals, patterned writing, as well as the provision of extended assessment time. The aim of the strategies is to build on a student's schema and interest.

The benefits of such models highlight the individualized and diverse needs of language learning students with special needs. As yet, guaranteeing unambiguous benefits across the board is not possible precisely because of the dearth of empirical research on instructional planning and curriculum design in this area. A very real consequence of this situation is the paucity of curricular materials available specifically geared to bilingual special education. Both fields of education have propagated methods on preparing either English language learners or special needs students. The main point to be internalized here is that materials must be integrated and specifically designed for English language learners *with* special needs. It is not enough that they receive "half of each curriculum" (Collier, 1995). Lack of curricular materials and trained personnel is still cited as the greatest barrier to providing services to English language learners with special needs.

So, what can teachers do to facilitate language learning for ELL students with a special need?

Of course, implementing well-informed instructional practices is one thing, but awareness raising, understanding of difficulties, and knowledge of differences and disorders are also an integral part of assisting the English language learner with disabilities.

In conclusion, we offer Hoover and Collier's (1989) recommendations as a point of departure to think about teaching ELLs with special needs:

1. Know the specific language abilities of each student.

2. Include appropriate cultural experiences in material adapted or developed.

3. Ensure that material progresses at a rate commensurate with student needs and abilities.

4. Document the success of selected materials.

5. Adapt only specific materials requiring modifications, and do not attempt to change too much at one time.

6. Try out different materials and adaptations until an appropriate education for each student is achieved.

7. Strategically implement materials adaptations to ensure smooth transitions into the new materials.

8. Follow some consistent format or guide when evaluating materials.

9. Be knowledgeable about particular cultures and heritages and their compatibility with selected materials.

10. Follow a well-developed process for evaluating the success of adapted or developed materials as the individual language and cultural needs of students are addressed. (Hoover & Collier, 1989, p. 253)

Conclusion

Understanding your English language learners can be daunting. They are different; they probably come from very different home environments from you, their teachers. Some of your students may be third-generation American and yet others may be newly arrived undocumented immigrants.

After reading Part 1, we don't expect you to now know everything there is to know about ELLs. We did not set out to provide you in these few short pages with an all-inclusive research-informed, all-encompassing treatise on ELLs in education. We have been circumspect, to be sure, in trying to introduce you to ELLs. There are plenty of ELL-specific books for that. It *was* our intent, however, to raise your awareness about the educational implications of having ELLs in your classroom. Our goal with this is to start drawing a picture of who an English language learner is and from this position help you think about the educational possibilities for your class.

Parts 2, 3, and 4 of this book are devoted exclusively to completing this picture. Not in a global sense, but finely etched within the parameters of your own content area.

What will be introduced to you in the pages to come will undoubtedly refer back to some of the points raised in Part 1. We have no intention of offering you static teaching recipes; instead we offer something akin to ideas, understandings, and skills that you can transfer to your own classrooms. Last, we refer you to Part 4 of this book, which offers you avenues for future professional development.

Part 2

Principles of Teaching and Learning in the Arts

In this chapter, we identify and summarize what arts teachers can learn from theorists, philosophers, and practitioners across the intersecting fields of education and English language learning with the teaching and learning of visual arts, music, drama, and dance. Specifically, the guiding principles for arts instruction will be articulated and theoretically situated within the research literature on creativity and relational pedagogy. Furthermore, an overview of the research literature offering insights into the nexus of English language learning and arts education will be provided. Purposeful connections teachers can foster for English language learning in arts classrooms will be embedded in these discussions.

2.1
The Nature of
Artistic Thinking

The nature of artistic thinking offers unique educational significances for learners and learning, and is fundamental to the education of all students. We draw on Eisner (2002; 2005) and Eisner and Day's (2004) scholarship to articulate interrelated principles of effective instruction permeating artistic thinking. These include:

- Meaning-making as fundamental to the creative nature of all human beings.
- Qualitative relationships as the necessary negotiation of a parts-to-whole integrity, engaging all sensibilities.
- Arts processes and thinking as fostering caring ways of living and being with others.
- Particulars of learners, teachers, and contexts as contributing to what, how, when, and why artistic learning occurs.
- Teachers as responsible for creating the necessary conditions and circumstances to occasion and support artistic learning.
- Multiplicities of all kinds embraced as productive for learning, with diversity, individuality, and the unexpected incorporated into the process.
- Process and product as interrelated, with assessment practices understood as resources in support of this interrelationship.
- Communication of ideas, sharing of perspectives, and imagination of possibilities, as a means of promoting understandings of one another, and of the world.
- Creation as ongoing and entailing re-creation and renewal, based on the assumption that there is always more to know and to learn for all involved.

Artistic thinking embracing these interrelated principles insists on opportunities for all students to see, to compose, to experience the qualitative relationships that emerge, and to make judgments in process. Content and form are understood as inextricably linked, inseparable. There are relationships among thinking and the materials, sounds, expressions, and movements to be encountered and negotiated by the visual artist, musician, thespian, and dancer. The act of creating meaning entails thinking within the "constraints and affordances" of these qualities (Eisner, 2002, pp. 236–238), responding to what is suggested and revealed. Such artistic thinking is what the arts teach and education ought to entail.

Visual arts, music, drama, and dance teachers need to invite students to participate wholly as creators. Concrete opportunities for discovery and invention will nurture artistic thinking. There is little room for exploring artistic thinking where rigid rules dictate the ways in which the arts should be represented. Artistic thinking comes from playing with possibilities, searching for relationships. The development of such thinking in situation permits possibilities to be included as engagement evolves. Without artful, playful engagement, it would seem that imaginative thought, requiring speculation and conjecturing about possibilities, might not be possible. Thus, artistic thinking demands student investment, and the visibility gained through ongoing sharing and critique holds tremendous potential for enlarging and informing all understandings. Teacher belief in the worthiness of artistic thinking translates into greater commitment to search for these considerations in one's teaching practices. This chapter therefore asks visual arts, music, drama, and dance teachers to remind themselves of the artist within, awakening the artist within each of their students.

2.2
Qualities Instilling Artistic Thinking

Art, music, drama, and dance classrooms are often found in remote corners of school buildings. They are not always easy to locate. We have all been lost a few times on sojourns to such rooms. One such sojourn takes us to visit Jen Deets' visual arts classroom[1]. On this day, her room is being painted and so her class has relocated to a basement room, even more remote and around a few more twists and turns in the hallway. As we enter the makeshift art room we are immediately aware of student investment in their work—heart and hand. Students are deeply absorbed in their thinking and barely look up as we enter. We do not recall the specifics of the assignment but purposefulness infuses the context with a serious, attentive energy that is palatable. Students are immersed in artistic process and we find ourselves drawn in and very reluctant to leave. The arts learning context transcends the physical space. Talking with students about their artistic engagement, listening to their interactions with others, watchful of their deliberations and judgments, the artistic process is made visible as artistic forms emerge. Students negotiate the materials they are working with and respond accordingly, adapting, changing, and creating. The physical learning space is always a contributing feature, but Jen very importantly opens an imaginary space for her students, fostering student investment in process. Such invested learning reveals the power of the form to inform. Eisner (1972) writes, "What is mediated through thought are qualities, what is managed in process are qualities, and what terminates at the end is a qualitative whole; an art form that expresses something by virtue of the way in which these qualities have been created and organized" (p. 114). The act of creation precipitates these qualities. Through adapting, building, changing, and making meaning, artistic thinking is engaged in a constant organizing and reorganizing encounter. Artists have intimate knowledge of these qualities. And, these are the qualities arts educators should embed within learning opportunities for their students to experience. We see benefits in language growth and comprehension for ELLs through occasioning such opportunities. These interrelated qualities instilling artistic thinking include:

Attentiveness: Teacher and student attentiveness is a willingness to be receptive to sensory qualities and relations, perceiving possibilities. Purposefully ensuring opportunities for close observation and time to dwell with and in learning situations enables everyone to see and act on potential that might not otherwise be seen.

Personal Investment: Teacher and student investment respects and encourages divergent ways of approaching learning. Acknowledging and valuing how knowledge grows from and is a reflection of lived experience invites everyone to see and experience multiple ways to know the world.

Emotional Commitment: Teacher and student emotional commitment within learning tasks reveals how learning entails discovery. The significance arising out of such discovery is neither an object or a concept, but a feeling or attitude that is an ongoing catalyst for participation.

Felt Freedom: Student and teacher felt freedom contributes to a spirit of inquiry. Learning opportunities must allow for liberties in the ways everyone chooses to participate. Learning needs space to wonder, question, and reconsider, importantly making room for the creation or invention of meaning, valuing mistakes, experimentation, projection and speculation.

Dialogue and Interaction: Teacher and student dialogues and interactions become the link to sense making. Teachers draw students into the depth and complexity of subject matter through dialogue and interaction. In this way, thought not only shapes outcomes, it is constitutive of them.

Attunement within Inquiry: Teacher and student learning is a venture. It demands alertness and participation. The organization for learning emerges from the negotiation of relations. Thus, the inquiry is always in the making, fluid and ever changing. As such, it requires questioning, openness to possibilities, and attentive listening and responding. Attunement throughout the inquiry itself determines the form or manner of representation as it evolves for each participant and for each lesson.

Enlarged Self-knowledge: Teacher and student self-knowledge are enlarged through deliberate opportunities to attend to other(s)—other materials, other ideas, other images, and other experiences. Empathetic understandings are fostered and deepened as relations between self and other are continually addressed through concretely negotiating among differences of all kinds.

(See Macintyre Latta, 2001, for further discussion of these specific qualities in relation to teaching/learning in classrooms and the writings of Dewey, 1934; Eisner, 2004; Greene, 2000.)

The interdependency of the qualities of attentiveness, personal involvement, emotional commitment, felt freedom, and dialogue and interaction offer directions for continued inquiry and generate greater self-knowledge, forming the learning contexts for artistic thinking to develop and flourish. Dewey (1934), Eisner (2004), and Greene (2000) claim it is impossible to separate these qualities from the entirety of the act of creating meaning. Artistic thinking is experienced as connected, all parts linked in relation to the vital movement of the whole, belonging to the self and situation within this movement of thinking. In this way the act of creating positions participants to be wholly involved. Embedding these qualities within arts experiences very importantly creates the much-needed mediating room and time for ELLs to navigate sense making on their own terms, and allows teachers room and time to gain insights into the particulars of these terms, thus, informing how best to support their language development.

2.3
The Primacy of Creativity and Relational Pedagogy to Arts Instruction

Much work over the last three decades on creativity calls into question the marginal role of the arts in schools all over the world (Abbs, 2007; Bowman, 2005; Bresler, 2004, 2007; Bruner, 1990; Csikszentmihalyi, 1997; Robinson, 1982, 2001; Seidel, Tishman, Winner, Hetland, & Palmer, 2009). Creativity and education scholars point to the curtailment of meaning-making opportunities for students and the specifics of what is being lost for learners and learning (Custodero, 2005; Eisner, 2005; Greene, 2000; Hostetler, Macintyre Latta, & Sarroub, 2007; Webster, 2002; Wiggins, 2002, 2009). These scholars argue that the arts have the potential to be mediums, instilling the power of creativity into our lives. They further argue that human beings are fundamentally creative and we see every reason to respect this inherent gift, working with the tremendous possibilities the arts hold for teaching/learning of all kinds. By valuing personal knowings, interpretations, and expressions, and relying on dialogue and participation as a means to this sense making, artistic experiences are felt and lived through as a whole. In so doing, the act of creating and the relations encountered can never be reduced to rules. Rather, judgments are made on an ongoing basis, always searching for a rightness of fit. The act of creating positions students between the content they are addressing, the ideas and concepts they are working with, and the form the search takes. And, it is within this in-between position that at some point the materials, sounds, expressions, and movements become a medium, precipitated through the act of creating. Dewey (1934) calls this "sensitivity to a medium as a medium" at "the very heart of all artistic creation and artistic perception" (p. 199). A movement of thinking ensues; it is a moving force holding a spirit worth attention. The situation and/or materials, sounds, expressions, and movements talk back, and students respond to the "back talk" (Schon, 1983). Such back talk suggests education is interdependent with the primacy of relations. In other words, teachers ought to be promoting interactive, deliberative, caring relationships between students and subject matter. The arts enable this as they offer practices that are inherently relational. Visual artists, musicians, thespians, and dancers concretely negotiate materials, sounds, expressions, movements, spaces, and time. Philosophers for centuries have turned to the arts as exemplary forms of such ontological reciprocity—the negotiation of self–other relations (see for example Dewey, 1934; Gadamer, 1960/1992; Hegel, 1964/1886; Kant, 1952/1790; Schiller, 1954/1795). Much current work on pedagogy claims that it is within this relational space of self and other that learning takes place (Biesta, 2004; Bingham & Sidorkin, 2004; Macintyre Latta, 2005; Noddings, 2003, 2005). Relational pedagogy positions participants to enter learning as creators, embracing the risks and opportunities.

Our goal in Part 3 of this book is to provide examples that will enable teachers and their students to locate the learning significances of creative work for themselves. These examples will assist teachers and their students to navigate with greater confidence the relational risks and opportunities for learning, creating meaning, and concomitantly creating greater self-knowledge.

For ELLs, the examples of arts experiences offer contextualized opportunities that foster greater participation through enhanced opportunities to practice and to attain greater language proficiency. These opportunities create the space needed to work through ideas alongside educators that are responsive and sensitive to students' varying comfort levels, cultural values, abilities, and specific details of individual learning circumstances. These opportunities also allow time to consider and to address the new culture immigrants and refugees find themselves navigating. For many, arts experiences can be healing, enabling ELLs to confront and to negotiate social, psychological, and emotional aspects that intersect with their learning and self-development. Concomitantly, these experiences engage educators in seeking the supports and resources needed to optimize learning.

2.4
Arts-Focused
ESOL Research

This section examines the research literature addressing arts-focused ESOL instruction, to identify ways in which this existing knowledge may support arts education as a means of engaging ELL students in language development and in subject matter in some of the ways presented and discussed in the previous sections.

While language acquisition is not our direct focus in this book, we acknowledge its importance in the academic and social success of ELLs. We explore arts education as a means of supporting English acquisition through its capacity to engage students in the production of language, and to enhance the motivation of students to communicate with their peers in English. Principles identified in Part 1 are key modes for engaging ELLs in arts education to support their English language development, and for engaging ELLs in authentic language use to support their participation in arts education.

Principle 1: Give ELLs many opportunities to read, write, listen to, and discuss oral and written English texts in a variety of ways.
Principle 2: Draw attention to patterns of English language structure.
Principle 3: Give ELLs classroom time to productively use their English.
Principle 4: Give ELLs opportunities to notice their errors and to correct their English.
Principle 5: Construct activities that maximize opportunities for ELLs to interact with others in English.

In these ways, the role of the arts educator in acting on these principles to create learning opportunities for ELL students to participate in interactions with peers, becomes essential to their progress towards English fluency and integration with peers in school. Four primary themes in the research literature reiterate this need:

Importance of Affirming Diversity

There is an abundance of research highlighting the importance of affirming diversity (Banks, 1995; Nieto & Bode, 2008) by recognizing and including the ethnic cultures and languages that students bring to school (Ada, 1988; Cummins, 2001; Cummins et al., 2005; Feuerverger, 1994; Igoa, 1995; Soto, 1997) through culturally-responsive and culturally-relevant curriculum (Gay, 2000; Ladson-Billings, 2001; Villegas, 1991). There are, however, many challenges to moving from the theory of recognizing and celebrating student diversity, to the practice of implementing policies and practices to meet the needs of the students and their families. Some of these challenges are addressed in this book as we explore ways in which engagement in arts education may support the implementation of policies and practices to engage students in learning activities that affirm diversity.

Need for Mainstream Teacher Education for ELLs

There is currently a lack of mainstream teacher education to prepare teachers to work with ELL students (Janzen, 2008), despite the importance of affirming diversity and the increasingly diverse student population. Research has found that teachers in mainstream classrooms are "largely untrained to work with ELLs; in fact, only 12.5% of U.S. teachers have received eight or more hours of recent training to teach students with limited English proficiency" (National Center for Education Statistics, 2002). Teachers generally expressed feelings of professional inadequacy in working with ELL students (Hamann, 2008; Verplaetse, 1998). In many cases, it could be said that educators and researchers are not even aware of what they do not know, and research and professional development to inform the work of mainstream teachers is a relatively recent phenomenon (Hamann, 2008). The perspectives of mainstream teachers on ELL inclusion might even be referred to as "markedly absent" (Reeves, 2006, p. 131). The discrepancies between states further add to the overall difficulties experienced by teachers as they attempt to gather resources to support their ELL students.

At the same time, there has been a shift away from "pull-out" programs where ELLs are provided with instructional support outside of mainstream classes by ESL teachers alongside other ELLs, towards "push-in" programs where ELL experts work with ELL students on an ongoing basis to support their participation in mainstream classes (Meskill, 2005). This move toward teachers working with ELLs in their mainstream classes and art educators working with language diverse students in their arts classes suggests an inter-mingling of teachers and ELL students that was not as prevalent in the past when ELL students were educated in ESL classrooms separate from their English-speaking peers. This shift has contributed to a growing need for mainstream teacher education for ELLs. More specifically, there is an enhanced need for professional development to gain knowledge about the intersection of ELL and subject matter instruction, and for new approaches and strategies to inform the work of teachers working with growing numbers of ELL students in their mainstream classes.

Value of Arts Education (Visual Arts, Music, Drama, and Dance) to Support Students' Language Development

The notable absence of professional development for mainstream teachers working with ELL students continues despite the recognized advantages of drawing on arts education as a means of engaging ELL students in language use towards proficiency, and as a means of engaging all students in learning about cultural and linguistic diversity.

Much of the existing research presents an argument for the integration of ELLs into mainstream arts education classes to encourage, and to support, the growth of language in rich, "authentic" contexts to challenge the development of language in varied ways that may occur in real life settings. Spina (2006) found that an arts-based curriculum provides significant cognitive advantages to ESL students by building on cognitive strengths inherent in bilingualism. Furthermore, not only does an arts-based curriculum facilitate the acquisition of English but these gains were made without sacrificing proficiency in the students' first language.

While research highlighting the advantages of arts education to support language development of ELL students is only beginning to take off, the potential of arts education as a means of supporting the language development of all learners has already been acknowledged. Arts-based writing practices in general (Grauer, 2005), and songwriting in particular (Cantor, 2006) have been recognized as inspiring learners through practices that support creativity. There has also been research documenting the generative ground of art making for language development revealed through student writing (Andrzejczak, Trainin, & Poldberg, 2005), and research examining the positive effect of pictures and prompts on the writing skill development of students in primary grades, by providing contextual and background information (Joshua, 2007). Costantino (2007) illustrated the role of image-based, nonlinguistic thinking (e.g., visual thinking, qualitative reasoning, and imagination) in interpreting and expressing understandings of works of art transcending spoken communication.

Given that it takes at least five years for ELLs to catch up to their monolingual English-speaking peers in academic language proficiency (Cummins, 1996), ELL students may fall behind in content area instruction when integration into mainstream classes is postponed until their English language proficiency is at grade level (Valdés, 2001). Furthermore, existing programs and assessment practices designed to support ELLs in their acquisition of English have sometimes been found to limit their academic progress by restricting their access to mainstream classes and exposure to grade-level instruction in courses that will move them towards entry into post-secondary education institutions (Valdés, 2001).

These findings suggest that the potential for linguistic and social gains are significant when ELL students are integrated into mainstream arts classes. Teachers may realize that through arts activities such as music, painting and other expressive mediums, language learners may begin to communicate verbally through free creative play (Goldberg, 2004; 2006). Moreover, "the art classroom may be the first place that immigrant students feel comfortable and capable in school" (Eubanks, 2002, p. 44). This finding highlights the importance of art teachers being able to adapt curricula and pedagogy quickly to accommodate their students, to understand the needs of ESL students, and to develop successful teaching strategies as important components of art teacher preparation.

Finally, the integration of ELL students into mainstream arts education also addresses the role of schooling in supporting the equal and equitable access of all students, regardless of culture, language, ethnicity, or race. Reeves (2004) stated that:

> For equality to be realized in educational opportunity, all students must have access to opportunities that are not just real, but authentic and participatory, and authentic and participatory educational opportunities should not require the normalization of students in white English-speaking monolinguals. Rather than the erasure of difference or the pretension that difference does not matter, schools should work toward a view of educational opportunity that represents their multiplicity. This participatory version of educational opportunity must be one that can be accessed through multiple pathways

that require neither the dissolution of high academic expectations nor the devaluation of non-dominant language and cultures.

(p. 62)

    Realization of the potential of engaging ELL students in arts education as a means of developing language skills further reinforces the argument for their inclusion into school curriculum. As we learn more about the benefits of art education as a means of supporting English language acquisition for ELL students and enhancing awareness and appreciation for diversity, we are also becoming more aware of challenges inherent to learning to design arts education programs to support the arts and language development of students with different academic and language backgrounds. More specifically,

- Eubanks (2002) and Echevarria, Vogt, and Short (2000) acknowledged the importance of adapting the curriculum and instructional approaches, respectively, to accommodate for ELLs.
- Milbrandt (2006) drew attention to the potential of art teacher education models in providing concrete opportunities to attend to differences in students and contexts.
- Henry (1999) argued that pre-service art teachers need to be able to "develop a repertoire of teaching strategies appropriate to the needs of all students" (p. 11), and stated that experience working with students who speak other languages during teacher preparation programs may help to better prepare pre-service teachers for the diversity they are likely to encounter in contemporary classrooms (Henry, 2007).
- Johnson (2002) emphasized that designing an arts-centered teaching and learning context requires attention to the creation of a classroom climate that facilitates intercultural knowledge and dialogue, an environment that supports intercultural sensitivity, awareness, and understanding. Particular attention to the following recommendations were noted:
    - the placement of images, artifacts, and artworks of culturally diverse artists in the classroom;
    - the organization and structure of the classroom such that it facilitates and enhances interaction between students and teachers;
    - an atmosphere that is supportive of the learning styles preferred by students, one that provides opportunities for students to learn through different cognitive styles.

    The existing research featured here provides support for the advantages of incorporating arts education with ESL instruction, and highlights the need for professional development to inform the work of mainstream teachers who work with ELL students.

Value of Arts Education (Visual Arts, Music, Drama, and Dance) to Enhance Access and Learning about Students' Experiences of Diversity

Research examples across the arts also illustrate the inherent potential within the arts for accessing student experience and engaging students in reflection and exploration of the nuances of interaction among individuals of varied backgrounds. The examples attest to the power of the arts as ways of learning. They highlight the potential of the arts as a resource not only to engage ELL students, but all students, in multi-dimensional ways of artistically expressing and sharing experiences to explore the nuances of interactions with peers and others, and as a medium for teachers to learn about these experiences in ways that are meaningful and safe for the students. Johnson (2002), in her work as a visual artist and educator, explores the capacity of the visual arts to translate difference into a common bond, and examines the power of art as a means of contributing to the development of intercultural competence in students. She identifies the following as ways in which an art-centered diversity education may facilitate the development of intercultural competence in students, by:

- exposing students to the voices, images, feelings, ideas, and experiences of diverse cultures;
- providing opportunities to broaden and to enrich students' cultural knowledge of diverse peoples;
- facilitating opportunities for students to communicate and to share knowledge and information across cultures;
- exploring the cultural, historical, psychological, and political roots of students' own identity and examining the complex intersections and interconnections of race, gender, class, ethnicity, religious belief, sexual orientation, ability, and age that comprise the American culture;
- developing critical thinking skills by providing students with activities that will enhance their capacities for imagination, intuition, reasoning, and evaluation, as well as contribute to achieving perspective, constructing and discerning relationships, and gaining self-awareness;
- developing skills to differentiate between "looking" at the surface of art and culture, and "seeing" beneath the surface to discover meaning and values in one's own culture and the culture and art of diverse peoples; and
- exploring the impact of aesthetic norms on our inclination to favor the familiar, and to narrow our vision of others.

Kuster (2006) and Dowdy and Campbell (2008) advocate for a partnership as a means of informing and enriching education about both the arts and culture. They highlight the interconnections between multicultural education and the arts, and elaborate upon ways in which multicultural theories may enrich arts education while art education enhances teaching about diversity. Gustafson (2000) provides specific accounts of ways in which engagement in the arts in diverse, urban settings has provided a glimmer of hope for many students and their families in highly meaningful ways.

Arts and Cognition

The existing work noted, thus far, offers ways in which the arts may provide the link that Garcia (2002) has identified as being critical to connecting the new English learning experiences of ELL students to their prior knowledge, as a means of consolidating their learning. The arts can be powerful vehicles for engaging ELLs and all students in meaning making of different kinds. The multisensory participation required in arts experiences challenges students to actively embrace this task, and allows for the necessary mediation for students to negotiate and to build meaning. The undergirding understanding of cognition as attention to the creative processes integrating thinking and feeling and the mind and the body, is based on a widened and deepened conception of cognition that emerged in the 1950s and early 1960s with what Efland (2004) called the "waning of behaviorism" (p. 71). Key thinkers examining and exploring relationships across the arts and cognition include Dorn (1999), Eisner (2002), Efland (2002), Gardner (2006), and Parsons (1998). There are important differences distinguishing these thinkers' perspectives. Most notably, Efland (2004) distinguishes Eisner's (2002) biological rootedness of the mind in the senses from Gardner's (2006) linking of the mind and associated multiple forms of intelligence to the workings of the brain. Nonetheless, all of these thinkers have in common a strong, shared commitment to the integral place and role of the arts in the overall development of the mind. They collectively insist that the arts ought to be present as important experiences within curricular practices concerning the education of all children. The arts engage mind, body, and spirit and "move minds" (Bresler, 2004), instilling active learning contexts to enhance ELLs' multi-literacy growth through holistic communicative processes.

In the following sections, we present ways in which visual arts, music, drama, and dance, respectively, may contribute to language development and comprehension of ELL students as well as intercultural awareness within all students.

Visual Arts Education

Visual arts education has attended to cultural integrity and personal identity in curriculum development and pedagogical practices for some time (Chalmers, 2002). A survey of the research literature emphasizes art education as a process of cultural construction, informing and enlarging perspectives, fostering greater self-knowledge (Efland, 2002; Irwin & deCosson, 2004), and inciting social action (Bresler, 2007; Eisner & Day, 2004; Stokrocki, 2005). The connective potential of art making through cultural memory, performance, and translation is highlighted in existing work (Irwin, Rogers, & Wan, 1999). More specifically, engagement in visual culture offers a means of gaining historical, social, contextual, and personal perspectives (Duncum, 2005; O'Donoghue, 2007; Tavin, 2005), while learning about varieties of multicultural art respecting diverse artistic cultures promotes a sense of belongingness and greater situated-ness of self in the world (Blocker, 2004).

As we learn more about the processes of implementing visual arts education programs, the potential of the intersection between arts education, language development, and intercultural awareness as learning opportunities becomes more apparent. Grauer and Irwin (2005) offered concrete examples of art-making processes informing and shaping lives while Henry and Costantino (2006) conveyed the potential of the visual arts to act as cultural mediators. Chen (2005) offered details of the impact of an art experience on student learning, by documenting ways in which a summer art experience in Taiwan helped students to bridge cultures and value the significances others bring. Wilson (2004) pointed to multiethnic and multi-arts perspectives as the new narratives for child art study.

Music Education

Music education for ELL students is also a growing field with greater attention being given to music as social practice. The music education field is currently facing a number of considerations (J. R. Barrett, 2007; Elliot, 2005, Goble 2010), with a move oriented toward more comprehensive, social, cognitively challenging, meaningful, embodied, resonant, and diverse musical experiences (Reimer, 2005). Music appreciation's important roles in engaging listening, improvising, and composing across music practices of playing and performance are increasingly understood as deeply connected to personal experience and knowledge in relation to social contexts (M. Barrett, 2007). Music education needs to be accessible to all and reinvest in the work of creativity. Bowman (2005) insists it is the music educator that must enable students "to cherish the risk and responsibility laden world of creative action, or leave it in the mysterious domain of geniuses" (p. 43). And similarly, Cohen (2002) advocates for musical creativity in teachers' practices and Jorgensen (2008) fleshes out the importance of imagination permeating all aspects of music teachers' practices.

The MayDay Group (n.d.) consists of a cross-section of thinkers from all over the world invested in "action for change in music education." The value of music in the general education of all people is voiced through seven action ideals that challenge educators to think about what ought to matter in music education (see http://www.maydaygroup.org/). Taking up this call to action, Frierson-Campbell (2006), in her book, *Teaching Music in the Urban Classroom*, includes practical strategies to support the work of teachers in urban school settings with students of diverse backgrounds in the instruction of music. She advocates for responsive, caring learning contexts that develop music appreciation. More specifically, McAnally (2006) discusses ways in which teachers may motivate urban music students by first ensuring safety, belonging, and confidence in the learning context to foster student willingness to engage in music learning. Mixon (2006) discusses the intricacies of building an instrumental music program stressing the need to build advocates and educate in support of student differences with colleagues and across the greater community. Similarly, Dolamore (2006) examines the challenges of building and supporting a string chorale program in an urban setting, identifying five core values of high standards, diversity of cultural and economic level, student-centered music curriculum, audience attention, and community awareness. Abrahams (2006) offers suggestions on ways in which choral conductors in urban schools may differentiate their instruction in choral rehearsal to support the needs of different students, allowing for greater student interaction and more time for learning through observation and deliberation. Green and Shapiro (2006) present ways in which music from different cultures may be used as a resource to learn about one another as well as about oneself, and Iken (2006) discusses the potential positive impacts of instrumental music education for students in urban school settings. Robinson (2006) examines the nuances of white teachers who are developing music programs in school communities consisting of students of color and the needs for greater learning relevancy for all learners. Within this context, the potentially transformative possibilities of music education for urban school settings consisting of students from diverse backgrounds are beginning to be recognized (Benedict, 2006). And the ways to authentically engage students in music learning are being sought. For example, Blair (2009) and Shively (2002) both look to the relevance of constructivist theorists for informing the teaching and learning practices of music education for learner agency, and Ruthmann (2008) seeks ways for teachers to value and respond to students' musical agency and compositional intent through purposefully designing composing experiences in more inclusive ways.

Drama Education

With respect to drama education, O'Toole and O'Mara (2007) describe the "slow process toward curricular establishment in Western educational systems" (p. 214) but note that struggles to move beyond drama as simply play and/or disruptive thinking are taking place. Curricular connections across drama and literacy skills and multiliteracies are growing alongside a strong body of literature that draws upon the use of drama and theatre as a means of exploring the experiences of youth, gaining insights into self and other(s). Representative examples include:

- Neelands and Goode (2008) purposefully include cultural connections in their handbook of available forms in theatre and drama. In so doing, they emphasize its role in facilitating understandings across differences such as class, gender, sexualities, race, ethnicities, etc.
- Gallagher and Lortie (2007) conducted a long-term drama research project with high school students to examine the social forces of inclusion and exclusion experienced by urban youth. Through this work, they illuminated the intersections of the personal and cultural lives of youth outside of school with the formation of social, academic, and artistic identities within school.

- Mienczakowski (2009) relays the emancipatory potential of theatre, in his examination of the use of theatre in research ethnography and new understandings of the dynamic across audience-performer-researcher.
- Goldstein (2003), in her critical ethnographic study of teaching and learning in a multilingual school, used drama with students as a means of exploring the complexities of relationships and policies pertaining to the language use of Chinese students in a Canadian high school.
- Conrad (2008) explored risky youth experiences through popular theatre, examining student participation to inform the development of a "participatory, performative research method." Similarly, Donmoyer and Yennie-Donmoyer (1995) reflected upon the use of Reader's Theatre as a mode of data collection that engages youth participation and reflection upon their own experiences.
- Finally, Saldana (1999) and Norris (2000) explored the use of research data and the lived experiences of the participants, as performance texts for youth theatre.

As illustrated in the examples presented above, the use of drama to engage students in reflection upon the experiences of others offers all students the opportunity to consider challenges encountered by peers different from themselves. Participation in these drama-based experiences offers students a venue to share personal experiences as well as to learn about the experiences of others in a safe context.

Dance Education

Embodied understandings of teaching and learning across disciplines has emerged as a current area of interest in the work of curriculum theorists (Bresler 2004; Macintyre Latta & Buck, 2008; Springgay, 2008). Dance education provides concrete opportunities for learning through the body and holds many insights for theorists. In particular, the mind-body integration that is critical in this work offers ways to explore nonverbal communication. The following teacher researchers have contributed to this developing area of dance education by identifying and examining issues of importance:

- Anttila (2007) emphasized how children can be agents in dance as active participators and creators.
- Bresler (2004) documented the role of embodiment in what it means to teach and to learn through the significances of multi-sensory engagement.
- Blumenfeld-Jones (1995) looked at the productive learning intersections of curriculum, control, and creativity through dance education.
- Hanna (2008) provided examples revealing dance education as a multisensory language for imagining and learning, with translation transcending oral language.
- Dils (2007) redefined dance appreciation as dance literacy nurtured by moving, observing, writing, discussing, and making dances. The union of thinking, sensing, memory, and experience helps participants to internalize and synthesize learning.
- McCutchen (2006) developed a comprehensive guide for teaching dance as art in education emphasizing the body's power and capacity to communicate through movement.
- Risner (2009) investigated dance education's associations with gender and gender roles, foregrounding how boys who study dance value the embodied creative and expressive qualities, sustaining their interest.
- Snow (2007) relayed dance as a language of accessibility offering a way of knowing, reflecting, and listening, storied through movement.

- Stinson (1997) relayed the power and learning significances of adolescent engagement in dance education.

These examples illustrate ways in which the potential of dance education as a means of engaging students in language as a multisensory experience are beginning to be recognized.

Overall, the arts illustrate the extent to which multiple perspectives are valued by highlighting many ways to live and be in the world. In this way, art making fosters deeper understandings of how students' artworks shape their lives and impact upon the lives of others. Existing research is encouraging in that it supports the partnering of English language acquisition with arts-based curriculum as a means of enhancing learner identity, the development of English language proficiency, cultural sensitivity, and the expression and skills in the arts. Recognition of the enormous potential of this work reinforces the critical need of resources to support teachers as they work to implement arts education for ELLs in mainstream classrooms. This book directly addresses this need for resources with the provision of instructional examples for pre-service and practicing teachers who work with diverse student populations. In the following section, we address the implementation of an arts curriculum for teachers of diverse student populations.

2.5
Enacting an Arts Curriculum

Artistic thinking teaches us to attend to process, to have confidence in learning through process, and to imagine a world that is necessarily interdependent with others. This book assumes artistic thinking is a necessity for all students and, indeed, for the health and survival of our future. Arts teachers need to ensure that the physical and imaginary learning contexts foster artistic thinking, positioning/inviting all students to participate wholly as creators. And, in doing so, learning opportunities demanding student engagement (see the interrelated contributing qualities outlined in section 2.2 of attentiveness, personal involvement, emotional commitment, felt freedom, dialogue and interaction, attunement within inquiry, and enlarged self-knowledge) through artistic processes of making and relating, perceiving and responding, connecting and understanding, will enable ELL students to find the time and space to negotiate and translate understandings, play with and speculate about possibilities. Their participation contributes to enlarging their understandings and communication capacities in the process. Through engagement in this process, ELL students will find respect, affirmation, and appreciation of individual and cultural uniqueness through artistic thinking. As a result, productive learning connections emerge for all the students involved. Teachers' lived understandings of the curriculum as a medium for artistic thinking, with assessment understood as the individual and collective accompaniment on an ongoing basis, are primary tenets permeating such enactment.

Curriculum as Artistic Medium for Teachers and Students

Pinar (2008) traces the roots of the term *curriculum* back to the Latin *currere,* referring to run. In doing so, he draws attention to its verb form. The curriculum, conceived as such, comes to form, as the arts do, "a complex mediation and reconstruction of experience" (Pinar, Reynolds, Slattery, & Taubman, 1995, p. 567). Dewey (1934) points out that, "medium signifies first of all an intermediary" (p. 197). The mediation and reconstruction Pinar (2008) and Pinar et al. (1995) distinguish forms the intermediary or medium, assuming content means little without deliberate student engagement. This is key to the nature of the curriculum as medium. It occurs through students' interactions with things; things typically called curriculum materials. As such, the curriculum becomes:

- a reciprocal medium, involving communicative interchanges among students and other(s). ELL students stand to benefit from such purposeful reciprocity;
- a connective medium, preceding meaningful learning. ELL students stand to benefit through the deliberative processes of seeking purposeful learning connectedness;
- a transformational medium, with self and other(s) changing in the process. ELL students stand to benefit from heightened cognizance of learning growth.

Therefore, positing the nature of the curriculum as a medium for artistic thinking views all curricular materials—programs of studies, curriculum guides, textbooks, clay, paint, newspapers, internet, interactive CDs, films, all technologies, tools, novels, music and musical instruments, imagery, objects, clothing and costumes, lakes, ponds, fields, street corners, and the list could go on—as materials for student engagement. Often, teachers find security in curriculum materials as a comforting source of activities and tasks. But, teachers as artists are curriculum makers, fostering students to be artists as curriculum makers too. So, rather than focusing on the external attributes of curricular materials, the focus of curriculum as medium becomes the process of traversing, through dialoging, and negotiating interactions across students and curriculum materials. To be clear, we are not advocating for an abandonment of artistic technique, skill, and aesthetic appreciation and critique. The teacher/artist across all forms of arts learning needs to approach curricular materials as arts materials. The teacher/artist is a curriculum maker working with techniques, skills, and exercises in appreciation and critique. Visual arts, music, drama, and dance teachers need to ask how curriculum materials can become mediums for learning. They also need to ask how individual students can each contribute to the collective movement of thinking. Answers to these questions will be found through actively negotiating the reciprocity, connectedness, and transformations igniting the movement of thinking, manifesting curriculum as an artistic medium for learning.

Teachers must continually build rich bases of content and pedagogical knowledge, as they perceive their way into, and not away from, curriculum as medium. Demands are made of teachers throughout the curriculum making process—perceiving, selecting, organizing and responding as they negotiate and renegotiate teaching/learning opportunities. We are reminded of the teacher's integral role as we return to Jen Deet's visual arts classroom. Jen is attentive, responding to the particularities that the lesson gathers together and calls forth. What becomes clear to us is the importance of Jen's understandings of herself as a curriculum maker within this context. She plays multiple roles. At times, Jen is providing instructions to the class as a whole. And at other times, she is much less visible, involved with small groups and individuals. A few moments later, Jen is leading an entire class discussion that then dissolves into individual study and consideration. Jen incorporates many non-directive teaching roles along with more authoritative teaching roles. Her teaching practice is an ongoing search for attunement, attending to curriculum as medium for sense making. The form for learning grows and takes shape through the interacting process. This demands everyone's full participation. Jen's actions speak to her willingness to engage in teaching/learning as a creative encounter. We observe that most students acquire this attitude too, as students perceive their way into artistic thinking and not away from it. The medium of curriculum in Jen's classroom forms as it lives through students' experiences. The curriculum is intentionally planned by Jen but, at the same time, is not entirely foreseen nor preconceived, thus, animated with movement and life. It is experienced differently for individuals and the class as a whole, but learning is actively occurring. Learning becomes visible and tangible through valuing personal understandings, interpretations, and expressions; involving the personal construction of meaning alongside relying on dialogue and participation as a means to this sense making; and entailing qualities that have to be felt and lived through as a whole. It is such artistic thinking that offers tremendous possibilities for ELLs working alongside all learners. Drawing students into the depth and complexity of subject matter cultivates a learning community invested in the individual/collective nature of this movement of thinking. So, all engage at different rates, in different ways, in leaps and bounds, and with stops and starts. It is a movement that demands students and teacher attend to process and not solely to end products. The movement is generative, attentive to particularities of context, and open to possibilities. Within artistic thinking lives a worthwhile direction, a medium, for teaching and learning that asks students and teachers to participate through adapting, changing, building, and making meaning together.

Assessment as Artistic Learning's Accompaniment

Artistic thinking relies on ongoing assessment to be an integral part of the process, supporting and enhancing learning (Boughton, 2004; Dorn, Madeja, & Sabol, 2004). Such means of assessment assumes that learning products cannot be separated from learning processes. The contemporary research literature documents relationships between assessment and all learning (e.g., Assessment Reform Group, 1999; Black & William, 1998a, 1998b; Shepard, 2000). And, while we agree that this attention is indeed worthwhile, the focus for teachers and learners often becomes the assessment product, such as a predetermined instrument, rather than the assessment process itself. Consideration needs to be given to the classroom assessment practices needed to actually form and inform learning. As artistic thinking is a creative enterprise, resisting imposed routine, demanding reason alongside ongoing judgments, considering alternatives and relations, and assuming openness and inventiveness, it lends itself to formative assessment practices that prompt and further learning. And, such formative practices are at the heart of Eisner's (2004) lifelong primary concern for educating artistic vision, calling for seeing with potential: "To succeed the artist needs to see, that is, to experience, the qualitative relationships that emerge in his or her work and to make judgments about them" (p. 5). Formative assessment practices offer the reciprocity, connectedness, and transformational potential creating the participatory dynamic integral to artistic thinking.

Activities intended to scaffold learning, enabling teachers and students to see with potential within learning processes—including deliberation, brainstorming and questioning opportunities; charting what one knows, how one knows it, and what one might like to know; concept maps; debates and discussions; experimentation, and speculative exercises—are all examples of formative assessment practices. But, simply using these practices does not ensure educators and their students see the pedagogical implications of such scaffolding or understand their responsive roles in the utilization of formative assessments (Delandshire, 2002; Shepard, 2000; Stake, 2004). Shepard (2000) identifies strategies of *dynamic on-going assessment, prior knowledge, feedback, transfer, explicit criteria, self-assessment, and evaluation of teaching* that need to be closely attended to and vividly portrayed regarding the concrete use of such formative assessment practices in the process of learning. In Part 3 of this book we are cognizant of these formative assessment practices and how they must be worked out in teachers' practical actions alongside their students. We also see much potential within formative assessment practices for making ELL thinking visible and therefore serving as a springboard for teachers to engage and further ELL, and all students', learning. Five key overlapping features that address this potential within formative assessment practices are as follows:

1. Teachers and students attend primarily to the experiences and understandings that are present in learning situations as the necessary place to begin learning. These givens comprise the raw materials of artistic thinking, alive in the students, teacher, and subject matter themselves. Teacher recognition of these raw materials and purposeful search for relationship building, connecting students, teacher, and subject matter is the work of artistic thinking. For ELLs the opportunities to make prior knowledge visible enables communicative abilities and also enables teachers to see much more specifically the sense making of these learners, provide constructive feedback, and envision how they might value and engage these ideas with other learners.

2. Teachers and students seek evidence of learning processes in learning products with a willingness to examine the specifics of individual student understandings and utilize these understandings as the basis to assess and negotiate ongoing reciprocal practices intended to grow student thinking. Teachers and students look for evidence of internalization of concepts, documenting attention to the particularities of what students bring to (and gain from) the specific learning situation, and provide ways for participants to convey the directions and forms their engagement takes. Opportunities to give expression to ELLs' sense-making processes through continual back and forth interactions and deliberations, deepens understandings as ideas are revisited, changed, and adapted in different ways and circumstances, transferring, expanding, and strengthening expressive capacities.

3. Teachers and students recognize that learning can be documented differently and that there is much to be gained for everyone through paying attention to the multiplicity of understandings. Seeking such opportunities for ELLs affirms and values personal experiences and interpretations. In turn, this builds confidence and contributes to building a community of learners that concretely practices how others enable everyone's thinking through dynamic embedded assessment. Teachers and students learn to take pride in validating and enlarging personal thinking, very much facilitated by the collective concern.

4. Teachers and students are comfortable with learning represented through multiple textures of understandings. For ELLs, opportunities to make personal understandings visible in a trusted context that respects and supports this vulnerable learning ground are paramount.

5. Teachers and students attend to the creation of student meaning, engaging in ongoing teacher/student conversations concomitantly on individual and collective bases. Entering into the discourse relationships suggests an organization and form for continued inquiry, way-making in a constant interchange between teachers and students. Opportunities for ELLs to concretely experience that personal sense making contributes to the collective sense making can be empowering and transforming (see Boughton, 2004; Dorn et al., 2004; Macintyre Latta, Buck, & Beckenhauer, 2007; Macintyre Latta, Buck, Leslie-Pelecky, & Carpenter, 2007 for further discussion of formative assessments in relation to teaching and learning).

These five features of formative assessment fold into each other, and ask teachers and students to reorient their readings of artistic learning artifacts from asking, "What is known about predetermined concepts or terms?" to "What does this artifact reveal about the learner and her/his understandings?" Therefore, student expression is seen as articulating particular relational understandings at play, directly connected to the specifics of the learning task. Formative assessment artifacts need to cohere process-product-learner. Teachers must perceive them as the "coherent fabric" (Dewey, 1910/1978, p. 83) expressing the interaction of student and subject matter. Thus, coherence demands an attentive gaze, seeking relationships that sum up and carry forward. Students' tentative understandings need to be validated and prompted. Students' further understandings entail coming to understand differently and with more substance and depth. This cohering process manifests as a repetitive movement. But, it is a repetition that is dynamic and generative rather than simply repeating the same over and over again. Dewey (1934) calls this "esthetic recurrence" (p. 166), distinguishing it from mechanical recurrence. Mechanical recurrence focuses on isolated parts and thus away from the whole. Esthetic recurrence, however, looks to the individuality present in each learning artifact seeking personal learning connections but also reaching out to the relations, associations, and interactions with other individuals and across the whole, expanding and transforming everyone's understandings. Esthetic recurrence involves teachers and students attending to the manifesting relationships rather than specific elements in learning artifacts recurring. These recurrences present themselves in different contexts and with differing learning consequences so that every recurrence is "novel as well as a reminder" (Dewey, 1934, p. 169). Discerning these relationships is the indispensable condition of attending to the artistic thinking processes. This capacity to perceive relationships among parts is what teachers will be asked to interpret and act upon in Part 3 in relation to formative assessment.

Conclusion

We conclude Part 2 by emphasizing that learning processes and products must affirm and manifest the vitality of each other through formative assessment practices. A heightened awareness to building relations between students and subject matter ensues. Teacher confidence to act on this awareness comes from artistic thinking itself. Dewey (1910/1978) notes that "the teacher's own claim to rank as an artist is measured by his [sic] ability to foster the attitude of the artist in those who study with him [sic]" (p. 288). Stirring such artistry in teachers and students is critical to the formative nature of all learning.

Part 3

Teaching the Arts—Visual Arts, Music, Drama, and Dance

Seidel, Tishman, Winner, Hetland, and Palmer (2009) insist that quality arts experiences are "fundamentally tied to what happens in the room where arts learning takes place" and thus are integral to the search for quality arts experiences (p. 87). They further relay this as an important shift of attention toward enabling teachers to create arts learning experiences that are invested in students' learning. Thus, we begin here with the introduction of arts learning experiences in visual arts, music, drama, and dance, drawing from the work of practicing arts teachers.

3.1
Introduction

Jodi Heiser is a practicing visual arts educator in the Ralston School District in Nebraska, located in the Midwest of the USA[1]. Ms. Heiser is committed to providing the highest quality visual arts experiences possible for all of her students. She takes tremendous pride in these efforts and advocates for the necessity of the arts in education. Such advocacy efforts insist that visual arts education is understood by her students, colleagues, and greater community to be demanding of serious study and participatory engagement. One way she models this is through the use of over-arching themes across each teaching year. Her most recent theme is, *Art around the globe: Understanding art as a human capacity.* Her classroom is organized in part as an art museum exhibiting varied art products of specific units of study with accompanying artist statements articulating the learning connections students are making. A large world map reveals the many places, cultures, and experiences these connections have elicited for students with sticky notes, flags, and arrows documenting the tales. Ms. Heiser finds students genuinely interested and invested in these connections. Students seem to value sharing with and learning from others, continually situating themselves in ongoing discussions given their personal backgrounds and experiences. Ms. Heiser describes how a recent immigrant student from China assigned to one of her classes paid close attention on his first day in the classroom to works of art and learning connections regarding the art of his home country. The next class, he arrived with a carved jade necklace of a dragon from China to share with the class. Though his communication efforts were not in fluent English, there was shared interest in the dragon necklace and its connections to the new student's life experiences. Ms. Heiser was able to build on this interest, and a common understanding that cultivated an important opening for continued investment in communication was achieved. This initial point of interest contributed to the new student gaining more confidence as he talked with the class about some of his life experiences in China.

Ms. Heiser's commitment to making room for every student to learn instills respect and responsibility as ways to live and to be in her art classroom. The physical space of her classroom welcomes differences of all kinds and students seem to appreciate the sense of belonging they find. The learning context of the classroom is a contributing factor, in that it feels inviting and comfortable, with students feeling valued and affirmed. An example of the significance of such contexts is a group of Latino students conversing in Spanish as they design peace posters inspired by Pablo Picasso's works of art. They include Spanish words on their peace posters, and translate these words for their peers as they share the designs for critique and discussion. Another student explains how an art assignment caused her to ask questions and to take a stance on a community issue. This student is now taking action beyond the art room, by organizing a fund to support a cause she first became interested in through art work. As colleagues and the greater community attend to the happenings of the art classroom, they can see how artistic thinking translates into diverse and interesting art forms, alongside increasing the strength of student identities and valuing the participation of others, contributing to the overall art experience.

Ms. Heiser is not at all ordinary and, yet, she is representative of most arts teachers we meet. She is passionate about the arts in learning and the learning in the arts. Her students can see and feel this passion within the learning situations their teacher has created. Ms. Heiser also teaches for a school district facing the growing complexities typical of schooling today. Critical issues in Ralston and other Nebraska schools represent a microcosm of issues currently facing schools in other parts of the United States and beyond (Sarroub, 2008). Selected communities throughout Nebraska (and the Midwest) are deemed refugee-designated sites by the U.S. government due to their relatively stable economies and low unemployment rates. As a result, Nebraska has experienced a dramatic increase in immigrant and refugee groups in the past two decades. Public schools, community agencies, childcare centers, and other education settings are charged with the challenging task of educating an increasingly diverse student population. These challenges are coupled with the geographic and economic diversity that are characteristic of Nebraska. Over half the population is located in rural areas and small towns of less than 25,000 residents. The economic status of counties within the state ranges from among the nation's most affluent to its poorest. While Nebraska has historically ranked among the highest achieving states in terms of academic test scores, policy makers are increasingly concerned by the emergence of "the other Nebraska"—more specifically, student populations separated by language, poverty, ethnicity, and race, who are often much less academically successful than the mainstream population.

As a result of demographic complexities, arts educators in Nebraska have found themselves sometimes feeling isolated and continually grappling with ways to invest in students' artistic thinking, as they encounter pre-production through intermediate fluency ELLs alongside diversity of many kinds. The intricacies of challenges teachers face in meeting the needs of ELLs mainstreamed into a regular arts classroom resonate with those of arts teachers, nation-wide and beyond. Ms. Heiser tells us she is not willing to compromise the visual arts content and associated thinking. She seeks ways to ensure that the conditions and practices for teaching and learning in her classroom enable ELLs and all learners to be drawn into the depths and complexities of subject matter. She insists that this is difficult and nuanced work but explains that it is these contingencies that hold the creative vitality and pleasure alive within teaching for herself and for her students.

In Part 3 (Sections 3.2–3.5), we describe learning experiences for middle and high school visual art, music, drama, and dance teachers sharing Ms. Heiser's commitment to the arts in education and education in the arts for all students. We also encourage teachers from other disciplines to look to these arts experiences for potential ways to integrate the arts into a cross-section of content areas and to generate rich learning opportunities for ELLs alongside engaging all learners. The arts experiences offer connections to the principles for ELL instruction and the corresponding stages of ELL performance outlined in Part 1. The experiences are intended to convey: (a) how to teach ELLs English through the arts, and (b) how to teach art, music, drama, and dance content to ELLs who are at different levels of English language proficiency. We chose topics that are adaptable across grade levels and easily modified for differing contexts, multiple levels of understandings, and varied approaches to learning. Currently, content area teachers do not necessarily use their full repertoire of pedagogical practices to wholly engage and support ELLs in (a) and (b). We intend to show with a varied range of examples how (a) and (b) can be achieved through what arts teachers already know and strategies they already use.

This book is about mainstreaming, inclusion, and reaching out to all students. It is also about using strategies that help ELLs to engage fully in an arts curriculum. Each experience will consider how an arts teacher can modify a lesson to meet the needs of ELLs at various stages of language acquisition, emphasizing the important contributions of context, the role of the teacher in the learning context, and the role of curriculum enacted as a medium for artistic sense making. We will convey how information and research expounded in Parts 1 and 2 of the book inform the learning experiences described. The format of the learning experiences is designed to highlight their potential for the cross-fertilization of artistic ideas, support the generation of language learning opportunities, and maximize their usefulness to the reader. As such, the learning experiences are deliberately designed to attend to Doll's (2009) four curricular qualities of richness, relatedness, recursiveness, and rigor. Embedding these qualities within the arts experiences to follow is, of course, dependent on a teacher's enactment, as Thornton (2005) and Seidel et al. (2009), among others, note. But, they are purposefully intended to provide the experiential ground that is "rich and complex for all learners, engaging them on many levels and helping them learn and grow in a variety of ways" (Seidel et al., 2009, p. iv).

The learning experiences are accompanied by related questions and formative assessment practices aligned with the approach to second language acquisition explicated in Part 1 (refer back to Part 1 for the theory underlying this approach). The four levels of this approach—preproduction, early production, speech emergence, and intermediate fluency—are outlined in Table 3.1. Although the teaching strategies overlap across the four levels, they serve as a useful guide for fostering ELL speech emergence. As Cruz, Nutta, O'Brien, Feyton, and Govoni (2003) explain, this approach "equips teachers to deal effectively with ELL students and to select appropriate teaching strategies" (p. 15).

Arts instruction needs to be meaningful at all levels of speech emergence. Of course, this level of engagement is most difficult to achieve at the preproduction level. But, as language can be naturally combined with demonstrating, modeling, viewing, listening, hands-on practice, and the visibility of others as they engage in these practices, arts classrooms hold much potential for ELLs across all levels of speech emergence.

The potential within arts learning for ELLs stems from shared, participatory artistic processes across all forms of artistic thinking. Given that all human beings are fundamentally creative, arts education builds upon this capacity, deepening and enlarging students' capacities for artistic expression (see Part 2.3 for further discussion and references). Artistic processes, common across the arts, that enable students to access opportunities to communicate creative thinking include: making and relating; perceiving and responding; and connecting and understanding, continually imagining anew (Eisner, 2002). These artistic processes are embedded within the arts experiences presented in this part of the book. The artistic processes of making and relating, perceiving

TABLE 3.1 Four levels of speech emergence

	Preproduction	Early production	Speech emergence	Intermediate fluency
ELL linguistic ability	"Silent" period Pointing Responding with movement Following commands Receptive vocabulary up to 500 words	One- or two- word responses Labeling Listing Receptive vocabulary up to 1,000 words Expressive vocabulary 100-500 words.	Short phrases and sentences Comparing and contrasting Descriptions Receptive vocabulary up to 7,000 words Expressive vocabulary 2,000 words	Dialogue Reading academic texts Writing Receptive vocabulary up to 12,000 words Expressive vocabulary 4,000 words
Teaching strategies	Yes/no questions Simplified speech Gestures Visuals Picture books Word walls K-W-L charts Simple cloze activities Realia TPR	Questions that require: yes/no; either/or; two-word response; lists of words; definitions; describing Reader's theater Drama Graphic organizers	How and why questions Modeling Demonstrating Cooperative learning Comprehension checks Alternative assessments Simulations	Brainstorming Journal writing Literary analysis Problem solving Role playing Monologues Storytelling Oral reports Interviewing and applications

Source: Cruz, B. C., & Thornton, S. J. (2009). Teaching social studies to English language learners. In T. Erben, B. C. Cruz, & S. J. Thornton (Eds), Teaching English language learners across the curriculum series. New York: Routledge.

and responding, and connecting and understanding are inter-related and foster opportunities for internalization and integration. They are best developed as being interdependent on one another, "packing and unpacking meaning" (Hanna, 2008, p. 493). Thus, these artistic processes are generative in that they provide a needed space for ELLs to engage language in ways that support, nurture, and develop proficiency in the target language. Artistic processes supporting language development and cultural understanding in students will be interwoven through examples presented here. As such, we emphasize that the strength of these processes lies in their potential to support the creation of a relational space, both artistically as well as linguistically. Using case experiential examples from each of the arts—visual arts, music, drama, and dance—we suggest the lived consequences and significances for ELL learners and all learning through shared artistic processes asking students and teachers to actively engage in making and relating, perceiving and responding, and connecting and understanding, imagining anew. These concrete examples are intended to inform the instruction of specific arts forms, and to transcend arts forms extending beyond to cross-disciplinary teaching/learning connections and possibilities.

We do not regard the learning experiences that follow to be complete lesson plans but, rather, springboards for teachers to adapt to fit the particulars of their students and contexts. As teachers plan, we encourage the use of ELL-sensitive practices. A template developed by Dr. Joyce Nutta that takes into account students' varying levels of language proficiency serves as an excellent guide (Table 3.2). It reminds teachers to plan for language objectives as well as arts learning objectives. Each experience suggests ways to integrate these objectives to maximize learning opportunities.

It is advisable to refresh your understandings of levels of language acquisition discussed in Part 1 before proceeding further into Part 3. Another wonderful resource that offers access for you to hear and see English language development examples can be found on the University of South Florida's online database developed by Erben, Sarieva, and Zoran (see http://esol.coedu.usf.edu/elementary/ELL/credits.html). These examples feature students representing each of the language levels and include annotated audio to enable users' understandings of second language acquisition theory. You will also find speaking, reading, and writing samples of ELLs across differing backgrounds, ages, and grade levels with case studies for further insights. The online databases can be found at:

> http://esol.coedu.usf.edu/elementary/index.htm
> http://esol.coedu.usf.edu/middleschool/index.htm
> http://esol.coedu.usf.edu/highschool/index.htm

"Teaching Tips" are included throughout Part 3 to prompt further teaching ideas and connections, to enable teachers to effectively work with ELLs in arts classrooms.

Teaching Tip

The webcasts at www.colorincolorado.org/webcasts offer an exciting new way to learn about teaching ELLs. Each webcast features a 45-minute video program, which includes recommended readings and suggested discussion questions. A PowerPoint presentation accompanies the video.

Each of the learning experiences included in Part 3 clearly notes the levels of language acquisition met, with some experiences meeting all levels, and others more specifically designed with certain levels of language ability in mind. Ideas offered are intended to serve as springboards

TABLE 3.2. Lesson plan with ELL modifications

Lesson plan	Preproduction	Early production	Speech emergence	Intermediate fluency
Content objective: Should be valid for all language levels				
Language objective: The goal should be one level above students' present level				
Preparation: What materials can you identify to provide comprehensible input for each level?				
Procedures: How are you going to provide comprehensible input in your delivery?				
What strategies will you use?				
Assessment: How are you going to assess at each of the language levels?				
Home-school connection: What activity can you use to connect with all learners' home cultures?				

Source: Cruz, B. C., & Thornton, S. J. (2009). Teaching social studies to English language learners. In T. Erben, B. C. Cruz, & S. J. Thornton (Eds), Teaching english language learners across the curriculum series. New York: Routledge. Modified by B. Cruz and S. Thornton, from a grid created by Dr. Joyce Nutta, University of South Florida.

for arts educators to adapt and to change, fitting the specifics of their ELLs, other student needs, and contexts. In other words, the arts experiences that follow are fodder for readers' imaginations, to re-imagine them in various ways, and for multiple purposes. These arts experiences are intended to extend across multiple class meetings, allowing students to revisit ideas and deepen understandings. They are deliberately designed to be accessible by supporting and engaging a wide range of understandings, and challenging all involved. Critical guidance from arts teachers is assumed. Teacher judgment and expertise is, thus, encouraged as experiences can be modified and are highly dependent on specific circumstances and connections being made to previous learning and directions for further learning. The primary instructional strategies are identified with guiding questions and accompanying formative assessment practices to facilitate teachers' ease of use. National standards for visual arts, music, drama, and dance are embraced across all experiences with room for teachers to align specific local and/or national standards to particular experiences.

Teaching Tip

Check out the suggestions for incorporating the standards into artistic thinking at the following websites:

National Standards for Arts (visual arts, music, drama, and dance) Education (http://artsedge.kennedy-center.org/teach/standards/)

National Standards for Art Education (http://www.arteducators.org/olc/pub/NAEA/advocacy/)

National Standards for Music Education (http://www.menc.org/resources/view/national-standards-for-music-education)

National Standards for Theatre Education (http://www.aate.com/content.asp?contentid=124)

National Standards for Dance Education (http://ndeo.org/content.aspx?page_id=22&club_id=893257&module_id=53060)

The sections that immediately follow (3.2–3.5) outline how the artistic processes of making and relating, perceiving and receiving, and connecting and understanding might unfold in visual arts, music, drama, and dance case experiential examples. Three themes, "Total Control Can Be the Death of a Work", "Responsive Matters of Perception", and "Examined Lives in Relation—A Fusion Dinner Party", form the framework for the cases across all examples. Common generative "texts" also permeate all examples. We use text to refer to resources and materials incorporated into the content as generative vehicles for student engagement. These texts are purposefully selected to position students to interact and to deliberate with them and each other. These texts are intended to serve as dialogical mediums to substantively engage students with the content, assuming varying levels of understandings. These texts can be used to introduce the content, but alternatively, these texts can also be used at multiple points in a lesson to revisit ideas, to deepen students' thinking, and to reorient the direction for learning. Generative activities of this kind might be among those supported by Gee (2000, see Jensen, 2008) as a move toward pedagogical principles that allow for a shift toward multimodal literacy through the inclusion and use of multiple means of presenting and generating new understandings of content materials. Cantor (2006) might refer to these as an example of a "fearless innovation," an arts-based experience that inspires learners through the provision of support for creativity. Finally, Brown and Pleydell (2005) argue for the use of varied sensory experiences in the process of new language development to support the creation of multiple imprints on the learner's memory. The common themes and generative texts running through the visual arts, music, drama, and dance case examples are intended to prompt cross-fertilization across disciplines and interests, suggesting multiple ways that educators and their students might work with these ideas, and extending far beyond the confines of the case examples. Therefore, readers are encouraged to read across the visual arts, music, drama, and dance case examples to foster arts experiences and insights for the particulars of their classrooms.

The incorporation of arts journals (either electronically, traditionally, or a combination of both means) is encouraged throughout as a formative assessment vehicle to document students' sense-making in process. Journal entries are purposefully incorporated into arts experiences to serve as indicators of individual and collective understandings so teachers and students can determine directions for furthering everyone's learning. Thus, the journal's intent is to enable students to make their thinking more visible and to allow teachers and others access to this thinking. Journal entries should also be shared with peers to promote dialogue and interaction as deemed fitting by students and teachers. Student responses to each other's journal entries can be incorporated as is fitting for each learning context. Teachers must deliberately incorporate time to attend to and to respond to each journal on a regular basis, modeling the necessary seriousness and commitment for all students. In these ways, the journals become windows into student thinking, providing the ground for initiating, developing, and continuing the learning conversation with students on an individual and group basis. See Table 3.3 for students' expectations for teachers' responses to journal entries.

Through such continuous engagement, ELL students will find the time and space to negotiate and translate understandings requiring speculation and conjecturing about possibilities, enlarging their understandings and communication capacities in the process. Teachers will also gain greater access to all students' work and thinking, and thoughtfully translate this information purposefully into future learning efforts.

Teaching Tip

Arts journal entries need to be dated and organized chronologically. Expectations for entries should be kept simple, and openness to multiple ways to document specific entries is assumed. Students must understand that their teacher will read their journals regularly as a means of communication about student thinking and learning. Teachers must respond back to students in their journals in an ongoing expected interchange. These responses can be brief and in the margins of the journal. It is the regular feedback from teachers that cultivates the needed context for furthering learning. Arts journals, incorporated as such, provide important access to students' learning, enabling teachers to get to know ELLs (and all students) and to grow their thinking. Given that ELLs at varying levels of proficiency will likely engage in this activity differentially, it is important to acknowledge the proficiency of the student by providing support for students to participate actively. For example, teachers may offer lower level ELLs the option of verbally recording their journal entries into a digital recorder or having their journal entry dictated to a teacher, teaching assistant, or a classmate. Students at lower levels of proficiency might also be provided with support in the form of journal entries that are partially written such that they are able to complete the entry by filling in missing words.

As part of the process of developing the ideas presented in this book, a group of 10 practicing arts teachers met regularly and generated the experiences that follow. It was an enjoyable and invigorating exercise, and we hope the ideas translate into engaging, productive learning

TABLE 3.3: Students' expectations for responsive journaling by teachers

- Teachers will read and respond to my journal regularly.
- Teachers will expect me to formulate ideas and attempt to develop these ideas as thoughtfully as I can.
- Teachers will address my questions and offer ideas to extend and challenge my thinking.
- Teachers understand that journal assignments will vary in length and in the ways I may present my thinking.

opportunities for all teachers who use this book. The arts case examples that follow include specific activities that some of the participating teachers have found to be very effective in their classrooms. Although these teachers are individually credited throughout, all ideas were extended through our collective conversations. The resulting arts experiences chronicle the many connections each participant contributed. All participating teachers recognized the potential of these ideas to inform their future practices in classrooms, and expressed appreciation for the integrated nature of the ideas. We look forward to hearing about the many ways these ideas will be shaped, the directions these ideas will take, and the many connections that teachers and their students will make. We very much encourage all teachers to "try things out, reflect, hypothesize, test, play with things" (Noddings, 2006, p. 284). That is the primary intent of the arts case examples for the remainder of Part 3. See Table 3.4 for key questions to ask when structuring such experiences.

TABLE 3.4. Structuring arts learning experiences

Have you attempted to engage students' background knowledge and previous learning experiences?

Have you enabled students to make connections to previous learning pushing forward into new learning?

Have you provided enough structure so that students can see purpose in the lesson and focus on the relevant tasks?

Have you made expectations clear?

Have you provided concrete opportunities for active learning?

Have you provided ways for students to revisit ideas and enlarge their understandings?

Have you created time for students to express their thinking, time for reflection, and time for input from others and reformulation of ideas?

Have you allowed students to be the creators of their own meanings, looking back and looking ahead, formulating their own questions, and setting up their own inquiries, applying and furthering their own understandings?

3.2
Visual Arts Experiences to Engage ELLs Alongside All Learners

Greene (1995) talks about teaching for "openings," as finding "ways of being dialogical in relation to the texts" (p. 116) engaged together. These openings then become paths to pursue further learning. Visual arts experiences focusing on making and relating, perceiving and responding, and connecting and understanding through attention to these processes, open learning paths for students to follow and to negotiate. These paths position students to attend to the creating process from within, always imagining anew. Making and relating, perceiving and responding, and connecting and understanding in visual arts experiences involves manipulating different media toward varying expressive ends. The forms that emerge are a reflection of the visual, aural, emotional, and kinetic judgments made during the process. Such attention puts one in ongoing dialogue with content, demanding alertness and questioning. Such attention, however, necessitates openness to possibilities by both students and the teacher. It is a dialogic process that is inquiry-guided, and responsive to the features encountered and the relations that transpire. Making and relating, perceiving and responding, and connecting and understanding involve students playing with the parts-to-whole relationship in order to achieve an artistic form. A trust in the process is needed. Students make decisions within the making and relating, perceiving and responding, and connecting and understanding process. Finding ways to value this process of thinking from within enables students to better articulate the meaning making processes. As a result, a heightened cognizance of this process in self and others ensues, with students engaged in analyzing and assessing increasingly complex visual relationships. Participation in these concrete activities creates time for ELLs to dwell and to attend closely to their thinking, negotiating and articulating understandings. Thus, openings are created to deliberately foster artistic thinking, gaining content knowledge alongside language and social growth in ELLs through their engagement in conversation about a topic that might not otherwise arise among ELL students due to cultural mores or perceived challenges of interactions about abstract concepts. Teachers may draw upon the generative nature of the topic to differentiate instruction as well as explore the theme in ways beyond what might develop in the context of a regular school day, and engage students in continued interchange as they draw upon knowledge from diverse cultures, experiences, and understandings to inform the conversation.

Visual Arts, Theme I: "Total Control Can Be the Death of a Work"

Generative Text

Rivers and Tides is a film documenting the elemental sculptural forms in the making by Scottish artist Andy Goldsworthy (2004). The imagery of the film gives physical and material expression to his statement, "Total control can be the death of a work" (Scene 4), providing a vivid and tangible portrayal of artistic thinking in process.

About the Text

The DVD of *Rivers and Tides* (Goldsworthy, 2004) can be viewed in its entirety, or teachers may choose to introduce Goldsworthy's elemental sculptures though specific scenes that are accessible on the DVD in short segments. It is 90 minutes in length but the scenes offer a way for students to watch one or more excerpts of about 15 minutes each. Alternatively (or in addition), images of Goldsworthy's sculptural forms are available in Abram books (http://www.abramsbooks.com/#) and on the web, see (http://www.morning-earth.org/ARTISTNATURALISTS/AN_Goldsworthy. html), (http://www.flickr.com/groups/andygoldsworthy/pool/), and google images (http:// images.google.com/imghp?hl=en&tab=wi).

Scene 4 of the DVD, *Rivers and Tides, Feelings of Uncertainty* (Goldsworthy, 2004), depicts the artist seeking his artistic materials as he negotiates his way about the landscape. Viewers come to see how his sculptural forms are site-specific. Viewers increasingly see how Goldsworthy's knowings of the site and the particulars of the land are a necessity. The scene depicts Goldsworthy watching, listening, touching, and attending to colors, textures, shapes, patterns, weather conditions, and existing features of the terrain, gaining knowledge of the land. Control is never imposed. Goldsworthy meets and works with tensions, resistance, and discord as inherent within the process, expected along the way, and as being productive to his art making.

Case Example # 1: Site-Specific Art's Relations to Place

Before students enter the classroom, take an empty picture frame and hang it in the art room so that it frames a space on the wall that otherwise would not draw much attention. Begin class with a discussion about the features and qualities that are framed and the relations created and suggested. Compile a list of these findings for all to see. Repeat this exercise again, framing another space on the art room walls, ceiling, or floor. Collectively (or in small groups) discuss how these framed spaces can, or cannot, be understood as art forms.

Provide extra support for ELL students whose language is at earlier levels of development (and other students for whom these activities may be novel) by introducing the idea of items and surfaces being influenced by inherent features and qualities. Give some examples of features and qualities of the framed item/surface by noting them to the students and pointing them out. Ask students questions to guide their observations—What colors do you see? What kind of mood do the colors express? How about the size of the item/surface? How would the item/surface look if it were smaller or larger? Compare the size of one aspect of the item/surface with another. Do you think the colors make the size of the item/surface seem larger or smaller? How about the shape of the item/surface? Would it look differently if this corner were rounded or if one side had a rough edge? How about these lines? Do they make the item look softer? Harder? Sharper? How do the lines shape your ideas about the texture of the item/surface? And so on. Encourage other students to contribute their ideas about the features and qualities, and to identify them in the item/surface. Frame another item/surface in the classroom, and model the activity again. Encourage students to work together in pairs or in small groups to identify features and qualities of items and surfaces in the classroom and then give students the opportunity to present their findings to the rest of the class. ELL students may also benefit from the use of graphic organizers, labels, visuals, and modified teacher talk that might include redundancies, simplifications, repetitions, circumlocutions, and flash card translations of key terms. Then, give students the following instructions:

1. In 30 minutes or less, locate five to ten examples of found art using a digital camera lens as a frame rather than the picture frame that provided preliminary practice.
2. Take a digital picture of each example.
3. Bring examples of found art back to the art class to share.

Set the parameters for locations to search and remind students of the necessary focused use of time. Distribute digital cameras and have students embark on the task. As students return to the classroom, have each one upload 2–3 images to create a PowerPoint slide show of everyone's found art images. The PowerPoint slide show provides an opportunity for each student's found art to be highlighted and discussed. Guessing the specific locations of each example of found art will intrigue students. Attention should be given to the similarities and differences across all the images. ELL students will be encouraged to draw upon technology resources to assist them in the making and presentation of the PowerPoint presentation. For example, students will be made aware of functions such as language settings on the computer that can be changed to the home language used by the ELL to provide scaffolding in English language learning, and to enhance engagement and participation through enhanced access to English and possibilities for translation of ideas into English from the home language.

In addition to using modified sentence structures to ease comprehension of beginning ELL students, it is important for teachers not to assume that teacher talk with accommodations will be easily understood by ELL students. In fact, it is critical for teachers to constantly identify ways of contextualizing language used, and to develop alternative visual, textual, oral, auditory, etc. ways of presenting materials.

Following this exercise, introduce the Scottish artist, Andy Goldsworthy. Have students watch Scene 4 from the DVD, *Rivers and Tides* (2004), paying particular attention to what Goldsworthy might mean by his statement, "Total control can be the death of a work." Have this statement written on the board for all to refer to. After watching Scene 4, have students address the following questions in their art journals and then in small groups relay what they saw and heard.

Journal Entry

- What words describe Goldsworthy's attitude and engagement?
- How does Goldsworthy find and respond to his artistic materials? In what ways do the materials speak?
- What is the role of the surrounding environment to Goldsworthy's work?
- Why is place of importance?
- How does Goldsworthy treat the materials and respond as the work is created?

. . . .

Ways of accommodating students at different levels of English proficiency

Using some large rocks as actual examples for students to physically examine, engage ELLs as follows:

Preproduction: Pointing to a rock's characteristics and naming them.
Early Production: Comparing and contrasting the qualities of specific rock examples.
Speech Emergence: Describing the environment Goldsworthy works within and naming the conditions and materials that become his art forms.
Intermediate Fluency: Articulating the relations found in the environment to Goldsworthy's art forms and his making processes.

Teachers may accommodate for the many nuances and different levels of proficiency of ELL students by using differentiated instructional techniques in the context of a lesson.

Facilitate these small group discussions as necessary. Attend to important insights that groups generate. Bring these insights to a large group discussion that synthesizes the reverence Goldsworthy (2004) demonstrates for what is found and encountered in the environment, the integral role of play and his acknowledgment that something is already at play, and his responsive thinking movement that is animated by the spirit of place. Have students state in a written sentence or two in their journals what they believe Goldsworthy means by his insistence that total control can be the death of a work. Place a copy of each student's statement inside/outside/around the framed space on the art room wall.

Teaching Tip

Sequence content to anticipate misunderstandings and challenges by providing concrete exercises that allow ELLs preliminary access to the main ideas and intents of the primary learning tasks or projects. These efforts will enable ELLs' understandings and therefore learning success.

Journal Entry

Control can be the death of an artwork in that . . .

. . . .

Ways of accommodating students at different levels of English proficiency

Preproduction: Freeze some of the frames of the DVD, point to various items seen in the frames, and say the words out loud. Have students repeat the words as a means of building familiarity with the words and building vocabulary.

Early Production: Use the same photos from the frames of the DVD, and have students write out the vocabulary on index cards. Have students make drawings and use words in their home language to help them to remember the words for future use.

Speech Emergence: Describe what is seen in one of the frames to a classmate, and have the classmate guess which frame they are speaking about. Encourage the classmate to ask questions to verify that they have chosen the correct frame. Write the phrase, "control can be the death of an artwork," on the board and have students look up the words. Discuss and have students draw what this phrase might mean.

Intermediate Fluency: Write the phrase, "control can be the death of an artwork," on the board and have students look up the words. Discuss what this phrase might mean. Provide some examples of instances in your own life when this phrase might have been appropriate, and encourage students to articulate examples in their own lives when they believe that "control can be/ was the death of an artwork". Recount what they saw in the DVD as being examples of the phrase.

Discuss with students how the contemporary art works of Andy Goldsworthy are situated within the issues raised by other land artists and their continued concerns for the perceived artificiality and commercialization of art at the end of the 1960s in America. Exponents of land art rejected the museum as the setting of artistic activity and developed monumental landscape projects that were beyond the reach of the commercial art market. Assign students (individually or in small groups) to examine the art forms of a cross-section of the artists engaged in this work currently and in the past (see some suggestions in the teaching tip to follow). Students will note in their art journals one representative image they each find of such work and a brief description of it and the artist.

Journal Entry

Title of image:
Description of image:
Artist background:
Additional information:

• •

Ways of accommodating students at different levels of English proficiency

Preproduction: Write in title of image, and choose from two adjectives which of the adjectives would be better suited to the image. Encourage students to write out the words on cards, to include pictures, and to refer to their home language as strategies to help them remember the new words.

Early Production: Write in title of image, and choose adjectives from a list of four adjectives those which would best describe their perceptions of the image. Encourage students to include pictures, and to refer to their home language as strategies to help them remember the new words. Include additional facts that they find about the image.

Speech Emergence: Write in title of image, and write sentences including adjectives that they feel would best describe their perceptions of the image. Encourage students to conduct mini interviews with classmates and teachers in the school community, and to write what others say about the image in their journals. Encourage students to share what they have found by reporting these findings.

Intermediate Fluency: Write in title of image, and write sentences including adjectives that students feel would best describe their perceptions of the image. Encourage students to include additional facts that they find about the image and the background information about the artist, and to share any additional information they find with a small group of fellow-students.

Teaching Tip

Many ELL students (particularly those at the Level 1 and 2 stages) may have difficulty participating in some of these activities without language support. Scaffold the participation of ELL students by providing vocabulary support in the form of definition lists, word walls, or small group meetings to go over new language, and guided reading and writing to support efforts to read about and to write about topics that other students in class are studying. Encourage ELL students to keep the vocabulary lists with them and to refer to the lists as needed as they work on activities with their peers. These lists might also be helpful for non-ELL students, particularly when the language for an activity is different from what they might use in everyday situations.

Teaching Tip

Representative American land artists include Carl Andre, Alice Aycock, Betty Beaumont, Eberhard Bosslet, Lucien den Arend, Agnes Denes, Jan Dibbets, Harvey Fite, Michael Heizer, Junichi Kakizaki, Richard Long, Walter de Maria, Robert Morris, David Nash, Dennis Oppenheim, John Pfahl, Andrew Rogers, Robert Smithson, Alan Sonfist, James Turrell, Nils Udo, Bill Vazan, and Elisabeth Wierzbicka Wela.

Non-American land artists include the British Chris Drury, Andy Goldsworthy, Richard Long, and the Australian Andrew Rogers.

Discuss the intents of land artists and their primary concerns through the images of their works. Ask each student (or small groups of students) to share each selected artist's image and convey a description of it. Discuss the role of a photo record associated with these works and connect back to the documentation of Goldsworthy's sculpting process. Have students then move to a site-specific setting for their own land art creations. The site could be on school grounds where a temporary fence could be used to create the necessary space. Snow can be a wonderful medium. The sites, of course, could take many other forms and places. If no site is available, sand can be utilized in trays or boxes. Have students frame their own working space on site and then complete an observational record of the features, inhabitants, and relations mediated by and shaped within the space. This observational data should be documented in students' art journals.

Journal Entry

Features observed:
Inhabitants observed:
Relations observed:

· ·

Ways of accommodating students at different levels of English proficiency

Preproduction: Present a pre-recorded video clip of a site that can be shown numerous times to students. Point out features the first time the video is shown, and have students say them, and write them out on index cards to add to their personal dictionary.

Early Production: Present the pre-recorded video clip of a site to students. Have them identify features they see the first time. Then replay the video to see whether they are able to remember the ones they identified the first time, as well as identify new features. Have the students write out the words on index cards to add to their personal dictionary.

Speech Emergence: Present the pre-recorded video clip of a site to students. Have students identify features they see the first time, and then dictate to a teacher or another student their observations about inhabitants observed.

> Intermediate Fluency: Have students identify features they see the first time, and then replay the video to see whether they are able to identify additional features they missed the first time. Have the ELL students describe to a teacher or another student their observations about inhabitants and relations observed while the teacher or student writes what the student is saying.

Ask students to share their site observational records with a partner and compare findings. Have students then begin to work with what their site suggests for creating an art form. If they bring in outside materials to incorporate into their works, they must be able to articulate why they found them to be necessary and fitting. The primary goal is to use what is given in each site as the artistic materials to engage and construct with responsively. The work is to be completed within a set time of approximately one class period. A photo record of the completed art forms and ongoing documentation of nature's reclaiming of the site of each form will be displayed in the art room in student-chronicled timelines. Tracking these timelines, attending to the specific changes, will serve as a further vehicle to prompt continued class discussion of control and process in art making. Relations to environmental art may emerge, and if so, have students check out environmental artists, such as a group of Finnish artists (http://www.environmentalart.net/natur/index.htm) and the Green Museum comprising artists concerned with connections across the arts and ecology (http://www.greenmuseum.org/archive_index.php).

Summation

Visual arts case example #1 asks students to attend closely to meaning-making processes through the theme "Total Control can be the Death of a Work." A film documenting the artistic processes of Scottish sculptor Andy Goldsworthy (2004) serves as a generative responsive text. In the visual arts experience, students gain understandings of site-specific art and its relation to place and participants alongside visual art terminology. Students are engaged in concretely navigating personal meanings of the creative process and its found expressive qualities, communicating these qualities through their own artwork. Opportunities to acknowledge and respect individual visual art approaches and interpretations are key, positioning students to work interactively and collaboratively throughout, purposefully listening to, attending to, and gaining ideas from others. ELL students discern encoding and decoding word relationships and construct understandings through associations across oral and visual communication alongside varied interactive and collaborative interchanges.

Additional Selected Resources

Film/DVD

Goldsworthy, A. (2004). *Rivers and tides: Working with time*, DVD. Directed by Thomas Riedelsheimer. Mediopolis Films.

PBS. (2001). Art 21—Art in the twenty-first century, Season 1, Place (http://www.pbs.org/art21/series/seasonone/place.html).

PBS. (2007). Art 21—Art in the twenty-first century, Season 4, Ecology (http://www.pbs.org/art21/series/seasonfour/ecology.html).

Books

Andrews, A. (Ed.). (2006). *Land art: A cultural ecology handbook.* London: RSA.

Beardsley, J. (1998). *Earthworks and beyond: Contemporary art in the landscape.* New York: Abbeville.

Boettger, S. (2002). *Earthworks: Art and the landscape of the sixties.* Los Angeles: University of California Press.

Grande, J. K. (2004). *Art nature dialogues: Interviews with environmental artists.* New York: State University of New York Press.

Kaye, N. (2000). *Site specific art: Performance, place, and documentation.* New York: Routledge.

Kwon, M. (2004). *One place after another: Site-specific art and locational identity.* Cambridge: MIT Press.

Lailach, M. (2007). *Land art: The earth as canvas.* Hohenzollernring: Taschen.

Natural World Museum. (2007). *Art in action: Nature, creativity, and our collective future.* San Rafael, CA: Earth Aware.

Sonfist, A. (2004). *Nature—The end of art: Environmental landscapes.* Florence, Italy: Gli Ori.

Internet Sites

Earth Artists, an interdisciplinary network of artists, focused on ecology (http://www.earthartists.org/)

Earth Day activities (http://eelink.net/pages/EE+Activities+-+Earth+Day)

Eco-art (http://avant-guardians.com/environmentalities.html)

Ecological restoration initiatives (http://www.ecologicalrestoration.info/gallery3.asp)

Environmental artist Josh Keyes (http://www.joshkeyes.net/)

Middle Eastern environmental artist Ahmad Nadalian (http://www.wwwebart.com/nadalian/index.htm)

Monumental land art provides access to imagery of well-known large earthworks (http://www.daringdesigns.com/earthworks.htm)

Our Earth as Art (http://earthasart.gsfc.nasa.gov/index.htm)

Visual Arts, Theme II: "Responsive Matters of Perception"

Generative Text

A slam poem, *Love*, is authored and performed by a high school student, Lucas Hines[1], giving expression to the young man's ongoing considerations about what it means to be in love. Access the performance of the slam poem at: http://cehs.unl.edu/mlatta/poem.htm.

About the Text

The student's poem on love is situated within a quickly evolving movement of slam poetry occurring over the last 25 years. Poetry found this new outlet in 1984 through Marc Smith, a Chicago construction worker experimenting in front of an audience with forms for poetry readings. Slam has since moved from the margins to mainstream, and from a local to global phenomena, revitalizing poetry. A slam is a poetry competition where poets perform original work alone or in teams with audience engagement as judges. These poems represent diverse topics and purposes, including comedic, dramatic, personal, and political. A slam poet aims for audience connection. And, with this emphasis on performance, slam poets share their identity, their convictions, and their embedded understandings through spoken word, body language, and stage presence. Poetry slams are now found everywhere in the United States and have expanded to other countries including Australia, Austria, Bosnia-Herzegovina, Canada, the Czech Republic, Denmark, France, Germany, Macedonia, Nepal, the Netherlands, New Zealand, Singapore, South Korea, Sweden, Switzerland, and the United Kingdom.

Visual Arts Case Example # 2: Impressions in the Making

Engage students in an opening exercise that entails distinguishing between recognizing and seeing art works using John Dewey's (1934) distinction that looks beyond categorization (see Teaching Tip p. 80). To do so, provide students with a series of images of art works across sculptures, drawings, paintings, prints, and mixed media, and ask them to account for what they recognize in terms of media, style, technique, and categorization of the works, and then what they see that transcends these considerations. Students should record this information in their visual arts journals as the images are viewed.

Journal Entry

Recognition/Seeing

1.
2.
3.
4.

. . . .

Ways of accommodating students at different levels of English proficiency

Preproduction: Point to the colors (or shapes) of objects in the works of art, and have students repeat after you. Once it seems that most of the students are able to identify and say the colors, point to the colors and have the students say them and relay the feelings elicited.

Early Production: Describe the colors and shape of an item seen in one of the works of art, and have students identify the work you are describing. Switch roles and have students take turns describing the works of art while their peers guess the work they are referring to.

Speech Emergence: Model the process of examining each of the works of art, and describe features of each in detail, referring to color, shape, images, style, technique, etc.

Intermediate Fluency: Discuss the difference between 'seeing' and 'recognizing', and elaborate upon how this difference might be described for each of the works. Have students work together to discuss the differences as they refer to the works of art.

Teaching Tip

John Dewey in his 1934 text, *Art As Experience*, offers a useful way to distinguish between recognizing and seeing. He describes recognition as entailing categorizing, labeling, and separating while seeing entails connections to past and present with implications for the future. Have students think about and discuss how recognizing limits what one sees in others and in situations. Turn to local and global examples of race, culture, ableism, etc.

Have students discuss their findings in small groups, classifying the kinds of information that recognizing and seeing depend upon, and the relatedness that exists across them. Facilitate these small group discussions as necessary, and listen for ideas to bring to the large group discussion. Bring synthesis to a large group discussion by asking students to share where "seeing" ideas come from as they attend to each artwork. As this conversation unfolds, emphasize that seeing is always about interpreting, interdependent with the experiences and understandings (the matter) we each bring to any situation. Students will gradually understand that cognizance of these matters is the responsive work of perceiving.

Introduce the generative text of the slam poem by asking whether students have participated and/or performed as a slam poet. Ask about whether they have performed and/or participated in any other kind of performance. Encourage students to elaborate and discuss what is involved for the performer and for members of the audience. Evolve this discussion to include some of the history and traditions that slam poetry embraces that align with past art movements, such as Dada emphasizing playful spontaneity and contemporary performance art in which the actions of an individual or a group at a particular place and time constitute the work.

Ask students to attend the high school student's slam poem performance on love. Immediately following the viewing, have students write responsive words in their visual arts journals. Involve students in playing with these words so that the responsive page on their journal depicts words that carry meanings via the line quality, size, and other features, utilizing traditional writing tools or software generating word clouds via wordle at: http://www.wordle.net/.

Teaching Tip

ELLs will gain visible access to a cross-section of terms as the thematic word clouds are shared. Encourage all students to explain their choices in relation to the slam poem and thus enable ELLs (and other students) to enlarge and deepen language acquisition and comprehension.

Journal Entry

This word cloud was made using wordle: http://www.wordle.net/

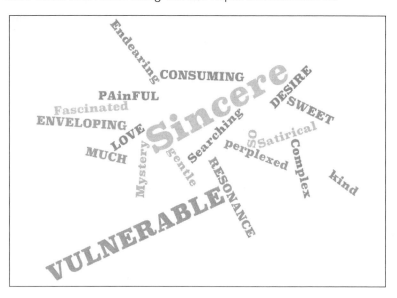

Ways of accommodating students at different levels of English proficiency

Preproduction: Identify words that describe a work of art, and then write each out on a whiteboard as you talk about the work. Have each student enter one of the descriptive words into the wordle program online to collectively create a word cloud. Have students add the word cloud to their personal dictionaries.

Early Production: Identify words that describe a work of art, and then write each out on a whiteboard as you talk about the work. Have each student enter one of the descriptive words into the wordle program online to collectively create a word cloud. Have students select another work of art, and work in groups to complete a second word cloud. Add both clouds to their personal dictionaries.

Speech Emergence: Work together to make a word cloud describing a work of art. Have students work in pairs to make their own word cloud, and then present the word cloud to their classmates.

Intermediate Fluency: Work together to make a word cloud of words describing a work of art. Have students work in pairs to make their own word cloud, and then present the word cloud to their classmates. Encourage students to play with size and color as a means of emphasizing some ideas over others, and then to describe these nuances to classmates when they present the word cloud.

Combine all of the words and phrases across class members to generate a collective response or word cloud. Together examine the collective response to consider the multiple emotions and personal understandings represented. Discuss what makes the poem's topic universal, considering love's relation to the human condition, transcending time, culture, and tradition. Invite students to share societal ideas about love across cultures, ethnicities, and across different time periods, as they have heard referenced by parents, teachers, and other members of North American societies as well as individuals from ethnic communities. Have students write about these ideas about love in their journals. Encourage them to elaborate upon societal expectations and mores about courting practices as well, and then to share what they have written with classmates in the form of a small group discussion.

Teaching Tip

Incorporate ways to engage ELL students in sharing knowledge about their place of birth and/or their ethnic cultures and communities if they express an interest or a desire to do so. Not only would this practice provide ELL students with opportunities to use their developing English to express lived experiences, it would also be an appropriate way of drawing upon this cultural expertise to enrich the curriculum of all students.

Have each student select one of their responsive words or phrases to the love poem, and locate visual art works that convey a similar impression. Students can access images at the J. Paul Getty Museum "explore art" site (http://www.getty.edu/art/gettyguide/), and collect and save these works of art from the Getty collection on their own bookmarked page. Involve students in sharing their bookmarked page with three to five other students, with each guessing the original word or phrase eliciting the collection. Have students record in their visual art journals the contributing elements and relations that the artists each use to convey a particular impression. As students record this information in their journals, walk over and visit with students on a one-to-one or small group basis to ascertain students' understandings and prompt and challenge their thinking.

Teaching Tip

Purposefully connect students' previous thinking to present thinking as you work on a one-to-one or small group basis. Students' thinking will be affirmed, and the role of the journals as a medium for continued conversation and embedded ongoing assessment opportunities are more fully understood by students. Continuous journaling practices will greatly enable ELLs by making their thinking visible and enhancing communication possibilities.

Journal Entry

Permeating Impression

	Artist's name	Title of work	Elements and relations
1.			
2.			
3.			

• •

Ways of accommodating students at different levels of English proficiency

Preproduction: Prepare small printouts of the works of art, and ask students to identify key elements that they like or dislike, and why. Have students write out the artist's name and the title of the work on one side of an index card, and then glue the completed print out pictures on to the other side of the index card. Encourage them to use the cards as flash cards, to increase independence in learning to make language associations.

Early Production: Have students write out the artist's name, and the title of the work, along with an image of the work printed up from the computer. Students can glue the image on one side of an index card, and the name of the artist as well as the title on the other side of the card, to help them converse about works of art.

Speech Emergence: Have students write out the name of the artist and the title of the work in their journal entries, and then talk about the elements and relations together to generate ideas.

Intermediate Fluency: Have students write out the name of the artist and the title of the work in their journal entries, and then talk about the elements and relations together to generate ideas. Have students work with two other classmates to complete the 'Elements and relations' column of their journal entry. Make an effort to pair students who are strong in English and in art, with those who are beginning English learners or who are not as knowledgeable in art.

Bring individual and small group findings to an entire class forum that considers how the love slam poem generated a conversation that engaged individual and collective thinking, enlarging everyone's perspectives and understandings.

Teaching Tip

Deliberately model the individual/collective thinking process by referring to particular student's ideas as prompting everyone's thinking. Ensure inclusion of all students over time as you attend to ways to value what each student brings to the collective sense making.

Teaching Tip

Teachers need to ask themselves, once they have created a lesson plan, "What aspect of English will my (ELL) students come out of this lesson knowing or being able to use?" Doing so will help teachers to focus the development of their lesson plans, as well as serve as a reminder to constantly assess their students' progress.

Revisit the slam poem as a class, looking for the elements of innuendo, playfulness, and satire. Discuss how visual artists might also use these elements and why. Have students research visual art examples reflecting social commentary, politics, and humor.

Teaching Tip

The J. Paul Getty Museum site has a past collection, *A Light Touch: Exploring Humor in Drawing*, which offers some historical examples of humor. See: http://www.getty.edu/art/exhibitions/light_touch/

In their visual art journals, have students note how selected artists powerfully use innuendo, playfulness, and satire to convey their passionate ideas. Students can sketch and combine words to describe their findings. Have students look further for local contemporary visual artists that are committed to social commentary, and examine their work for the elements that contribute to the overall artistic impression.

Journal Entry

Artist:
Artwork:
How does the artwork speak?

· ·

Ways of accommodating students at different levels of English proficiency

Preproduction: Prepare small printouts of the works of art. Alongside students, color elements that tell or reveal significances to them. Have students write out the artist's name, and the title of the work on one side of an index card, and then glue the completed print out pictures on to the other side of the index card. Encourage them to use the cards as flash cards, to increase independence in learning by discussing the works.

Early Production: Have students write out the artist's name, and the title of the work, along with an image of the work printed up from the computer. Students can glue the image on one side of an index card, and the name of the artist as well as the title on the other side of the card, to use as a platform for discussing the works of art with others.

Speech Emergence: Have students write out the name of the artist and the title of the work in their journal entries, and then discuss with the students ways in which the artist conveys messages through the style and techniques used in their work. Use this exercise as a way to provide opportunities for students to incorporate descriptive language. Begin with structures that students already use in their language and help them to identify ways of making their language more descriptive. Also discuss with them how different situations and contexts may call for the use of different kinds of language, and identify possible situations when descriptive language might be appropriate.

Intermediate Fluency: Students write out the name of the artist and the title of the work in their journal entries, and then discuss with the students ways in which the artist conveys messages through the style and techniques used in their work. Have students work with two other classmates to respond to the question about how the artwork speaks to them. Make an effort to pair students who are strong in English and in art, with those who are beginning English learners or who are not as knowledgeable in art. Another possibility might be to group together students from the same cultural background who are stronger in English and art with those who are at the beginning stages. Use this exercise as a way to provide opportunities for students to incorporate descriptive language. Begin with structures that students already use in their language and help them to identify ways of making their language more descriptive. Also discuss with them how different situations and contexts may call for the use of different kinds of language, and identify possible situations when descriptive language might be appropriate.

Compile a large visible list of the artistic devices employed across all examples accessed by students. Talk specifically about the role of lighting in art works as one specific artistic device. In pairs, have students access one of the past exhibitions of the J. Paul Getty Museum, *Radiant Darkness: The Art of Nocturnal Light* (http://www.getty.edu/art/exhibitions/radiant_darkness/).

Students can zoom in on the images, enlarge them, and read some background information on the artworks included in this exhibition that incorporate divine light, candlelight, firelight, and moonlight. Discuss as a class how the dominant impressions of the images from the exhibit convey a strong permeating impression similar to the slam poem's unifying emphasis on love.

Teaching Tip

ELLs' comprehension is enabled through the continued recursive movement of the lesson, going between images and written texts, alongside expected management and instructional routines. Look for evidence of synthesis and internalization of ideas in journals and prompt further connections. To further assist ELLs in participation in class discussions, it is often helpful to structure routines for discussion and to constantly re-employ these routines such that they learn what is expected of them. This may provide ELLs with a routinized structure in which to participate.

Discuss the important role of lighting in the art form of photography. Once again have students return to the J. Paul Getty Museum website but this time looking at the past exhibit of photographs created by Sigmar Polke, one of the most influential artists working in post-war Germany (http://www.getty.edu/art/exhibitions/polke/).

Individually and collectively have students consider Polke's use of juxtaposed images, multiple exposures, extreme close-ups, and under- and over-exposures, documenting his experimentation with photography.

Teaching Tip

ELLs' comprehension is enabled through the continued recursive movement of the lesson, going between images and written texts, alongside expected management and instructional routines. Look for evidence of synthesis and internalization of ideas in journals and prompt further connections.

Have students each bring a hat of their choosing to class. Relocate the class to the school theatre or a similar space that is spacious, quiet, and easily manipulated with light. The theatre's stage fosters imaginative engagement as an audience is envisioned and the performative expectation is felt. Give students time to roam and to gain a lived sense of the stage. Follow this by having students each leave their hats, arranged as they determine to be fitting, in their own space on the stage floor. With someone operating the light board, have students experience from the audience perspective how lighting changes the stage and the appearance of the hats. Provide access to cameras and have students return to the stage to take a series of photographs of their hat with the light that presents itself as the lighting continues to be altered. As students begin to consider tone, contract, shadow, and camera settings as they construct their photographs, have them also consider the role of different angles, perspectives, and distances. Back in the classroom, have students chronicle their photographing experiences in their visual art journals as they examine their photographs. Diagrams, maps, and drawings chronicling the experience can be used with or without words. (This photographic activity is adapted from the teaching practices of Chris Maly[2] at Lincoln High School in Nebraska).

Teaching Tip

Purposefully engage ELLs in pointing out the changes in their hat photographs so that questions can be asked and greater clarification can be reached to enable students to use this information to chronicle their photographic experience in their journals. Photonovela provides the technological capacity to support and foster language growth via photos. See: http://www.photonovela.com/instructions.php.

Journal Entry

How did lighting change what you saw in the hat? Chronicle the specific observations.

How did lighting cause you to respond in different ways? Chronicle the ways you adapted. What was unexpected? How did ideas emerge and develop?

· ·

Ways of accommodating students at different levels of English proficiency

Preproduction: Bring a hat to place on the stage, and take a photograph of the hat, with different kinds of lighting on the hat. Line the photos up, and have the students identify differences between the photos. State that the differences are due to differences in the lighting on the hat.

Early Production: Bring a hat to place on the stage, and take a photograph of the hat, with different kinds of lighting on the hat. Line the photos up and have students identify differences between the photos. State that the differences are due to differences in lighting on the hat. Have students bring their own hats to place on the stage, and repeat the same activity.

Speech Emergence: After students have taken photographs of their hats on the stage, encourage them to identify differences, and to talk about these differences in terms of lighting, in groups of three or four.

Intermediate Fluency: After students have taken photographs of their hats on the stage, encourage them to identify differences, and to talk about these differences in groups of three in terms of lighting. Guide students to discuss ways in which the lighting contributed to them responding in different ways.

Ask students to display five of their photographs of their hat for all to see. Facilitate a class discussion that considers each student's hat series and reflects on the students' discoveries as the hats were photographed and what each student tried to achieve across the varying conditions. Determine how features work together to create the strongest compositional impression. Conclude by discussing how the hat photographs can reflect a time, place, identity, culture, and mood much like slam poetry and social commentary art. For continued conversation, create a photomontage using one image from each student's hat series to display outside the classroom. A wordle "word cloud" could also be generated with students contributing words from their journal entry chronicling the specifics of their hat photographic experience to be displayed alongside the photomontage.

Summation

Visual arts case example #2 explores the intersections of personal experience, culture, and the unique qualities of the particular artistic media through the theme "Responsive Matters of Perception." A high school student shares his slam poem on love as a generative responsive text. A slam poem is a form of self-expression intended to leave an audience with a clear indication of a specific time, place, and culture. Slam poets perform their original pieces for others under time constraints, so communicating in ways that hold attention and convey personal convictions becomes the aim. The relations and connections created across the poet and the audience reveals insights into community issues and considerations. In the visual arts experience, students are asked to consider how art imagery is developed for a variety of purposes, and discuss their own intentions and the intentions of others in creating art objects. Students also consider the various sources of ideas and influences affecting arts imagery, and investigate and analyze how meaning is embedded in works of art. ELL students are positioned to find expressive language for imagery that intersects with aspects common and distinct across languages and cultures. ELL students will benefit from exploring multiple interpretations, gaining greater cognitive flexibility in the process of addressing English language ambiguities through seeking personal resonance.

Additional Selected Resources

Films—Slam Poetry

Delvin, P. (2004). *SlamNation—New educational edition*. Slammin' Entertainment. New York: New York Video Group.
Levin, M. (1998). *Slam*. Vancouver: Lion's Gate. Rated: R
Simmons, R. (2009). *Brave new voices*. Home Box Office, Time Warner Entertainment Company.

Films—Visual Art

PBS. (2007). Art 21—Art in the twenty-first century, Season 4, Romance (http://www.pbs.org/art21/series/seasonfour/romance.html).

Books

Algarin, M., & Holman, B. (1994). *Aloud: Voices from the Nuyorican Poet's Café*. New York: Henry Holt & Co.
Eleveld, M. (2003). *The spoken word revolution: Slam, HipHop, and the poetry of a new generation*. Bel Air, CA: Sourcebooks MediaFusion.
Glazner, G. M. (2000). *Poetry slam*. San Francisco: Manic D Press.
Hermsen, T. (2009). *Poetry of place: Helping students write their worlds*. Urbana, IL: NCTE.

Internet Sites

Slam Poetry
A Brief Guide to Slam Poetry (http://www.poets.org/viewmedia.php/prmMID/5672)
Contexts, Poets, Background Information on Brave New Voices (http://www.hbo.com/bravenewvoices/crew/index.html)
Living Word Project (http://livingwordproject.org/lwp_description.html)

Poetry Slam Incorporated (http://www.poetryslam.com/)
Saul Williams (http://www.poets.org/viewmedia.php/prmMID/5813)
The Nuyorican Poet's Café (http://www.nuyorican.org/)
Youth Speaks (http://youthspeaks.org/word/)

Art

Photography exhibit, *Where we live: Photographs of America from the Berman Collection* (http://www.getty.edu/education/for_college/berman_project.html)

Time Magazine photos (http://www.time.com/time/today-in-pictures)

Art Image Banks

Museum of Modern Art (MoMA) Guides for Educators (http://www.moma.org/modernteachers/guides.html)

Museum of Modern Art (MoMA) Lessons for Educators (http://www.moma.org/modernteachers/lessons.php)

Museum of Modern Art (MoMA) Prints and Illustrated Books (http://www.moma.org/collection/browse_results.php?criteria=O%3ADE%3AI%3A2|G%3AHI%3AE%3A1|A%3AHO%3AE%3A1&page_number=1&template_id=6&sort_order=1)

New York Public Library Digital Gallery—Arts & Literature (http://digitalgallery.nypl.org/nypldigital/explore/dgexplore.cfm?topic=arts)

The World Wide Web Virtual Library (http://www.chart.ac.uk/vlib/images.html)

Visual Arts Data Service—An online resource for visual arts (http://www.vads.ac.uk/)

Visual Arts, Theme III: "Examined Lives in Relation—A Fusion Dinner Party"

Generative Text

Filmmaker Astra Taylor converses with some of today's most influential thinkers within selected contexts, fitting to each one. The thinking each shares is chronicled in her film, *Examined Life*, Zeitgeist Films, 2008. The film reveals the multiple perspectives from which the world can be seen and lived. In this way, the film becomes the text to re-imagine the perspectives gained and to stage a fusion dinner party. A fusion dinner party intentionally invites meetings across differences. Envisioning, creating, and enacting a fusion dinner party serves as a further generative vehicle for a visual arts experience.

About the text

Viewing the entire DVD of the film, *Examined Life* (Taylor, 2008), gives the fullest access to Astra Taylor's intent to invite and to foster conversation on what it means to live right. Alternatively, or in addition, short overviews of the film can be accessed at: http://www.nfb.ca/film/examined-life-trailer/ and http://www3.nfb.ca/webextension/examined-life/

The persistent questions throughout the film are: how does one live the examined life and why should we invest in doing so? The film reveals that the ways we answer these questions are shaped by our various worldviews. Thus, the film confronts and asks viewers to challenge the values, assumptions, and beliefs connected to one's worldview. The cross-section of contemporary philosophers, including Cornel West, Avital Ronell, Peter Singer, Kwarne Anthony Appiah, Martha Nussbaum, Michael Hardt, Slavoj Zizek, Judith Butler, and Sunaura Taylor, provide intersecting and opposing ideas that engage viewers and invite them to join the conversation. In doing so, viewers will find themselves interacting and deliberating about the film's surfacing issues of courage, responsibility, ethics, power, privilege, indifference, social justice, gender, ableism, and politics, and what this might entail for notions of citizenry and democracy in an increasingly globalized world.

A fusion dinner party is purposefully designed and enacted to embrace differences in perspectives (Lorraine Cockle[3], teacher in Calgary, Alberta, Canada offers the idea of the dinner party, which we adapted). The film, *Examined Life* (Taylor, 2008), serves as a generative text providing the "food for thought" from multiple perspectives for the fusion dinner table settings and conversation. Akin to a fusion menu at a restaurant that brings the table ware, cooking, and traditions of several cultures together, the fusion dinner conversation is intended to surface differences, seek insights from one another, and prompt new connections and possibilities. Students are asked to examine their own lives in relation to selected historical and contemporary artists. In doing so, the relations across the arts and society will be foregrounded for all to connect and grow understandings.

Teaching Tip

Have students create operative guides for the Fusion Dinner Party conversations through:

- Thinking of the best group conversations they have been involved in. What things happened that made these work?
- Thinking of the worst group conversations they have been involved in. What went wrong and why?
- Listening for common themes, shared experiences, and features of conversations that seem important to all.
- Drafting guidelines for conversations that comprise the operative modes everyone agrees to practice.

Related ideas and more insights for fostering student participation in discussions are further expanded by Stephen D. Brookfield in his book, *The Skillful Teacher: On Technique, Trust, and Responsiveness in the Classroom*, published in 2006 by Jossey-Bass, San Francisco.

Teaching Tip

Students resist participating in conversations or class discussions if:

- fearful of looking foolish;
- feeling unprepared;
- trust is lacking in the teaching/learning situation;
- student thinking is not welcomed;
- teachers do all the talking;
- talking is not valued;
- disinterested in subject matter; and
- classmates resist and curtail participation of others.

These factors are a concern for all students, and may be heightened in ELL students, especially if they were academically competent in their home countries and are now struggling with building their English language skills from a basic level of proficiency.

Visual Arts Case Example # 3: Women Artists in Conversation

Initiate this experience by referring to Socrates' statement, "The unexamined life is not worth living" (Plato, Apology 38, in Taylor, 2003). Contextualize the discussion, providing some background on the significances of Socrates as a major Greek classical philosopher who continues to influence thinking today. Note that because of previous political associations with an earlier regime, the Athenian democracy put Socrates on trial, charging him with undermining state religion and corrupting young people. The speech he offered in his own defense, as reported in Plato's Apologhma (*Apology*), provides reminders of the central features of Socrates' approach to philosophy and its relation to practical life. Even after the jury has convicted Socrates, he refuses to accept exile from Athens or a commitment to silence as his penalty. He insists that public discussion of the great issues of life and virtue is a necessary part of any valuable human life. Socrates chooses death over abandoning philosophy, and the jury is glad to grant him that wish. Some students will have knowledge of the Socratic method, so involve them in sharing what they know about it and/or have directly experienced. Clarify for all students the emphasis on questioning to continually challenge oneself to consider the values and assumptions undergirding personal beliefs. Introduce the notion of a personal worldview as embedded in everyone's actions and thinking. Ask students to provide some examples from their lives in relation to the larger community. The political and social issues of contemporary life offer many illustrations at local and global levels. Explain to students that all of us take actions daily but that our cognizance of our worldview is not always present. Return to Socrates' statement asking everyone to question and to examine our lives as we live them.

Use the questionnaire (see Table 3.5) that asks students to consider their personal worldview. Have students complete the seven question questionnaire individually first and then move to small groups to share and discuss their responses, loosely modeling the Socratic method of questioning to prompt conversation. Emphasize that there is not a right or wrong answer to these questions and that the purpose is to generate a thoughtful conversation. Show Figure 3.1 (see p. 93) as an

TABLE 3.5. Personal worldview questionnaire

For each of the following statements, circle the response that best reflects your opinion on the issue.

1. View of human nature: People are naturally good.	Strongly disagree	Disagree	Neutral	Agree	Strongly agree
2. View of the good life: People should just try to have fun by pursuing leisure activities and not worry about work and accomplishing great things.	Strongly disagree	Disagree	Neutral	Agree	Strongly agree
3. Equality with others: All humans are equal, and no one should get special privileges.	Strongly disagree	Disagree	Neutral	Agree	Strongly agree
4. Responsibilities to others: We should care for others first, and worry about ourselves second.	Strongly disagree	Disagree	Neutral	Agree	Strongly agree
5. Relationship between the individual and the state: Individual rights are more important than the rights of society.	Strongly disagree	Disagree	Neutral	Agree	Strongly agree
6. Relationship of humans with nature: Preserving nature is more important than using its resources to support human activity.	Strongly disagree	Disagree	Neutral	Agree	Strongly agree
7. Sources of ethical wisdom: The truth about what is morally right or wrong is found in an objective authority and not in each individual's personal beliefs.	Strongly disagree	Disagree	Neutral	Agree	Strongly agree

Note: To modify for varying English language skills, read aloud and discuss the seven issues in small groups with an appointed leader.

Source: Alberta Education, Copyright © 2007, *Personal Worldview Questionnaire*, http://www.learnalberta.ca/content/sssm/html/exploringworldview_sm.html. Reproduced with Permission.

image for students to keep in mind as they engage in conversation. The aim is to have students practice greater cognizance of genuine attention to others and the role of others in the formulation of our own ideas. Participation thus asks all involved to listen and to attend closely to each other, and to bring these insights and perspectives back to bear on their own thinking. Foster and support these small group conversations as necessary. Allow enough time for students to see and to feel the participatory thinking involved. Bring the conversation to the large group by taking a close look at the seven questions on the questionnaire and asking students where they see evidence of these questions in our lives today. Examples are easily accessed through turning to the current political scene, evidencing tensions concerning privilege, poverty, and power.

Teaching Tip

Consider supporting the participation of ELL students who may not yet have the skills to complete the questionnaire individually by having students work in pairs or in small groups. In general, alternate group work, pair work, and individual work so that students have experience with different kinds of work situations, and different people. Remind students that you will be grouping them in different ways deliberately with the intention of providing them different kinds of experiences, and that part of their work in school is learning to work with many kinds of people who have learning needs and styles different from their own.

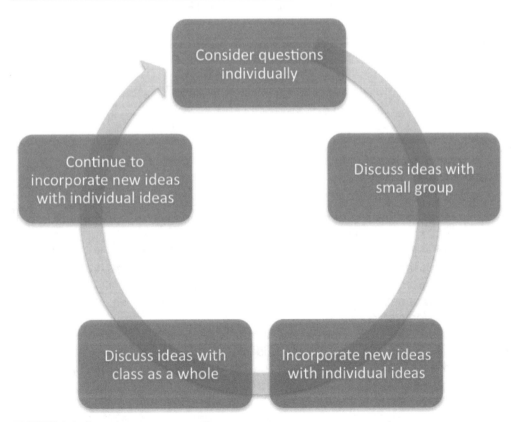

FIGURE 3.1: Learning as conversation.

Introduce the film *Examined Life* (Taylor, 2008), and the filmmaker's project in conversation with contemporary thinkers. Astra Taylor, the filmmaker, purposefully selects particular thinkers to engage them in conversation about their worldviews. Have students each research one of the contemporary thinkers to provide a brief overview of the people to be met via the film. Identify each thinker and have students contribute their findings so that a composite description is recorded and visible for each thinker. See listing of thinkers on p. 49.

Teaching Tip

Create a series of large silhouette drawings of Auguste Rodin's famous sculpture, *The Thinker*. As one of the most parodied works of art in the world, *Le Penseur* has inspired people worldwide for over 100 years. Often used as an icon of philosophy and the mental disciplines, it seems fitting to display these silhouettes in the classroom, and to use them to record the information on each contemporary thinker showcased in the film *Examined Life*.

View the film *Examined Life* (Taylor, 2008) as a class. It is 88 minutes long. To accommodate available class time, the film is easily divided into shorter viewing segments. Excerpts from the film could also serve as catalytic material without necessarily viewing the entire film. Following the viewing of the film, have students respond in their visual art journals, considering what they each think the film conveys about what it means to live the examined life.

Journal Entry

Develop an interpretive rendering in narrative, poem, or image form (or combination) in response to the film *Examined Life*.

. . . .

Ways of accommodating students at different levels of English proficiency

Preproduction: Have students watch the film and identify as many vocabulary words and ideas as possible. Encourage the students to write the words and ideas in any language they are able to, and then go back after watching the film to translate the words and ideas into English with the help of a dictionary or a classmate, if they need assistance. Have students write some words on to index cards to add to their personal dictionaries. Prepare the script of the video for ELLs to read along with video when attending to it and for reference later.

Early Production and Speech Emergence: Write the title of the film *Examined Life* on the board, and explain to the students that they will be watching the film. Discuss what they think the film might be about, based on the title. Provide students with a summary with some of the main ideas, and encourage students to watch for these ideas as they are watching the film. Have students work in groups with others who are native (or native-like) English speakers

> to prepare a poster for the film, as a means of exposing students to a wider range of English language.
>
> Intermediate Fluency: Provide a summary with a few main ideas and encourage students to watch for ideas as they are watching the film. Ask students about what they saw in the film, encouraging them to elaborate upon details. Have students work in groups with others who are native (or native-like) English speakers to prepare a brief narrative of the film, and then present the piece of work to a group of other students or teachers in the school.

Have students follow up on their renderings in their visual art journals by selecting one of the following:

- An article to read on the film in the New York Times (http://www.nytimes.com/2009/02/22/movies/22lim.html?_r=1);
- An interview transcript with Astra Taylor to read (http://www.ifc.com/news/2009/02/interview-astra-taylor-on-exam.php);
- An interview to listen to with Astra Taylor on NPR's *On Point* (http://www.onpointradio.org/2009/03/living-philosophy-the-examined-life).

Students should respond further in their visual arts journals to what additional insights they gained from the selected source.

Journal Entry

Identify information source:
Additional insights gained:

• •

Ways of accommodating students at different levels of English proficiency

Preproduction: Model the process of picking out new vocabulary words from an abbreviated version of one of the written sources, and write them out on to index cards. Have students pick out ten new words, and write them out on to index cards for their personal dictionary.

Early Production: Have students identify ten new vocabulary words from an abbreviated version of one of the written sources. Show students how to look up words in a dictionary. Have them write the words out on to index cards, along with the definitions, and examples of how they might use the word, to add to their personal dictionary.

Speech Emergence: Have students identify five new facts from one of the sources listed above. Have students work with other students who also examined the same source, and share these facts to form a composite of the source featured.

Intermediate Fluency: Have students identify five new facts from one of the sources listed above. Have students work with other students who also examined the same source, and share these facts to form a composite of the source featured. Present the composite to the rest of the class, and respond to questions others may have.

Involve students in small group conversations with each participant noting their favorite thinker from the film and why. The journal responses should enable these conversations. Bring synthesis to the conversations thus far by reiterating how philosophy generates conversation, and how the film generates conversation; then consider how all art works might generate conversation. Mention that Rodin's sculpture of *The Thinker* continues to do so. After this discussion, look back at a significant art installation in the 1970s by Judy Chicago that deliberately incited/invited conversation.

Introduce Judy Chicago's room-sized installation of *The Dinner Party* as an icon significantly marking women's achievements and valuing women's experiences in history throughout Western civilization. The following websites provide images from the permanent home of the installation in the Elizabeth A. Sacker Center for Feminist Art at the Brooklyn Museum of Art in New York City:

> http://www.brooklynmuseum.org/eascfa/dinner_party/home.php
> http://www.newyorkcool.com/archives/2007/May/arts-judychicago.htm

Share the images with students as the installation is discussed. Situate the installation in the execution time of the late 1970s with Chicago completing the project in 1979. Have students ascertain her intents to counter the erasure of women's achievements and why this installation is considered iconic. Include information on how the installation was viewed by more than one million people, travelling to 16 exhibition sites in six countries. Emphasize that as more and more people participated, the conversation grew, becoming increasingly multiplex. Ask students to describe what they see in the images of the installation. Have them consider the triangular shape of the table and other symbolism found in the piece as a whole. Additionally, students should know that a basic description includes 39 place settings with each conveying the contributions of a notable woman from history across the fields of science, medicine, literature, the arts, mythology, government, religion, and women's rights.

Individually have students select one of the photographed table settings from the website noted above and examine it closely. In their visual art journals, students should sketch the specific table setting and record the name of the woman, where and when she lived, her accomplishments, and any other information found to be personally significant, using the Internet as a research tool. Additionally, have students surmise the worldview of the woman selected for study, and situate her within the context of her time and place.

Journal Entry

Identify one woman artist at Chicago's Dinner Party:
Sketch the associated place setting:
Details and accomplishments:

· ·

Ways of accommodating students at different levels of English proficiency

Preproduction: Sketch a place setting, and label each of the items of the place setting. Discuss the kinds of foods each item may be used for, and engage students in conversation about how the items may differ, depending on the culture, society, and the kinds of foods a person is eating.

Early Production: Introduce phrases that might be helpful if the students were invited to a dinner party. Have students practice these phrases in pairs. Set up a table for students to use for practicing.

Speech Emergence: Introduce phrases that might be helpful if the students were invited to a dinner party. Have students practice these phrases in a group of five or six classmates, role playing as if they were at a dinner party themselves.

Intermediate Fluency: Introduce phrases that might be helpful if the students were invited to a dinner party. Have students practice these phrases in a group of five or six classmates, as if they were at a dinner party themselves. Brainstorm possible responses beforehand, but also encourage students to elaborate.

Once this task is completed, have students share their findings to gain greater insights into some of the women of Judy Chicago's multimedia project. Ask students to consider the project in relation to worldviews that might be held by Judy Chicago and each woman represented, and how these views were (and continue to be) challenged, disrupted, and confronted through the installation.

Engage students in collectively naming visual artists that come to mind. Compile a list for everyone to see. Typically male artists such as Picasso, van Gogh, da Vinci, Michelangelo, Rembrandt, Wyeth, and Warhol, dominate a listing. Note the absence of (or few) women, and the need for greater attention and awareness of women artists and also artists of color, both Eastern and Western, various sexual orientations, and including alternative ways of working and non-traditional art forms. Relate this exercise to Chicago's intents for *The Dinner Party*.

Plan for a dinner party as simple as providing pizza and salad to more complex endeavors asking students to prepare an authentic dish appropriate to the selected artist. Provide each student with a formal invitation (see Table 3.6) to continue Chicago's commitment to women's contributions and experiences throughout history by participating in a fusion dinner party. Define fusion and set the specific purposes for this dinner party to fit the teaching and learning needs of your classroom. For example, women artists might be contemporary and local, or of a particular culture or time period. Or, confine students' selections to women artists in a particular media or reflecting a particular issue. The formal invitation will set the theme for the fusion dinner party and outline the parameters for participation. Creating a dinner table with settings fitting for the gathering artists is the overall goal. The following website provides links to a cross-section of women artists, and could be used to identify a theme for the fusion dinner party: http://www. princetonol.com/groups/iad/links/artists.html. The following website offers a timeline of notable women from multiple disciplines and interests through history prior to 1599 to contemporary times: http://frank.mtsu.edu/~kmiddlet/history/women/wh-timeline.html

The visual arts journals should be used to chronicle the selection of the artist and the evolution of the place setting designs reflecting the theme and the selected artist's worldview.

Teaching Tip

Clarify new vocabulary and tasks by selecting words that will be understood alongside demonstrating, modeling, viewing, hands-on practice, and visibility of peers' work, providing multiple examples and points of entry to illustrate key points.

TABLE 3.6. Sample visual arts invitation, fusion dinner party

---

YOU ARE INVITED to a FUSION DINNER PARTY

Who— [NAME OF SCHOOL[VISUAL ARTS CLASS is hosting the dinner and all students in the class are invited.

Where— Art room.

Why— To continue the conversation Judy Chicago started, foregrounding women's contributions throughout history to our world.

When— [The date and the time of the dinner.]

What— [Specific instructions regarding the place setting design expectations.]

How— Materials and resources to inform the traditions a selected artist draws upon and the influences present in her art, expanding everyone's thinking and artistic practices.

Journal Entry

Chronicle your progress as you move through steps one to four of the design project:

1. Select a woman artist, given the theme of the party.
2. Document what this woman contributes to the theme.
3. Design and create a table setting, purposefully selecting media, features, and symbols conveying your interpretation of the selected women artists' contributions and experiences reflecting her worldview.
4. The multi-media table setting should include a plate, utensils, glass/cup, napkin, and place mat (noting the name of the artist) with everything fitting within a 14 inch square space.

· ·

Ways of accommodating students at different levels of English proficiency

Preproduction and Early Production: Explain to students that they will be learning about a woman artist by gathering as much information about her as possible, and then pretending to be her at a dinner party. Select one artist together as a group, and work with the students to gather information about her. Identify important information that needs to be found, and help the students to find this information from sources that have been shortened and simplified to suit their language skills. Guide the process of making the table setting for this artist, making sure to include utensils, plates, a napkin, etc. Have them include the information they find on the place setting so that they are able to refer to it during the dinner party. Role-play their participation in the dinner party to introduce the idea, and to give students the opportunity to learn the language

they might need. Work with ELL students to write or to read through prepared scripts that will support their participation in this activity. Place these
students into different groups when it is time to do the détente dinner party,
so that each may use the information gathered at their table.

Speech Emergence and Intermediate Fluency: Explain to students that they will
be learning about a woman artist by gathering as much information about
her as possible, and then pretending to be her at a dinner party. Have students work together in small groups to gather information about the artist.
Provide guidance about the kinds of information they might need (in the form
of guiding questions or points that they need to address), to help students
to focus their search. Also encourage them to share information they have
found as they work through the activity. Model what students need to do
to prepare the place setting, and have them write the information about
the artist on the place mat so that they are able to refer to it during the
role-play segment of the activity. Role-play their participation in the dinner
party to introduce the idea, and to give students the opportunity to learn the
language they might need during the dinner party. Place these students into
different groups when it is time to do the détente dinner party, so that each
may use the information gathered at their own table.

Support the development of these design ideas by setting regular conference dates to check
on the progress of locating and documenting a selected woman artist. Individual or small group
accountability is fostered through such efforts, and a particular student's thinking can be showcased as examples for and/or used to prompt others in their designing process. Take photographs
of everyone's work in progress to chronicle the design process in stages and post for all to see.
This effort will further motivate students while also valuing the designing experiences of each
student, and providing a catalyst for new ideas, materials, and approaches to the project. Keep this
attention to process as visible as possible to encourage students to be cognizant of it in their own
work, and in the work of their peers. Work in small groups and on an individual basis to point out
common considerations and differences as students create their table settings.

As the date for the dinner party gets close, collectively decide on the shape of the dinner table
given the theme and the student-generated ideas and designs. Use the similarities and differences
arising as the project develops to inform these decisions. It may or may not seem important to
predetermine the placement of each attendee at the party. Involve students in making these calls
throughout the evolution of the project. And, get students to invest in setting the operating guidelines for the détente dinner party conversation to ensure common understandings, expectations,
and modes for action.

Teaching Tip

Signs of creative behavior include increased animation and physical involvement,
challenging ideas, astute observations and questions, and willingness to search for
alternatives and explore new possibilities.

On the day of the fusion dinner party, arrange the large table as predetermined to house all table settings and a chair for each attendee. Cover the table with butcher paper to create a unified surface. Have students place their settings on the table accordingly. Before students take a seat at the table, have students circle the table to carefully examine each place setting and identify each artist. Have them also look at the table design as a whole, looking for the collective statement(s) generated. Once again, record each setting and the entire table in a photographic record to be displayed later. Invite everyone to sit down at their place setting and share food, enjoying and celebrating the accomplishments of the women artists gathered via the table settings and the efforts of the entire class. Conclude with each student sharing their insights about the woman artist they highlighted through the table setting design. Following these accounts, have students relay the common pervading themes and important differences, distinguish concerns and influences, and ascertain the roles of others in the lives of these woman artists. Ask each student as a contemporary artist to select one of the topics generated from the fusion dinner party conversation to develop a responsive artwork that reflects their personal statement. For example, these might include statements about justice, liberation, respect, and care. The details and expectations of this response piece should fit the curricular needs of your students and the given contexts and it may create opportunities to look at the work of local artists.

Teaching Tip

Emphasize with students that though a project may come to an end, you expect them to revisit the ideas, as all new learning is informed by previous learning. Students should be encouraged to make these connections in all learning tasks and teachers should affirm and foster these efforts.

Teaching Tip

Consider repeating an activity that was particularly novel to students, such as a fusion dinner party, if it seems that students struggled with ways in which they were expected to participate. Change the dynamics of the interactions at the dinner party by inviting other people, but keep the overall structure similar so that students are able to benefit from the experience of already having gone through it once before. Repetition would be particularly helpful to ELL students who are at beginning levels of proficiency, who may struggle with understanding as well as production of language.

Summation

In the visual arts case example # 3 students consider various worldviews through the lens of a young filmmaker's documentary as a generative text. The documentary juxtaposes various contemporary philosophers talking about their beliefs and prompts deliberation and debate. Visual arts relations to personally held worldviews are examined and their capacity to elicit deliberation and debate are considered. Judy Chicago's art installation, *The Dinner Party*, serves as an in-depth example. Students enact their own dinner party. Women artists from a particular time period, place, genre, culture, issue, etc. meet for conversation over dinner. Students increase their understandings of the contributions of various women artists past and present to the contemporary field of visual art, and demonstrate awareness of context, history, and traditions on art forms and media. Students convey the influences and impacts of the visual arts on daily life and the power of visual arts to create, alter, and reflect culture through designing and making a table setting embodying their understandings of a particular woman artist's works. The completed table with all settings provides a means to consider the visual arts as a vehicle for cultural production, transmission, and translation. ELL students have important negotiating opportunities to reason, interpret symbols, analyze images, and organize this information in order to grow artistic appreciation, convey personal understandings, and visibly contribute to and extend collective understandings.

Additional Selected Resources

Films

PBS. (2007). Art 21—Art in the twenty-first century series (http://www.pbs.org/art21/).
Taylor, A. (2008). *Examined life*. Toronto, ON: Zeitgeist Films (http://www.zeitgeistfilms.com/film.php?directoryname=examinedlife&mode=downloads).

Books

Brookfield, S. D. (2006). *The skillful teacher: On technique, trust, and responsiveness in the classroom*. San Francisco: Jossey-Bass.
Chicago, J. (2006). *Through the flower: My struggle as a woman artist*. Mustang, OK: Authors Choice Press.
Chicago, J. (2007). *The dinner party: From creation to preservation*. London: Merrell.
Clark, L. L. (2008). *Women and achievement in nineteenth-century Europe* (New approaches to European History). Boston, MA: Cambridge University Press.
Copeland, M. (2005). *Socratic circles: Fostering critical and creative thinking in middle and high school*. New York: Stenhouse.
Farris, P. (Ed.). (1999). *Women artists of color: A bio-critical sourcebook to 20th century artists in the Americas*. Westport CT: Greenwood.
Greer, G. (2001). *The obstacle race: The fortunes of women painters and their work*. London: Tauris Parke Paperbacks.
Grosenick, U. (Ed.). (2006). *Icons: Women artists in the 20th and 21st century*. Los Angeles, CA: Taschen.
Hannel, G. I. (2009). *Highly effective questioning: Challenging the culture of disengagement in the K-12 classroom* (Kindle ed.). Amazon Digital Services: Workshops in Questioning.

Internet Sites

Black history teaching resources at Smithsonian Museum (http://www.smithsonianeducation.org/educators/resource_library/african_american_resources.html).
March is Women's History month (http://www.princetonol.com/groups/iad/links/artists.html)
National Museum of American History (http://americanhistory.si.edu/).
National Museum of Women in the Arts (http://www.nmwa.org/).
National Women's History Museum (http://www.nwhm.org/?gclid=CIut7LXlxpwCFSduswodCU HFIg).

Smithsonian National Museum of African American History and Culture (Future Museum) (http://nmaahc.si.edu/).

Who is Rodin's Thinker? (http://www.artcyclopedia.com/feature-2001-08.html).

Women Beyond Borders: A Cross-Cultural Exhibition Connecting Women at the Onset of the 21st Century (http://www.womenbeyondborders.org/main.htm).

Women's history teaching resources at Smithsonian Museum (http://www.smithsonianeducation. org/educators/resource_library/women_resources.html).

Worldview sampler (http://www.teachingaboutreligion.org/WorldviewDiversity/worldview_ sampler.htm)

3.3
Music Experiences to Engage ELLs Alongside All Learners

Music experiences focusing on artistic thinking processes of making and relating, perceiving and responding, and connecting and understanding open dialogical spaces for students to critically engage their own expressive works and the expressive works of others. Such thinking is active, a process of attending to sensory qualities and relations, cognizant of the multi-sensory engagement necessary within all acts of making music. Thus, the processes of artistic thinking actively shape the act of responding. The negotiating room in-between allows for thinking and feeling through wondering, questioning, analyzing, and reconsidering, manifesting the responsive creation or invention of musical meaning. Participation in such music experiences heightens students' awareness of the composing process and students' capacity to articulate these personal connections. Students learn to use and to develop musical language in meaningful ways. Making and relating, perceiving and responding, and connecting and understanding experiences provide mediums for developing greater self-confidence and capacity in music alongside greater self-knowledge in relation to others. Growth is fostered across all students through opportunities for exposure to musical works shaped by different understandings, cultural influences, and interactions with peers and teachers. The development of language skills in ELL students is enabled through the deliberate creation of room for students to concretely play, voice, and navigate understandings through music. Additionally, the provision of interesting musical stimuli engages students in the sharing of ideas, and manifests opportunities for students to draw upon their language skills to express their thinking and cultural knowledge (Johnson, 2002). In this way, music can inform and enhance teaching about issues of diversity (Kuster, 2006) by inspiring learners through musical experiences that encourage the artistic thinking integral to creativity (Cantor, 2006).

Music, Theme I: "Total Control Can Be the Death of a Work"

Generative Text

Rivers and Tides is a film documenting the elemental sculptural forms in the making by Scottish artist Andy Goldsworthy (2004). The imagery of the film gives physical and material expression to his statement, "Total control can be the death of a work" (Scene 4), providing a vivid and tangible portrayal of artistic thinking in process.

About the text

The DVD of *Rivers and Tides* (Goldsworthy, 2004) can be viewed in its entirety or teachers may choose to introduce Goldsworthy's elemental sculptures though specific scenes that are accessible on the DVD in short segments. It is 90 minutes in length but the scenes offer a way for students to watch one or more excerpts of about 15 minutes each. Alternatively (or in addition), images of Goldsworthy's sculptural forms are available in Abram books (http://www.abramsbooks.com/#) and on the web, see (http://www.morning-earth.org/ARTISTNATURALISTS/AN_Goldsworthy. html), (http://www.flickr.com/groups/andygoldsworthy/pool/), and google images (http:// images.google.com/imghp?hl=en&tab=wi).

Scene 4 of the DVD, *Rivers and Tides*, *Feelings of Uncertainty* (Goldsworthy, 2004), depicts the artist seeking his artistic materials as he negotiates his way about the landscape. Viewers come to see how his sculptural forms are site-specific. Viewers increasingly see how Goldsworthy's knowings of the site and the particulars of the land are a necessity. The scene depicts Goldsworthy watching, listening, touching, and attending to colors, textures, shapes, patterns, weather conditions, and existing features of the terrain, gaining knowledge of the land. Control is never imposed. Goldsworthy meets and works with tensions, resistance, and discord as inherent within the process, expected along the way, and as being productive to his art making.

Music Case Example # 1: Sounds of Place

Initiate this experience by asking students to make a sound using anything they have access to for 20 seconds. Insist that students begin and end at the same time. Record the sounds created on a recording device and then play it for students to hear again. After identifying what each student used to create a specific sound, discuss sound as invisible waves moving through the air. The vibrations disturb the air molecules with each vibration making its own wave in the air—spreading out from the object or thing that made the sound. Have students then close their eyes and listen to a series of sounds created with devices found within the classroom. For example, tapping on a window with a pen, pulling open a desk drawer, turning on an electronic device, etc. After listening to each sound, have students guess as to its origins. Students should note these guesses in their music journals. As the sounds' origins are identified, discuss the guesses made.

Journal Entry

Guess #1:
Guess #2:
Guess #3:
Guess #4:

· ·

Ways of accommodating students at different levels of English proficiency

Preproduction and Early Production: After having identified the source of the sounds, write out the responses so that students are able to copy them into their notebooks. The responses, in turn, are examples that students may refer to as they attempt to learn connections between the sounds and the sources of the sounds in the exercise. Pair students up so that they are able to have a second opportunity to hear the sounds and then to state their sources.

Speech Emergence and Intermediate Fluency: Have students select items to use, and have them take turns making sounds while their partner or group mates attempt to identify the source. When thinking of accommodations, it is helpful for teachers to reflect upon some of the following points: what accommodations are made in process, content, and product? What accommodations does the teacher make for teaching, and what do ELLs make in learning? Reflecting upon these points will help the teacher to focus attention on goals and objectives of learning activities over time.

Explain that the sounds found in the room are site-specific. Expand the discussion of site-specific sounds by having students listen attentively to some soundscapes from Mexico. The soundscapes can be found at: http://www.archivosonoro.org/?cat=Ambientenatural. This site is a sound archive promoting the importance of listening to one's surroundings. Mexico is the setting but the sounds represent the diversity and actuality to be found there. Teachers should translate the accompanying texts to ensure appropriateness for student use as the site is updated daily.

Teaching Tip

To enable deep listening, foster a context for students that is conducive to listening. Dim lights, close windows and doors, and allow students to find their own space to attend to the sounds away from desks, instruments, and other distractions.

Depending on the particulars of the students involved, have students listen to one or more of the many soundscapes on the site. Each soundscape is just a few minutes long, and relays varied sounds collected from a particular site. Individually, have students describe their listening experiences in their music journals.

Journal Entry

Identify sounds as you hear them:
What images come to mind?
What features capture your attention?
Other responses?

· ·

Ways of accommodating students at different levels of English proficiency

Preproduction: Have students listen to the soundscapes, and ask them to describe the sounds (e.g. soft, sharp, etc.), and then ask what about the sound gives it that quality. Replay the soundscapes to give students another opportunity to respond.

Early Production and Speech Emergence: Adapt the questions so that early production and speech emergence students may be more likely to be able to respond. For example:

- 'What do you hear?' rather than, 'Identify sounds as you hear them';
- 'What do you think of when you hear the music?' rather than, 'What images come to mind?';
- 'What did you like? Dislike?' rather than, 'What features capture your attention?'

Intermediate Fluency: Have students respond to adapted questions in pairs so that they are able to express their ideas without feeling the pressure to speak in front of a large group.

Then, in small groups have students discuss what they think they heard, images that came to mind, features, relations, and inhabitants that drew their attention, and their body/mind response to the exercise of listening. Facilitate these small group discussions as necessary. Attend to important insights generated by the group. Bring these insights to a large group discussion that synthesizes the findings and compiles a common list for all to reference. Have students in small groups then create a three to five minute audio-recorded soundscape that is site-specific. To do so, set the parameters for the sites to be visited, note the time to complete the task, and emphasize that the goal is to record the sounds that arise from an immersion experience of a particular setting. The listening exercise of the soundscapes from Mexico should serve as an example of the attentive listening that this task demands. Sites could include natural areas characteristic of the place, school related sites such as the swimming pool, gymnasium, main office area, hallways, sports activities, and off school sites such as cafes, stores, galleries, streets, and so on. Specifically, have students create soundscapes with a recorded three minute excerpt to share with the class. During the recording time they are to immerse themselves in the sounds of place and note in their music journals what they see, hear, and feel.

Journal Entry

Immersion experience

Seeing:
Hearing:
Feeling:

• •

Ways of accommodating students at different levels of English proficiency

Preproduction and Early Production: Focus on one of the words at a time (seeing, hearing, feeling), providing students with opportunities to hear the word, to repeat the word, and to use it in a sentence. Include pictorial cues to build further opportunities to use the words in an appropriate way.

Speech Emergence: Pair students up with someone with whom they feel comfortable, and have the students work through each of the three points together. Have them present their sentences to a group of three or four classmates.

Intermediate Fluency: Pair students up with a classmate with whom they work well. Have the students work through each of the three points together, and present their sentences to a group of three or four classmates. Encourage them to grow their list of possibilities by asking others how they responded to the initial word.

Recordings and journal observations are shared across groups for the features, relations, and inhabitants of each site. Following this discussion and sharing of recordings, introduce the Scottish artist, Andy Goldsworthy. Explain that the DVD documentary portrays the sculptor concerned with site-specific art making. Ask students to translate possible connections to site-specific sounds. Ask them to further consider what makes Goldsworthy's work "art" and how soundscapes might also become "art." Have students watch Scene 4 from the DVD, *Rivers and Tides* (Goldsworthy, 2004), paying particular attention to what Goldsworthy might mean by his statement, "Control can be the death of a work" (Scene 4). After watching Scene 4, have students relay in their journals and then in small groups what they saw and heard.

Journal Entry

- How do the artistic materials speak to Goldsworthy? What are the materials that speak to musicians?
- What is the role of context in art and music?
- Why is place of importance?
- How does Goldsworthy treat the materials and respond as the work is created? How would you describe the making/relating composing process undertaken by musicians?
- How does Goldsworthy work with time? How do musicians work with time?

· ·

Ways of accommodating students at different levels of English proficiency

Using some large rocks as actual examples for students to physically examine, engage ELLs as follows:

Preproduction and Early Production: Play the scene from the DVD, and have students only watch for the first viewing. For the second viewing, have them write down as many nouns as possible. Encourage them to make this initial list in their home language if it would be helpful, and then translate the words into English. The words and their translations can be added to their personal dictionaries. Students could also work in pairs with English-speaking peers.

Speech Emergence: Play the scene from the DVD and have students describe what they see. Write their ideas out in the form of a short list on the board so that the points can become a running commentary on a second or third viewing (with the sound from the DVD muted).

Intermediate Fluency: View the scene from the DVD again, and discuss what the students see. Explore together the role of context in shaping music and art, and expand the discussion to include how context shapes the music and art in Goldworthy's work.

Facilitate small group discussions as necessary. Attend to important insights that groups generate. Bring these insights to a large group discussion of how music is organized by arranging the sound waves so that the sounds work successfully together. The arrangements of sounds into notes, rhythms, textures, and phrases can be discussed and related as called for within specific teaching situations. The use of beats, measures, cadences, and form should be discussed in terms of providing musical organization and translating understandings. Synthesize the relationships students voice to site-specific music. Discuss Goldsworthy's statement that "control can be the death of a work" in relation to music making.

Teaching Tip

Be sure to recognize the differing learning styles of students in the planning of learning activities. In addition to incorporating a range of different kinds of activities to engage students' different learning styles, also use a variety of ways of grouping students together for work. While some ELL students may thrive on interaction with non-ELL students as a means of engaging them in the task at hand, and as a means of accelerating language and vocabulary development through exposure to language beyond what they might produce and understand themselves, others might appreciate opportunities to absorb new language in a receptive way by participating through listening to others express their ideas and/or watching others participate actively.

> **Teaching Tip**
>
> Break learning experiences into parts with associated expectations for students to follow through on, clearly expressed one part at a time. Each part can entail different expectations for students to complete but following through on a part-by-part basis keeps the task manageable for ELLs and all students.

To further understandings, introduce the radio show of *New Sounds* on WNYC, and ask students to listen to one or more segments of the hour-long excerpts of site-specific music. The radio show can be accessed at: http://www.wnyc.org/shows/newsounds/episodes/2007/06. The archived radio show number 2693, which originally aired on June 28, 2007, includes flutist Paul Horn's recordings in the Taj Mahal, Robert Fripp's soundscape for the World Financial Center, Alvin Lucier's *I'm Sitting in a Room*, using a room's resonance capacities, LaMonte Young's *Well-Tuned Piano*, and Paul Winter's recording in the alpine valley of Crestone, Colorado (these recordings are also available as audio CDs). Consider what the significances of site-specific music are for participating musicians and their audiences/listeners. Ask students to embrace these significances as they return to their selected sites from the earlier exercise and compose an immersion musical experience, specific to the site, that structures time to convey the texture of place in musical terms. This composition should incorporate some sounds collected from the initial visit alongside a fitting arrangement involving instruments and/or voices of approximately three minutes in length that uses sound expressively to convey a sense of place. As each composition is performed, ask students attending to the performance to note the impression the music gives them in their journals. Discuss these impressions with the musicians. Consider together what qualities and features most contributed to the effect, and what deterred or distracted from the effect. The performance of these for each other should also prompt relations to contemporary electronic/electroacoustic music.

Summation

In the music case example # 1, students experiment with ways to record their musical ideas and the musical ideas of others in relation to the specifics of place. The elemental sculptural forms of Andy Goldsworthy serve as a generative text to consider how site-specific art making relates to site-specific music making and how both can become art forms. Opportunities to experiment with a range of musical sound sources in relation to seeking expression to represent thoughts, images, and feelings, enlarging the classroom repertoire, are key to this exercise. Decoding and encoding music using a variety of sound sources and technologies will foster communication understandings and confidence. ELL students will concomitantly translate thoughts into music and music into thoughts. Thus, the concrete back and forth navigation provides encoding and decoding means for revealing what they know, and makes this thinking more visible and accessible to others as they interact, making associations across oral and musical communication.

Additional Selected Resources

Film/DVD

Goldsworthy, A. (2004). *Rivers and tides: Working with time*, DVD. Directed by Thomas Riedelsheimer. Mediopolis Films.

Books

Dworsky, A. L., & Sansby, B. (2001). *Hip grooves for hand drums: How to play funk, rock and world-beat patterns on any drum.* Minnetonka, MN: Dancing Hands Music.

Krause, B. (2002). *Wild soundscapes: Discovering the voice of the natural world.* Berkeley: Wilderness.

LaBelle, B. (2006). *Background noise: Perspectives on sound art.* New York: Continuum International.

Levin, T. (2006). *Where rivers and mountains sing: Sound, music, and nomadism in Tuva and beyond.* Bloomington: Indiana University Press.

Oliveros, P. (2005). *Deep listening: A composer's sound practice.* Bloomington, IN: iUniverse.

Roads, C. (2001). *Microsound.* Cambridge, MA: MIT Press.

Schafer, R. M. (1993). *The soundscape: Our sonic environment and the tuning of the world.* Bel Air, CA: Destiny Books.

Internet Sites

Bird and animal soundscapes (http://naturesound.org/Welcome.html).

Center of new music and audio technologies (http://cnmat.berkeley.edu/mic/soundscape_and_field_recording).

Field recordings become creative compositions using non-traditional instrumentation (http://www.archive.org/details/wh055).

Seeing with sound (http://www.seeingwithsound.com/javoice.htm).

Sound tracks (http://www.quietamerican.org/field_vietnam.html).

Talking about sound and music (http://cnx.org/content/m12373/latest/).

World forum for acoustic ecology (http://interact.uoregon.edu/MediaLit/wfae/home/).

Technological Supports

Soundscape generator in Python (http://boodler.org/).

Soundscape generator, Apple (http://www.essl.at/works/flow/download.html).

Music, Theme II: "Responsive Matters of Perception"

Generative Text

A slam poem, *Love*, is authored and performed by a high school student, Lucas Hines[1], giving expression to the young man's ongoing considerations about what it means to be in love. Access the performance of the slam poem at: http://cehs.unl.edu/mlatta/poem.htm

---

About the Text

The student's poem on love is situated within a quickly evolving movement of slam poetry occurring over the last 25 years. Poetry found this new venue in 1984 through Marc Smith, a Chicago construction worker experimenting in front of an audience with forms for poetry readings. Slam has since moved from the margins to mainstream, and from a local to global phenomenon, revitalizing poetry. A slam is a poetry competition where poets perform original work alone or in teams, with audience engagement as judges. These poems represent diverse topics and purposes including comedic, dramatic, personal, and political. A slam poet aims for audience connection. And, with this emphasis on performance, slam poets share their identity, their convictions, and their embedded understandings through spoken word, body language, and stage presence. Poetry slams are now found everywhere in the United States and have expanded to other countries including Australia, Austria, Bosnia-Herzegovina, Canada, the Czech Republic, Denmark, France, Germany, Macedonia, Nepal, the Netherlands, New Zealand, Singapore, South Korea, Sweden, Switzerland, and the United Kingdom.

Music Case Example # 2 Finding Fitting Musical Expressions

Locate students in a space that invites physical movement. With students seated in a circle, introduce rhythm as something that needs to be directly felt. To draw students' attention toward the nature of rhythm, play/sing excerpts for students (or have a selection of recordings for students to attend to) of a wide variety of music with varying rhythms. Ask students to move one of their arms on the floor as each music excerpt suggests. Keep this exercise in motion for a few minutes so that students gradually become more focused on how the music moves them. With students on their feet, repeat this exercise but have students walk as the music suggests to each of them.

Teaching Tip

Disrupt the usual classroom context from time to time. A new space or novel approach will foster new thinking and fresh student connections.

Engage students in discussion about how rhythm is created, drawing attention to patterns of accent, duration, and pause in relation to tempo and dynamics. Relate this discussion to rhythm in our everyday lives. Introduce the Canadian short film, *Hothouse 5: Orange*, and have students attend to it for the film artist's interpretations of the city's natural rhythms. It is available at: http://www.nfb.ca/film/hothouse_5_orange/

Teaching Tip

Multisensory student engagement in learning creates ways for ELLs to concretely experience language in related, repeated, and yet different, ways.

On a second viewing of *Hothouse 5: Orange* have students use any drums available (or the floor) to concretely navigate the rhythms. Have students then attend to the film a third time, but without any sound. With students working in small groups, facilitate involvement in creating their own accompanying rhythm, continuing to use the drums. Establish a tight time frame (approximately 30 minutes) to accomplish this task. Students will perform these rhythm tracks for each other alongside showings of the film. Following each performance, discuss how each group perceived, responded, organized, and created accompanying rhythm. Ask one or two groups to perform their rhythm track again but without the imagery of the film. Involve the remaining students in attending to the kinds of expressions suggested. Have students note these expressive ideas in their music journals with some accompanying lines, shapes, and colors that seem fitting.

Journal Entry

Ideas that come to mind	Lines, shapes, and colors that come to mind
1.	
2.	
3.	

. . . .

Ways of accommodating students at different levels of English proficiency

Preproduction and Early Production: Show the film *Hothouse 5*, and have students focus on just watching the film on the first showing. For the second showing, demonstrate the use of colors, lines, and shapes, using a variety of materials (e.g. colored pencils, oil pastels, paints, chalk, and crayons on a large sheet of paper). Take into consideration accent, duration, pause, tempo, and dynamics to express the natural rhythms of a city using these materials. Have students do this as well for the third showing.

Speech Emergence: Demonstrate on a large sheet of paper how colors, lines, and shapes may look different when using different materials (e.g. colored pencils, oil pastels, paints, chalk, and crayons). Take into consideration accent, duration, pause, tempo, and dynamics to express natural rhythms of a city using these materials while doing this. Have students do this as well, and then share what they have produced in pairs or in small groups.

Intermediate Fluency: Demonstrate the use of colors, lines, and shapes, by using colored pencils, oil pastels, paints, chalk, and crayons on a large sheet of paper to express natural rhythms of a city as seen in the film. Take into consideration accent, duration, pause, tempo, and dynamics. Have students work in pairs, describing to their partners how the work coordinates with what is seen in the film (it would be ideal to do this while students are watching the film as well, to attempt to 're-create' what the students experienced).

Teaching Tip

Provide opportunities for ELL students to view videos, listen to the lyrics of songs, or to examine artifacts before they are introduced in class or after they have been introduced so that they are able to work together with peers (other ELL students) to examine the content to ask questions and to learn relevant vocabulary and language related to the content material at a pace suitable to their learning. Use the song lyrics to create a cloze exercise for the students.

The Canadian film *Begone Dull Care* (1949) offers a vivid painterly interpretation of jazz music by the Oscar Peterson Trio in which Evelyn Lambart and Norman McLaren painted directly on film. See: http://www.nfb.ca/film/begone_dull_care_caprice_couleurs/.

Have students view this film and then spend time in small groups discussing if it is ever possible to replicate a composer's intentions, interpreting the music exactly as the composer did. Guiding questions for this discussion include:

1. How does what comes to your mind influence the act of making music?
2. What is the role of context, place, and audience in making music?
3. What is the role of various instruments with more than one musician playing?
4. What about the roles of musical technique and skill?

Bring the small group discussions to the large group to further examine the answers to these questions, referring back to concrete incidents from the series of exercises involving rhythm exploration. Talk with students about the need to find the rhythmic aspects that form and articulate, providing dynamics and phrasing within music integral to each performance.

Introduce the generative text of the slam poem by asking whether students have participated and/or performed as a slam poet. Ask about whether they have performed and/or participated in any other kind of performance. Evolve this discussion to include some of the history and traditions of performance that slam poetry embraces and explore ways in which they are related to music. Ask students to watch the slam poet perform his love poem, looking for the perceiving and responding features that contribute to the completed performance. Have students relay the features that enable the poet to discover the rhythmic aspects that form and articulate, providing dynamics and phrasing within the spoken words. Note these features for everyone to see. In music journals, have students consider the significances the topic of love plays within the poet's (and the viewer's) level of engagement with the slam poetry.

Teaching Tip

Purposefully reiterate musical terms. Students will become more familiar with the terms and begin to articulate their understandings as they incorporate them in the various ways the lesson calls for. Continually look for ways to affirm and grow these efforts.

Teaching Tip

Encourage ELL students to begin and to grow a glossary of musical terms that they are able to refer to throughout the year (and indeed, throughout their music education). This may be done in the form of flash cards with a ring to hold them together, or cards that are added to a box or plastic storage container so that they are able to focus on learning the content of a few cards at a time, and so that they are able to easily access them as they are needed.

Journal Entry

What features inform the poet's performance? How do you think the poet was feeling? What impressions does the performance elicit in you? Why do you think the poet created this slam?

• •

Ways of accommodating students at different levels of English proficiency

Preproduction: Show photos of people expressing different sentiments and emotions to introduce a range of feelings or have students create their own photos of varying human expressions. Introduce words for the sentiments and emotions by matching them with pictures of people expressing these sentiments and emotions. Show pictures of people involved in different kinds of situations, and have students incorporate bodily expressions alongside words to describe how the people are feeling using the words. Encourage students to refer to pictures and specific bodily expressions with the accompanying words for the sentiments and emotions.

Early Production: Explore the question, 'How do you think the poet was feeling?' Show photos of people expressing different sentiments and emotions to introduce a range of feelings or have students create their own series of photo expressions. Then ask students about how they think the poet was feeling when he wrote the slam poem. Encourage them to respond using words introduced in the photos.

Speech Emergence: Review the vocabulary for sentiments and emotions using photos expressing different emotions or pictures of people involved in different situations. Using a video or a clip of a cartoon or photos from a book or magazine would be helpful as well. Encourage students to use the words in sentences to express the emotions of the people in the photos (or videos or cartoons). Next, play a clip of music, and discuss how music may also be used to express emotions and sentiments.

Intermediate Fluency: Review a range of feelings and emotions using pictures, and encourage students to use the words in sentences to express the emotions of the people in the photos (or videos, cartoons, magazines, books, etc.), and to elaborate on why they might be feeling that way. Next, play a clip of music, and discuss how music may also be used to express emotions and sentiments.

Introduce a rhapsody as a one-movement musical work with some similarities to a slam poem. Both are episodic yet integrated, free flowing in structure, and feature a range of moods and tonality. Improvisation is needed across both art forms. Facilitate the entire class in exploring attempts to embody emotions and moods of specific situations in musical form through rhapsodies. As students attend closely to a few rhapsodies, ask them to consider the relations to slam poetry. Relations include movement, playfulness, and episodic structure, permeated by a primary theme. Let the discussion evolve and then introduce *Rhapsody in Blue*, a musical composition by George Gershwin, discussing his historical significance. As students listen to a recording, have them respond in their journals to a statement from Gershwin about this composing experience.

Teaching Tip

Expect journal entries to be varied in length and complexity. Get to know students so you know when to push, challenge, and support each student's thinking.

Journal Entry

Gershwin recalls composing ideas for *Rhapsody in Blue*:

"It was on the train, with its steely rhythms, its rattle-ty bang, that is so often so stimulating to a composer—I frequently hear music in the very heart of the noise… . And there I suddenly heard, and even saw on paper—the complete construction of the Rhapsody, from beginning to end. No new themes came to me, but I worked on the thematic material already in my mind and tried to conceive the composition as a whole. I heard it as a sort of musical kaleidoscope of America, of our vast melting pot, of our unduplicated national pep, of our blues, our metropolitan madness. By the time I reached Boston I had a definite plot of the piece, as distinguished from its actual substance"

(Cowen, 1998)

• •

Ways of accommodating students at different levels of English proficiency

Preproduction and Early Production: Talk with students about where they like to work when they have a lot of work to do or a creative project to undertake. The teacher could begin by saying something such as the following: "Yesterday, I had so much work to do." At this point, the teacher could begin making a list of work that needed to be done. Include pictures of the items in the list. Emphasize to students that the list is very long, with many tasks. Then, introduce the problem you experienced—that it was difficult to work at home for some reason (e.g., "because it was so noisy" or "it was very messy," etc.). Introduce the idea of finding an alternative place to work (e.g., "So, I went to the basement to work."), and offer a reason why this was not possible (e.g., "But it was too cold."). "Then I went to the family room. But it was too noisy." "Then I went to the bedroom. But there was no table to work at." Continue in this manner, and encourage students to add places around their homes, the school, or the neighborhood where a person might go to work. Include a large blueprint of the different parts of a home and perhaps even photos of the rooms, and name the different places in the house where you went to work.

Speech Emergence: Introduce the idea of creative work and engagement. Tell them about where you like to work and why, and encourage them to ask one another where they like to work.

Intermediate Fluency: Talk about the process of creative work and feelings and qualities encountered. Refer to Gershwin's description and qualities suggested. Tell the students where you like to work and why and encourage them to share with the class where they like to work. Encourage them to talk about a time when they felt immersed in the creative process.

Discuss student responses to Gershwin's statement about composing and listen again to the recording of *Rhapsody in Blue*. Have students attempt to distinguish movements or themes and attend to the rhythmic patterns and relations. Build on the discussion from the earlier exercises on rhythm. Layer the understandings generated by students into another viewing of a performance. The singers, *Naturally 7*, term their music "vocal play." Each member's voice becomes a musical instrument, from trumpets to drums, and an attentive multi-sensory playfulness ensues across the group members as they create songs. See: http://www.ted.com/index.php/talks/naturally_7_jams_fly_baby_with_an_orchestra_of_vocals.html.

In small groups, have students specifically discuss:

1. What is the vocal play dependant upon?
2. How would you characterize the play that is entailed?
3. Access a transcript of the lyrics to the song on the website and consider the lyrics' relations to the vocal play created.

Attend to the small group discussions closely and synthesize the findings as the class as a whole watches the *Naturally 7* vocal group perform *Wall of Sound* and considers the same questions again. See: http://bandweblogs.com/blog/2009/01/05/naturally-7-release-wall-of-sound-watch-video/.

Conclude this music experience by giving each student (or small groups of students) three to five notated measures from varied existing music selections. Students will read these measures and use instruments and/or voice to perform these measures as they see fit. They will then each play with these given measures to find ways to continue to develop the music rhythm, attending to patterns of accent, duration, and pause in relation to tempo and dynamics, for an additional three to five measures. Concomitantly, have students note words and phrases in their music journals that convey the permeating theme of their rhythmic play with music. Ask students to play with these words so that the responsive page on their journal depicts words that carry meanings via the line quality, size, and other features, utilizing traditional writing tools or software generating word clouds via wordle at: http://www.wordle.net/.

Journal Entry

This word cloud was made using wordle: http://www.wordle.net/

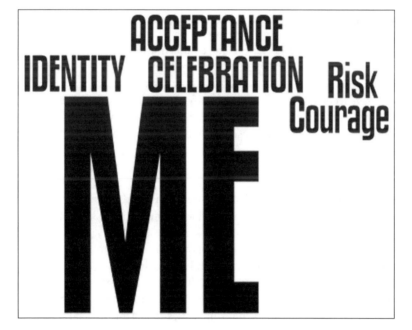

. . . .

Ways of accommodating students at different levels of English proficiency

Preproduction: Introduce the idea of a word cloud to depict ideas. Talk about instruments that may be part of a band, and identify the ones included in the vocal performance done by the singers of *Naturally 7*. Make a word cloud together using the names of instruments. Use a word cloud in association with an online translator.

Early Production: Introduce the idea of a word cloud to depict ideas. Talk about instruments that may be part of a band, and identify the ones included by the singers of *Naturally 7*. Have students make a word cloud together using the names of instruments, and share them with their classmates.

Speech Emergence: Introduce the idea of a word cloud to depict ideas. Talk about instruments that may be part of a band, and identify the ones included by the singers of *Naturally 7*. Have students make a word cloud together using the names of instruments, taking into consideration the use of size and color to emphasize some sounds or instruments over others. Play another piece of music and have students do another word cloud to reflect the new piece. Share the word clouds with their classmates.

Intermediate Fluency: Talk about how music can tell a story and express themes and ideas. Watch the vocal group *Naturally 7* perform Wall of Sound, and have students identify themes that they perceive as being important in this piece. Demonstrate how the theme words can be used to make a word cloud, and illustrate how size and color can be used to emphasize some sounds or instruments over others. Play another piece of music and have students do another word cloud to reflect the new piece. Share the word clouds among classmates.

The actual parameters and expectations for completion of the rhythmic music play will be dependant on students' musical knowledge and capacities alongside the teacher's intents and expertise, but everyone will benefit by setting time aside for students to perform their works for each other to engage feedback and critique. Identifying the origins of the measures of the music, and comparing and contrasting the students' interpretations with the original composition, reemphasizes the matters of perception for musicians and their audiences.

Summation

In the music case example # 2 students listen to traditional and contemporary music, and consider the roles that music plays across local and global communities. Students are asked to select music, and in doing so, analyze and respond personally to musical styles, forms, and genres. A high school student's slam poem enables students to analyze and to make decisions about the relationship between music and society, music and the environment, and music and other arts. The structure and purposes of a slam poem involve students translating how these structures and purposes might manifest across musical forms. In particular, a rhapsody as a one-movement musical work is examined as holding some similarities to a slam poem. The episodic, yet integrated, free-flowing structure, and attention to moods and tonality entailing improvisation are explored across both art forms. ELL students in collaboration with other students are involved in describing, analyzing, interpreting, and evaluating as all engage in composing similar rhythmic play and relations through music. All students evaluate their own musical insights and aesthetic responses in the context of critical commentary by their peers. All are asked to negotiate and to convey personal understandings to others, and to find fitting expression through the co-creation of music with others. In doing so, ELLs gain greater cognitive flexibility by addressing English language ambiguities in the process of seeking personal resonance.

Additional Selected Resources

Slam Poetry

Algarin, M., & Holman, B. (1994). *Aloud: Voices from the Nuyorican Poet's Café*. New York: Henry Holt.

Delvin, P. (2004). *SlamNation: New educational edition.* Slammin' Entertainment. New York: New York Video Group.

Eleveld, M. (2003). *The spoken word revolution: Slam, HipHop, and the poetry of a new generation.* Bel Air, CA: Sourcebooks MediaFusion.

Glazner, G. M. (2000). *Poetry slam.* San Francisco: Manic D Press.

Levin, M. (1998). *Slam.* Vancouver: Lion's gate. Rated: R.

Simmons, R. (2009). *Brave new voices.* Home Box Office, Time Warner Entertainment Company.

Internet Sites

A brief guide to slam poetry (http://www.poets.org/viewmedia.php/prmMID/5672).

Contexts, poets, background information on Brave New Voices (http://www.hbo.com/bravenewvoices/crew/index.html).

Living Word Project (http://livingwordproject.org/lwp_description.html).

Poet Heroes (http://myhero.com/myhero/hero.asp?hero=saulwilliams).

Poetry Slam Incorporated (http://www.poetryslam.com/).

Saul Williams (http://www.poets.org/viewmedia.php/prmMID/5813).

The Nuyorican Poets Café (http://www.nuyorican.org/).

Youth Speaks (http://youthspeaks.org/word/).

Music

National Film Board/Norman McLaren, Boogie Doodle (http://www.nfb.ca/film/boogie-doodle/).

PBS Music in Every Classroom:

    Africa: African arts and music (http://www.pbs.org/wnet/africa/tools/music/goals.html).

    American experience: Stephen Foster (http://www.pbs.org/wgbh/amex/foster/).

    American masters (http://www.pbs.org/wnet/americanmasters/database/database_music.html).

    American roots music (http://www.pbs.org/americanrootsmusic).

    Broadway: The American musical (http://www.pbs.org/wnet/broadway).

    Culture shock: The devil's music—1920s Jazz (http://www.pbs.org/wgbh/cultureshock/beyond/jazz.html).

    Great Performances: Educational resources (http://www.pbs.org/wnet/gperf/education/education.html).

    Jazz (http://www.pbs.org/jazz).

    The Blues (http://www.pbs.org/theblues).

STOMP Live (2007). New York: Marquee Merchandise (DVD).

STOMP study guide (http://www.stomponline.com/percussion.php).

Internet Sites

Harry Ransom Center, University of Texas at Austin: Teaching the American 20s (http://www.hrc.utexas.edu/educator/modules/teachingthetwenties/theme_viewer.php?theme=modern&section=new&subsect=3).

New York Public Library: A century of sound (http://www.nypl.org/news/treasures/index.cfm?vidid=9).

New York Public Library: The Rodgers and Hammerstein archives of recorded sound (http://www.nypl.org/research/lpa/rha/rha.html).

Rhapsody music catalogue (http://www.rhapsody.com/comedy-spoken-word/spoken-word/poetry-poetry-slam).

Sibelius Academy music resources (http://www2.siba.fi/Kulttuuripalvelut/music.html).

The classical musical pages (http://w3.rz-berlin.mpg.de/cmp/classmus.html).

Worldwide Internet music resources (http://library.music.indiana.edu/music_resources/).

For Teaching ELLs with Music

(http://www.eslpartyland.com/teachers/nov/music.htm)
(www.songsforteaching.com/esleflesol.htm)

Music, Theme III: "Examined Lives in Relation—A Fusion Dinner Party"

Generative Text

Filmmaker Astra Taylor converses with some of today's most influential thinkers within selected contexts, fitting to each one. The thinking each shares is chronicled in her film, *Examined Life*, Zeitgeist Films, 2008. The film reveals the multiple perspectives from which the world can be seen and lived. In this way, the film becomes the text to re-imagine the perspectives gained and to stage a fusion dinner party. A fusion dinner party intentionally invites meetings across differences. Envisioning, creating, and enacting a fusion dinner party serves as a further generative vehicle for a music experience enlarging historical and contextual understandings.

About the Text

Viewing the entire DVD of the film *Examined Life* (Taylor, 2008) gives the fullest access to Astra Taylor's intent to invite and fosters conversation on what it means to live right. Alternatively, or in addition, short overviews of the film can be accessed at: http://www.nfb.ca/film/examined-life-trailer/ and http://www3.nfb.ca/webextension/examined-life/.

The persistent questions throughout the film are: how does one live the examined life and why should we invest in doing so? The film reveals that the ways we answer these questions are shaped by our various worldviews. Thus, the film confronts and asks viewers to challenge their values, assumptions, and beliefs connected to one's worldview. The cross-section of contemporary philosophers, including Cornel West, Avital Ronell, Peter Singer, Kwarne Anthony Appiah, Martha Nussbaum, Michael Hardt, Slavoj Zizek, Judith Butler, and Sunaura Taylor, provide intersecting and opposing ideas that engage viewers and invite them to join the conversation. In doing so, viewers will find themselves interacting and deliberating about the film's surfacing issues of courage, responsibility, ethics, power, privilege, indifference, social justice, gender, ableism, and politics, and what this might entail for notions of citizenry and democracy in an increasingly globalized world.

A fusion dinner party is purposefully designed and enacted to embrace differences in perspectives (Lorraine Cockle[2], teacher in Calgary, Alberta, Canada offers the idea of the dinner party, which we adapted). The film *Examined Life* serves as a generative text providing the "food for thought" from the multiple perspectives of the fusion dinner table guests and conversation. Akin to a fusion menu at a restaurant that brings the table ware, cooking, and traditions of several cultures together, the fusion dinner conversation is intended to surface differences, seek insights from one another, and prompt new connections and possibilities. Students are asked to examine their own lives in relation to selected historical and contemporary musicians. In doing so, the relations across music and society will be foregrounded for all to connect and grow understandings.

Music Case Example # 3: Music with Staying Power

Talk with students about why music is often referred to as a universal language. Ask students to consider what makes music also a very particular language. A chart could be collectively organized and displayed to enable students to understand the celebration of cultural diversity that music inhabits and exhibits as well as the varying ways music translates and resonates with what is encountered in the world as individuals live in it. Engage students in considering the role of personal experiences, cultures, and contexts as these intersect with meanings and sounds.

Have students work in small groups to examine a particular song in depth. Select songs from a particular genre, time period, culture, or context. For example, the songs in the following list are considered influential songs of the 1960s and early 1970s, with their impact still felt today and traces evident in more recent music, including heavy metal, punk, disco, rap, hip hop, and techno.

- *Where Have All the Flowers Gone?*, Peter, Paul, and Mary, 1962.
- *Blowin' in the Wind*, Bob Dylan, 1963.
- *The Times They Are A-Changin*, Bob Dylan, 1964.
- *She Loves You*, The Beatles, 1964.
- *Satisfaction*, The Rolling Stones, 1965.
- *Turn! Turn! Turn!*, The Byrds, 1966.
- *California Dreamin'*, The Mamas and The Papas, 1966.
- *Yesterday*, The Beatles, 1966.
- *Nights in White Satin*, The Moody Blues, 1967.
- *Born to be Wild*, Steppenwolf, 1968.
- *Piece of My Heart*, Janis Joplin, 1968.
- *Dance to the Music*, Sly and the Family Stone, 1968.
- *Eve of Destruction*, P.F. Sloan/Barry McGuire, 1968.
- *Suite: Judy Blue Eyes*, Crosby, Stills, and Nash, 1969.
- *Fortunate Son*, Creedence Clearwater Revival, 1969.
- *Let It Be*, The Beatles, 1970.
- *Woodstock*, Joni Mitchell, 1970.
- *Black Magic Woman*, Santana, 1970.
- *Imagine*, John Lennon, 1971.
- *Stairway to Heaven*, Led Zeppelin, 1971.
- *Ohio*, Crosby, Stills, and Nash, 1971.
- *Chicago*, Crosby, Stills, and Nash, 1971.
- *American Pie*, Don McLean, 1971.
- *Aqualung*, Jethro Tull, 1971.
- *Won't Get Fooled Again*, The Who, 1971.

- *Time*, Pink Floyd, 1973.
- *I Shot the Sheriff*, Bob Marley and the Wailers, 1973.

Have students access these songs, listen to the music, and locate copies of the lyrics, attending to these closely. Following this exercise, involve students in finding out about the selected musicians, specific time period, and context, and considering what about the song creates the continuing impact.

Teaching Tip

The following websites will enable students to research the songs:
   http://www.songfacts.com/
   http://www.inthe70s.com/generated/lyricsmeaning.shtml

Teaching Tip

Incorporate opportunities for students to sing some of the songs and to watch videos of the time period during which the pieces were written, as a means of engaging students in the content of the music and as a means of setting the context for the music. Recognize, however, that learning the lyrics of songs may be difficult for some ELL students, especially those who are shy or who are not confident in their English language abilities. Providing a written copy of the lyrics, encouraging students to print out copies of songs they find on the Internet, and singing the songs together in a large group rather than individually will help the students to participate without putting them on the spot to perform.

Students should record all information gathered about their selected song into their music journals.

Journal Entry

Title of song:
Response to the lyrics and music:
Are you aware of music and words interacting to create meaning? Are multiple
   interpretations possible?
Do you think the song is a form of cultural expression? Explain.

· ·

Ways of accommodating students at different levels of English proficiency

Preproduction and Early Production: Have students write down the title of the
   song. Provide copies of the lyrics for students to refer to as they listen to a

recording of the song. Have them circle ten words that they know, and share them with other ELL students. Then, have them circle ten new ones that they would like to learn. Have the students take turns writing the new words on to the board, enlisting the help of others to learn the word. Have students write the new words on to index cards to add to their personal dictionary.

Speech Emergence: Have students write down the title of the song. Provide copies of the lyrics, with some words and phrases missing, for students to fill in as they listen to a recording of the song. Encourage them to share their responses with one another, in an attempt to have all of the blanks completed, before listening to the piece again in its entirety.

Intermediate Fluency: Have students write down the title of the song. Discuss with the students whether they think the lyrics are an expression of culture; encourage them to elaborate upon their responses. Encourage students to add to the lyrics using their own words, but following the same structure and music. Share what they have written with others in the class, while listening to the song again.

Have each student group create a web page that links to the selected song and lyrics, provides background on the musicians, and offers the group's interpretations of the song's influences and impacts. Alternatively, student groups could each create a music video to share with the class their interpretations of the particular song and musicians.

Groups should share their web pages or music videos, selected songs, and findings with the entire class, and collectively discuss the influences at the time and impacts on contemporary music. Consider together the staying power of these songs and how the messages within each song evoke responses that are deeply felt and shared by many. The following questions may be used to guide discussion of each group's work:

- What is the main theme or message of the lyrics of the song?
- What emotions are elicited from attending to the song?
- Do you see/hear literary/poetic devices incorporated by the songwriter?
- Do you see/hear reference to historical or cultural understandings?
- What aspects contribute to the song's meaning? Describe and analyze use of the musical elements such as the instruments, the vocal style, melody, and rhythm.
- Are issues raised in the song relevant today?
- How does the web page or video reflect the expressive intents of the song?
- How does the web page or video represent the mood of the song?

Depending on the level of engagement and understandings of students, some very interested students may benefit from listening to Susan McClary, a Professor of Musicology at the University of California, Los Angeles. She is a specialist in the cultural criticism and critical theory of music, focusing specifically on the European and Western popular canons and an avid pianist and harpsichordist. The following links provide access to her thinking regarding interpreting music and the role of context in understanding music. Teachers will definitely gain questions to pose to their students from accessing Susan McClary's talks, whether or not they have their students listen to them. See:

http://www.artistshousemusic.org/videos/interpreting+music+as+a+performer

http://www.artistshousemusic.org/videos/why+cultural+context+matters+to+understan
ding+the+music+you+play

Introduce the notions of interpretation and context to students as making up one's worldview. Have students each complete the questionnaire, Table 3.5 (see p. 92), as a means of exploring and reflecting upon their personal worldviews. Ask students to form small groups to share and discuss their worldviews. Emphasize that there is not a right or wrong answer to these questions and that the purpose is to generate a thoughtful conversation. Show Figure 3.1 as an image for students to keep in mind as they engage in conversation. The aim is to have students practice greater cognizance of genuine attention to others and the role of others in the formulation of our own ideas. Participation thus asks all involved to listen to and to attend closely to each other, and to bring these insights and perspectives back to bear on their own thinking. Foster and support these small group conversations as necessary. Allow enough time for students to see and to feel the participatory thinking involved, paying particular attention to scaffolding ELL students' participation through vocabulary development and support, and to encourage them to share their ideas with peers. Bring the conversation to the large group by taking a close look at the seven questions on the questionnaire and asking students where they see evidence of these questions in our lives today. Current political questions will provide varied local and global examples.

To examine the notions of interpretation and context in music in more depth, have students view the performances of contemporary musicians, Eric Lewis, Caroline Lavelle, and Nellie Mckay. These are accessible at:

http://www.ted.com/talks/eric_lewis_strikes_chords_to_rock_the_jazz_world.html
http://www.ted.com/talks/caroline_lavelle_casts_a_spell_on_cello.html
http://www.ted.com/speakers/nellie_mckay.html

Eric Lewis performs a piece on the piano titled *Chaos and Harmony*, and he breaks new ground by cutting across the music genres of jazz, rock, and blues. Caroline Lavelle plays her cello and sings *Further than the Sun*, drawing on classical and contemporary influences. Nellie Mckay plays the piano and other instruments as she offers poignant political statements and social commentary. In addition to each performance, the sites offer transcripts of the lyrics and interviews with the musicians as well as links to related information. These three musicians offer very different musical accounts of interpretation and context but should form a rich conversing ground for discussing how these manifest worldviews through each musician's performance and audience response.

Introduce the generative text of the film *Examined Life* (Taylor, 2008), and the filmmaker's project conversing with contemporary thinkers. Astra Taylor, the filmmaker, purposefully selects particular thinkers to engage them in conversation about their worldviews. Have students each research one of the contemporary thinkers to provide a brief overview of the people to be met via the film. Identify each thinker and have students contribute their findings so that a composite description is recorded and visible for each thinker. View the 88-minute film *Examined Life* as a class. Alternatively, the film is easily divided into viewing segments, and even viewing one or two segments will prompt much thinking. Have students select their favorite thinker from the film, and identify and discuss this decision in their music journals. Furthermore, ask students to surmise which music genre or cross genres would best characterize the thinking portrayed if translated to a musical score.

Journal Entry

Favorite thinker from *Examined Life*:
Why?
Music genre/cross-genre characterization:

· ·

Ways of accommodating students at different levels of English proficiency

Preproduction and Early Production: Introduce the term, 'favorite,' and talk with the students about some of your favorite things; be sure to include the name of your favorite film and talk about why it is your favorite. Ask students to think about their favorite films, and have them ask one another what their favorite films are. Encourage them to be specific, and to ask one another to elaborate on what they like about their favorite film.

Speech Emergence: Introduce the film *Examined Life*, and tell students about how the filmmaker will be interviewing different philosophers. Provide a short description of each of the philosophers that the filmmaker is interviewing, and have the students identify their favorite.

Intermediate Fluency: Introduce the film *Examined Life*, and tell students about how the filmmaker will be interviewing different philosophers. Provide a short description of each of the philosophers that the filmmaker is interviewing as background information for them to refer to while watching the film. It might also help students to connect the description to the philosophers if they are shown a photograph of the philosopher. Show the film, and then discuss with the students who their favorite philosopher is.

Involve students in small group conversations, with each participant noting their favorite thinker from the film and why, comparing the selected music genres. The journal responses should enable these conversations. Bring synthesis to the conversations thus far by reiterating how philosophy generates worldview conversations, and how the film generates worldview conversations, and then consider how music generates such conversations. Compile a visible listing of common themes surfacing across all texts, such as justice, liberation, respect, and care.

Invite students to a fusion dinner party where they each bring the examined life of one contemporary musician to the table. Provide each student with a formal invitation (see Table 3.7) that involves the selection of a contemporary musician that each student predicts will have staying power. Each student must examine the life of this musician to develop a case for the nature of this staying power. To provide some possible examples and to promote student thinking about potential musicians, have students look at the article "The Examined Life," published in the *Houston Press* June 1, 2006 by Jack Silverman. The article reveals that the music of Neil Young and Alejandro Escovedo both reflect life-changing happenings and speak locally and globally to common themes of humanity. See: http://www.houstonpress.com/2006-06-01/music/the-examined-life/

Support the development of student ideas toward realizing the dinner party, setting conference times individually to monitor and prompt the formation of each student's selection of a particular

TABLE 3.7. Sample music invitation, fusion dinner party

YOU ARE INVITED to a FUSION DINNER PARTY

Who— [NAME OF SCHOOL] MUSIC CLASS is hosting the dinner and all students in the class are invited.

Where— Music room.

Why— To foster conversation foregrounding contemporary musicians' contributions to, and impact on, our world.

When— [The date and the time of the dinner.]

What— Examine the life of one contemporary musician who you predict will continue to influence the music world 30 years from now. At the dinner table represent this musician through:

- Selecting one song/piece that reflects the nature of the musician's work and a means to share the song/piece at the dinner table;
- Documenting and sharing biographical and contextual information;
- Surmising the musician's impact and why;
- Optional: dressing and acting as you imagine the musician to be.

How— Materials and resources to inform the traditions a selected musician draws upon and the influences present in her/his music, expanding everyone's thinking and musical practices.

---

musician, representative song, means to share the song, and specifics contributing to staying power. Use Figure 3.1 to talk with students about the nature of conversation in preparation for the fusion dinner party.

Teaching Tip

Monitoring student progress entails attending to the formulating of ideas, the quality of the particular work, the ways in which a student responds to and values the works of others, and the ways the student generally approaches and participates in class. Students' journals can be useful vehicles for chronicling this information and monitoring progress.

Plan for a dinner party as simple as providing pizza and salad to more complex meals, asking students to prepare an authentic dish they speculate as being appropriate to the selected musician. The day of the fusion dinner party, arrange a large table with table settings and a chair for each attendee. Cover the table with butcher paper to create a unified surface. Invite everyone to sit down to share food, enjoying and celebrating the accomplishments of the musicians gathered via the efforts of the entire class. Conclude with each student sharing some aspect representing the music and their insights about the examined life of the musician they brought to the dinner table conversation. Following these accounts, have students relay the common pervading themes and important differences, distinguish concerns and influences, and ascertain the roles of others in the lives of these musicians and the potential connecting power within music for sharing understandings and transforming lives.

Summation

In the music case example # 3 students consider philosophical worldviews and their roles across the arts and in music in particular. A film documentary with a cross-section of philosophers in conversation holding varied worldviews serves as a generative text. Students are asked to engage in their own conversation, becoming musicians from a particular time period, genre, culture, issue, etc. meeting over dinner. Students discover why specific musical works were created, and consider the source of ideas and reasons for musical decisions. Interpreting the works of one specific musician, each student demonstrates understandings of the power of music to shape, express, and communicate ideas and feelings throughout history, re-presenting these ideas in voice and/or instrumental modes brought to share at the table. The gathering of musicians provides a means to share interpretations, explore a variety of influences on music and musicians, and consider music as a vehicle for cultural production, transmission, and translation. ELL students have important negotiating opportunities to reason, interpret rhythms and phrasing, and listen to and analyze musical movements. They are encouraged to take this information into consideration in their music appreciation and music-making processes, gaining greater expression and interpretation capacities, conveying personal understandings to others, and contributing to collective understandings.

Additional Selected Resources

Films

PBS program, music (http://www.pbs.org/arts/arts_music.html)
Taylor, A. (2008). *Examined life*. Toronto, ON: Zeitgeist Films. (http://www.zeitgeistfilms.com/film.php?directoryname=examinedlife&mode=downloads)

Books

Bennett, A., & Peterson, R. A. (Eds.). (2004). *Music scenes: Local, translocal, and virtual*. Nashville, TN: Vanderbilt University Press.
Hannel, G. I. (2009). *Highly effective questioning: Challenging the culture of disengagement in the K-12 classroom* (Kindle edition). Amazon Digital Services: Workshops in Questioning.
Ratiner, T. (2009). *Contemporary musicians: Profiles of the people in music*. Farmington Hills, MI: Gale Cengage.
Shehan Campbell, P., Drummond, J., Dunbar Hall, P., Howard, K., Schippers, H., & Wiggins, T. (Eds.). (2008). *Cultural diversity in music education: Directions and challenges for the 21st century*. Queensland: Australian Academic Press.
Simon, L. (2009). *Wish you were here: An essential guide to your favorite music scenes—from punk to indie and everything in between*. New York: Harper Paperbacks.

Internet Sites

Classroom website development (http://www.wmich.edu/teachenglish/subpages/technology/classwebsite.htm).

Contemporary music, twentieth and twenty-first century (http://www.zeroland.co.nz/contemporary_music.html).

Contemporary musicians list (http://music.aol.com/artists/adult-contemporary).

EFL/ESOL/ESL songs and activities (http://www.songsforteaching.com/esleflesol.htm

ESL Lounge (http://www.esl-lounge.com).

Learn English Through Song (http://www.letslets.com/teach_english.htm).

Music of countries and cultures (http://www.sbgmusic.com/html/teacher/reference/cultures.html).

Music types (http://www.mustcreate.org/kid_home/kids4_4.shtml).

Musician sites (http://www.mustcreate.org/kid_home/kids4_5.shtml).

National Museum of American History (http://americanhistory.si.edu/index.cfm).

Shehan Campbell, P., Thinking globally, acting locally: Cultural diversity in music education, with video links to a representative selection of world music and related issues (http://www.artistshousemusic.org/articles/thinking+globally+acting+locally+cultural+diversity+in+music+education).

William and Gayle Cook Music Library, Indiana University School of Music, *Worldwide Internet music resources* (http://www.libraries.iub.edu/index.php?pageId=90).

Worldview sampler (http://www.teachingaboutreligion.org/WorldviewDiversity/worldview_sampler.htm).

3.4
Drama Experiences to Engage ELLs Alongside All Learners

Drama experiences that are focused on making and relating, perceiving and responding, and connecting and understanding open dialogical spaces for students to: gain awareness of the roles of the dramatic arts in creating and reflecting understandings; build respect for the contributions of individuals and cultural groups to the dramatic arts in local and global contexts; and highlight the value of the dramatic arts as a medium for documenting human experience and expression, and examining the relationships across the arts, societies, and life. Greater self-awareness and wider/deeper insights are gained through attending to other(s)—other materials, other ideas, other images, and other forms of expression. In the process, empathetic and more informed understandings are fostered. Relations between self and other are continually addressed as personal connections and understandings are negotiated. Goldberg (2004) refers to such negotiations as offering needed spaces to explore possibilities and to develop ideas. Such spaces reduce socio-educational pressures, including constraints such as extreme shyness, fear of failure, and perceived language inadequacies that may hinder active participation by ELL students in regular classroom contexts. Thus, language learners may feel liberated to communicate nonverbally, alongside verbal communication, through dramatic arts experiences. By offering a broad range of ways in which students may connect and understand themselves in relation to others, teachers may help ELL students to overcome constraints to communication in the target language through participation in drama experiences such as those presented here in this section.

Drama, Theme I: "Total Control Can Be the Death of a Work"

Generative Text

Rivers and Tides is a film documenting the elemental sculptural forms in the making by Scottish artist Andy Goldsworthy (2004). The imagery of the film gives physical and material expression to his statement, "Total control can be the death of a work" (Scene 4), providing a vivid and tangible portrayal of artistic thinking in process.

About the Text

The DVD of *Rivers and Tides* (Goldsworthy, 2004) can be viewed in its entirety or teachers may choose to introduce Goldsworthy's elemental sculptures though specific scenes that are accessible on the DVD in short segments. It is 90 minutes in length but the scenes offer a way for students to watch one or more excerpts of about 15 minutes each. Alternatively (or in addition), images of Goldsworthy's sculptural forms are available from Abram books (http://www.abramsbooks.com/#) and on the web (http://www.morning-earth.org/ARTISTNATURALISTS/AN_Goldsworthy.html), (http://www.flickr.com/groups/andygoldsworthy/pool/), and Google images (http://images.google.com/imghp?hl=en&tab=wi).

Scene 4 of the DVD, *Rivers and Tides, Feelings of Uncertainty* (Goldsworthy, 2004), depicts the artist seeking his artistic materials as he negotiates his way about the landscape. Viewers come to see how his sculptural forms are site-specific. Viewers increasingly see how Goldsworthy's knowings of the site and the particulars of the land are a necessity. The scene depicts Goldsworthy watching, listening, touching, and attending to colors, textures, shapes, patterns, weather conditions, and existing features of the terrain, gaining knowledge of the land. Control is never imposed. Goldsworthy meets and works with tensions, resistance, and discord as inherent within the process, expected along the way, and as being productive to his art making.

Drama Case Example # 1: Contextual Matters of Site-specific Theatre

Have students gather into a circle, an arm's length away from each other, around the teacher and begin with some breathing and relaxation exercises to focus everyone. Follow these exercises by presenting a hula-hoop (or another fitting object, keeping in mind culturally responsive teaching) to students as a catalyst for imaginative engagement. (Chris Maly[1], a drama teacher at Lincoln High School in Nebraska contributed this suggestion, finding it to be very conducive to motivating and focusing students' attention). Demonstrate the hula-hoop in action and then ask each student to re-imagine what the hula-hoop could be. Provide an example or ask students to suggest some ideas to prompt everyone's engagement. Have students demonstrate its new use while others guess what the hula-hoop has become. Typical ideas include a frisbee and a steering wheel. But, insist that there is no duplication of ideas, so, gradually the hula-hoop suggests more interesting and unanticipated ideas. Depending on the class size, students may get more than one opportunity to re-imagine the hula-hoop. This activity immerses students in process, as the hula-hoop and the ideas generated involve students concretely in making and relating ideas. Have students note in their drama journals their *Top 5 hula-hoop re-imaginings*.

Journal Entry

My top five hula-hoop re-imaginings:
1.
2.
3.
4.
5.

· ·

Ways of accommodating students at different levels of English proficiency

Preproduction and Early Production: Have students draw their hula-loop imaginings, and demonstrate them in pairs.
Speech Emergence and Intermediate Fluency: Have students draw, describe, and demonstrate their hula-hoop imaginings in a group.

As students jot these down, pull out a backpack previously packed with items selected to suggest the characterization of its fictitious owner. Suggestions of items to include might be reading material, grooming item, hat, food wrappers, movie stub, and a shoe. Explain to students that in this imaginary exercise you want them to envision this particular backpack's owner, with the understanding that you just found it in the corner of the room. Without unpacking the backpack, ask students to look at the backpack carefully and write some descriptors in their drama journal that might suggest something about the owner.

Journal Entry

How do you imagine the backpack owner?

Clues:
Descriptors:

· ·

Ways of accommodating students at different levels of English proficiency

Preproduction: Pack a backpack for a day at school, and say the words of the items as you unpack the backpack. Have students repeat the words. Use the words in sentences, modeling how you might use the words when speaking with a friend or peer. Have students make sentences using the words as well, encouraging them to use the vocabulary in ways that might reflect how they would speak with their friends or peers. Help them by providing vocabulary and providing grammatically correct structures that they are struggling with.

Early Production: Pack a backpack for a day at school. Say the words of the items as you unpack the backpack, and have students repeat the words. Take some of the items away and have students guess the missing items. Do the same thing with a backpack that has been packed for a holiday, or a day at the beach. Use the words in sentences, modeling how you might use the words when speaking with a friend or peer. Have students make sentences using the words as well, encouraging them to use the vocabulary in ways that might reflect how they would speak with their friends or peers. Help them by providing vocabulary and providing grammatically correct structures that they are struggling with.

Speech Emergence: Have students plan for a day at school, on holiday, on a hike by packing a backpack. Students can work in pairs to identify items, and then to write sentences (or say phrases) about why they need each of the items.

Intermediate Fluency: Have students draw items for a backpack, and then have them guess what the owner of the backpack is doing based on the items. Have them make assumptions about the owner of the backpack based on the kind of outing they are planning and the items they are bringing with them.

Have students share their descriptors and then begin to examine the backpack by opening up side and front pockets and identifying any findings. Begin to compile a list of descriptors for the owner based on the clues and partial information located. Continue to compile this list as more and more of the backpack is unpacked, eventually arriving at a composite character description. Ask for a volunteer to attempt to model this character's imagined persona. With the volunteer student in the center of the circle of remaining students, continue to engage students in thinking about their composite character. Using costumes and props close by, consider clothing, and dress the volunteer student accordingly. Discuss how the character would carry the backpack, how she/he would move, and hold their body. Consider facial expression and eye contact, and have the student become the character moving about the room for a minute or so. Retrace the imaginative exercise collectively to recall how these ideas and images were formed. In drama journals, have students each note key features or combinations of features that enabled their growing characterization of this fictitious person.

Journal Entry

Backpack Detective

Key indicators about the owner include:

Ways of accommodating students at different levels of English proficiency

Preproduction: Show students a backpack that has been packed for a student. Work with students to identify adjectives that might describe the person who owns the backpack, and have the students repeat the words.

Early Production: Show students a backpack that has been packed for a student. Identify some adjectives that might describe the owner of the backpack, and have the students repeat the words. Have students offer suggestions about how the owner will use each of the items in the backpack.

Speech Emergence: Have students work in pairs to describe the owner of different backpacks (elementary school student, hiker, traveler, university student, etc.) with the contents displayed outside the backpack. Have students write a short paragraph about each owner, using descriptive words.

Intermediate Fluency: Have students work together to describe the owner of different backpacks (elementary school student, hiker, traveler, university student, etc.) with the contents displayed outside the backpack. Have students present each of the owners of the backpacks to a small group of classmates, reading from a short, descriptive paragraph about each owner.

Introduce mime, explaining that this art form challenges the performer to communicate primarily through body language. Ask students to work in pairs for the next 10 minutes to mime how the composite character (just created) might return to the room to look for her/his backpack. Have student take turns in pairs being the backpack owner and someone else who inadvertently is present within this situation. Enable students as necessary and look for some student interpretations to discuss with everyone. Encourage a few pairings to share their mime with the class as a whole. Discuss how others read gestures and body language incorporated in mime. Have students develop a sketch in their drama journals of the composite "backpack" character that takes the shape (or combination) of a drawing, poem, or written description.

Journal Entry

Character sketch (drawing, poem, written description, or combination)

Ways of accommodating students at different levels of English proficiency

Preproduction: Have students draw the owner of a backpack, showing the contents of their backpack displayed beside it.

Early Production: Work with the students to make a list of contents from the backpack where the contents have been displayed beside it. Help students to brainstorm a list of adjectives that might be used to describe a person who owns each of the items from the backpack. Have students write a poem consisting of adjectives about the owner of the backpack.

Speech Emergence: Have students work in groups to present a set of mimes

depicting the owners of five or six different backpacks. The audience members
will be matching the mimes to the different backpacks.

Intermediate Fluency: Have students work in groups to present a set of mimes
depicting the owners of five or six different backpacks. The audience members will be matching the mimes to different descriptions that the students
have written about the owners of the backpacks.

Teaching Tip

As students work in their journals, touch base with students one-on-one to prompt
connections and monitor understandings. Purposefully target different students
each class so that all students are reached regularly.

Revisit the hula-hoop and backpack exercises, fostering a class discussion that examines how
the ideas that were generated from these exercises emerged. Introduce site-specific art forms as
working with the characteristics of a particular place. Ask students to attend to the site-specific
sculptures of Scottish artist, Andy Goldsworthy. Have students watch Scene 4 from the DVD
Rivers and Tides (Goldsworthy, 2004), paying particular attention to what Goldsworthy might
mean by his statement, "Control can be the death of a work" (Scene 4). After watching Scene 4,
have students address the following questions in their journal and then in small groups, relaying
what they saw and heard.

Journal Entry

- How do the artistic materials speak to Goldsworthy? How does this translate
  to theater? Think about how the hula-hoop and backpack materials spoke.
- What is the role of context?
- Why is place important?
- How does Goldsworthy treat the materials and respond as the work is
  created?
- Are there some parallels with your experience with mime?
- What words describe Goldsworthy's engagement? How does a mime artist
  engage with their art form?

· ·

**Ways of accommodating students at different levels of English
proficiency**

Preproduction: Explore the idea of the role of context in shaping what we know
about others. Place the contents of a backpack alongside items that would
depict different places where the owner might be (e.g., the beach, a mountain hiking area, an elementary school, a big city). Say the words of the
items and the names of the places, and have students repeat the words.
Have them do this in pairs, after modeling step by step what you would like
students to do.

Early Production: Explore the idea of the role of context in shaping what we know
about others. Place the contents of a backpack alongside items that would

depict different places where the owner might be (e.g., the beach, a mountain hiking area, an elementary school, a big city). Have students repeat the
names of the places and the items, and make sentences about what they
might be doing in the location. The teacher could demonstrate to students
what is expected of them by modeling sentence types to be repeated.

Speech Emergence: Explore the idea of the role of context in shaping what we
understand. Place the contents of a backpack alongside items that would
depict different places where the owner might be (e.g., the beach, a mountain hiking area, an elementary school, a big city), and have students make
assumptions about what the owner is doing.

Intermediate Fluency: Explore the idea of the role of context in shaping what we
understand. Place the contents of a backpack alongside items that would
depict different places where the owner might be (e.g., the beach, a mountain hiking area, an elementary school, a big city), and have students make
assumptions about what the owner is doing. Highlight that the contents of
the backpack are the same but that the places are different. Explore ways
in which these differences shaped their responses about what the owner of
the backpack was doing and who the owner might be like. Relate this to
ideas about the hula-hoop and backpack activities.

Facilitate small group discussions as necessary, by putting into place structures that encourage students to contribute to discussions in ways that reflect what they are comfortable contributing, depending on their level of language proficiency and individual personality. This may be done by establishing turn taking practices whereby all students are encouraged to contribute, to encouraging students to refer to written materials to support their oral language participation in discussions. It is important to keep in mind that although students may not seem to be actively participating, as might be the case during the characteristic ELL silent period at the beginning levels, they may be absorbing language nonetheless. Attend to important insights that groups generate. Bring these insights to a large group discussion that synthesizes the reverence Goldsworthy demonstrates for what is found and encountered in the environment, the integral role of play and his acknowledgment that something is already at play, and his responsive thinking movement that is animated by the spirit of place. Discuss the translation to site-specific theater as using the properties, qualities, and meanings found on site to reveal the complexity of relationships of self and others in the world. Have students state in a written sentence or two in their drama journals what they believe Goldsworthy means by his insistence that control can be the death of a work and how this might be akin to site-specific theater.

Journal Entry

Control can be the death of a theater project by ...

• •

Ways of accommodating students at different levels of English proficiency

Preproduction: Review vocabulary from the DVD *Rivers and Tides, and* have the
students use the words in sentences in a school or community context. The

vocabulary could be introduced by providing students with a list of vocabulary words to listen for as they watch the DVD for the first time, and then pausing the DVD to talk about the meaning and use of the new word. Replay the segment of the DVD where the word was used, so that students are able to hear how the word is used in context before having students use the word in their own sentences.

Early Production: Review vocabulary from DVD *Rivers and Tides*, and have students write sentences that will support a conversation where they are asking a classmate or peer about hobbies, interests, and extra-curricular activities.

Speech Emergence: Revisit the idea that too much control can be the death of a work. Have students refer to incidences in their own life when they think this might have been the case. Have students share these ideas with a partner.

Intermediate Fluency: Revisit the idea that too much control can be the death of a work. Have students refer to incidences in their own life when they think this might have been the case. Have students share these ideas in a small group, and encourage them to make connections to how too much control might contribute to the death of work in theater.

Teaching Tip

Encourage students to create an electronic dictionary of vocabulary words they are likely to use. Help students to develop the habit of alphabetizing words as they add new ones to the dictionary, and to organize them according to subject or topic area, so that they are able to find new vocabulary words quickly. Encourage students to refer to these cards and to use the vocabulary as needed. It is important to recognize, however, that despite attempts to encourage independence in the students as they learn new vocabulary, it is likely necessary for the teacher to constantly use new vocabulary and to contextualize new vocabulary within known sentence structures or to use known vocabulary within new sentence structures, in order for the new language to be consolidated.

Brainstorm potential sites for site-specific theater with students. Talk about the authenticity that might be gained and how audiences might be engaged in these performances.

Teaching Tip

The *Chicago Walkabout Theater* has abstracts available online regarding two site-specific performances—one that took place in a laundromat, and one that took place in a series of public restrooms. These abstracts include the intents in relation to a particular space, time, and community. See: http://www.walkabouttheater.org/history/history.html.

Knowhere Productions is a Saskatchewan-based Canadian theater company that is invested in site-specific theater. Their website of a particular project using *The Weyburn Mental Hospital* founded in 1921 as the site, provides a window into how site-specific theater can draw upon history, artifacts, peoples' memories of events, and details and understandings of past and present to provide insights into mental health, alongside foregrounding local and global issues. Have students access the website to discover the "material traces" and "explore the actualities of a dense history" through *The Weyburn Mental Hospital* site-specific theater project, performed in August and September of 2002. See: http://uregina.ca/weyburn_project/pages/sitespec.html.

In their drama journals, have students draw a map of their explorations of the hospital and their associated responses and questions.

Journal Entry

Map documenting web trip through *The Weyburn Mental Hospital*

Responses:
Questions:

· ·

Ways of accommodating students at different levels of English proficiency

Preproduction: Enlarge a map of the hospital, and give students a 'tour' by pointing out the different places identified on the map. Have students repeat the words.

Early Production: Enlarge a map of the hospital, and give students a 'tour' by pointing out the different places identified on the map. Have students draw a map of their school or their home, and share it with their classmates.

Speech Emergence: Have students draw a map of their school building, and share it with a partner. Engage students in giving directions to another student to help them to find their way around the school.

Intermediate Fluency: Have students draw a map of their school building or the school neighborhood community. Students may role-play, taking turns asking for, and giving, directions to go from one place to another. In addition, students may write out directions for another student to follow, in order to locate a person or an item.

Discuss together what the contributing factors are that make *The Weyburn Mental Hospital* a particularly rich site for such theater.

Teaching Tip

The parts-to-whole relationship across learning experiences needs to be constantly negotiated by the teacher, assessing student understandings and levels of participatory thinking throughout. Constantly seeking opportunities to reinforce concepts from varying perspectives ensures greater continuity for all involved.

Define a tableau. In groups of three to five, have students create a tableau based on an idea, theme, or significant detail from *The Weyburn Mental Hospital* project. Students should collaborate to perform a tableau of bodies frozen as if caught in the midst of action, suggesting what the characters are doing and how they are interacting with others and their environment. After a practice time of approximately 30 minutes, have students perform these for each other. Keep a record of each tableau using a digital camera. Have the audience share their responses to each tableau and discuss these with the performers. Talk with students about connections to performance art and related purposes. Place digital images and representative responses on display where they will generate continued conversation and debate.

Summation

In the drama case example #1 students translate qualities present in given materials and situations into gestures and actions, giving expression to personal lived understandings of these qualities. Opportunities to practice selecting, organizing, and creating dramatic work that communicates individually and collaboratively notions that are difficult to express and to find fitting words will challenge all involved. Attending to a film or images of the sculptural forms in the making of Andy Goldsworthy serves as a generative text for students to consider how context matters to the evolution of art forms and drama in particular. ELL students will gain important opportunities for situated practice encoding and decoding with language, actions, and meanings folding into and reinforcing each other, using feedback to refine their own dramatic work. The features of site-specific theater are explored through examples engaging all students in navigating contextual considerations that form and inform such works.

Additional Selected Resources

Film/DVD

Goldsworthy, A. (2004). *Rivers and tides: Working with time*, DVD. Directed by Thomas Riedelsheimer. Mediopolis Films.

Books

Allain, P., & Harvie, J. (2005). *The Routledge companion to theatre and performance*. New York: Routledge.
Barranger, M. S. (2005). *Theatre: A way of seeing*. Emeryville, CA: Wadsworth.
Houston, A. (2007). *Environmental and site-specific theatre*. Toronto: Playwrights Canada.
Kaye, N. (2000). *Site specific art: Place and documentation*. New York: Routledge.
Pearson, M., & Shanks, M. (2001). *Theatre/archaeology: Disciplinary dialogues*. New York: Routledge.
Prendergast, M., & Saxton, J. (Eds.). (2009). *Applied theatre: International case studies and challenges for practice*. Bristol, UK: Intellect.
Schechner, R. (2000). *Environmental theater*. New York: Applause Books.

Internet Sites

Ramlila—the traditional performance of the Ramayana (http://www.unesco.org/culture/ich/index.php).
St. Louis-based site theater company (http://www.onsitetheatre.org/index.html).

Drama, Theme II: "Responsive Matters of Perception"

Generative Text

A slam poem, *Love,* is authored and performed by a high school student, Lucas Hines[2], giving expression to the young man's ongoing considerations about what it means to be in love. Access the performance of the slam poem at: http://cehs.unl.edu/mlatta/poem.htm

---

About the Text

The student's poem on love is situated within a quickly evolving movement of slam poetry occurring over the last 25 years. Poetry found this new venue in 1984 through Marc Smith, a Chicago construction worker experimenting in front of an audience with forms for poetry readings. Slam has since moved from the margins to mainstream, and from a local to global phenomena, revitalizing poetry. A slam is a poetry competition where poets perform original work alone or in teams with audience engagement as judges. These poems represent diverse topics and purposes including comedic, dramatic, personal, and political. A slam poet aims for audience connection. And, with this emphasis on performance, slam poets share their identity, their convictions, and their embedded understandings through spoken word, body language, and stage presence. Poetry slams are now found everywhere in the United States and have expanded to other countries including Australia, Austria, Bosnia-Herzegovina, Canada, the Czech Republic, Denmark, France, Germany, Macedonia, Nepal, the Netherlands, New Zealand, Singapore, South Korea, Sweden, Switzerland, and the United Kingdom.

Drama Case Example # 2: Relations at Play, Shaping and Reshaping Dramatic Forms

Jock Love Poem
by Lucas Hines
(Note to the reader: this is not how I talk)

I love you.
Like so much, that I don't even have like words.
I love you like a beautiful sunrise over the beautiful horizon
of love.
I love you more than you will ever admit.
I love you more, no I love you more, no I love you more.
I'm not hanging up, you hang up. I'm not hanging up, you hang up.
BECAUSE I LOVE YOU SO MUCH!

I love you like a fairytale. I can be your knight in shining armor.
I love you so freaking much, Dude.

I love you like if I didn't love you, I would be like, dead.
I love you like I need you to breathe.
I love you, I love you, I love you. I still love you, I love you more, I still love you more.
I got a secret, I love you.
I love you this much (holds hands spread out)
I love you like dogs love bones.
I love you like I would sing a song for you.
I've got great news, I love you.
I mean I couldn't paint a picture of how much I love you.
If love could fly us to the moon, we would be on the moon sometime in the future.
I would totally risk everything, because I love you.
I want to kiss you on the lips, because I love you.
I love you like if you looked in the dictionary under the definition of love, you would totally see me and you.

I love you like I'm trying to own the definition of loving you.
Do you know what love is? I do! It's how I feel about you.
Why did the chicken cross the road? BECAUSE I LOVE YOU. Duh!
Angels aren't as pretty as you.

I luv you, I heart you, ILY, XOXOXO I love love you, TE AMO (I love you in Spanish)
Je t'aime (I love you in French) Because I love you in different languages is how much I love you.

When its cold outside, I still love you.
I love you like you're the glue that holds my heart together.
She loves me, she loves me not, she loves me, she loves me not, she loves me, I love you more.
I love you so much that I cannot stop thinking about you, and I love it!
I want to get old with you. Because I love you.
2+2= I love you
I am so in love with you, that it is dangerous how much I love you
I love you so much that I'm trying to cry a little bit, because if you saw the tear, you would know how much I love you.
Darlin, Sweety, Sugar, Pumpkin, Smookems,
I love you. And I wrote you this poem because I love you. Alot
Like alot alot.

Introduce the written text of the slam poem by high school student Lucas Hines. Have students read through the text of the poem, first silently and then out loud, playing with tone, dynamics, and phrasing. Foster students' concentration as they immerse themselves in the text of the poem by turning lights down and ensuring the use of a room large enough for students to find their own space to hear and respond to their own voice. Visit each student and observe, affirm, and redirect as needed. Take note of differences and similarities across students' interpretations so that you can purposefully return to these examples in discussions to come. Allow time for students to really engage the poem. Have students record in their journals words and images that come to their minds through the poem. Ask students to play with these descriptive words, as they did with the oral text, so that the responsive page in their journal depicts words that carry meanings via the line quality, size, and other features, utilizing traditional writing tools or software generating word clouds via wordle at: http://www.wordle.net/.

Journal Entry

This word cloud was made using wordle: http://www.wordle.net/

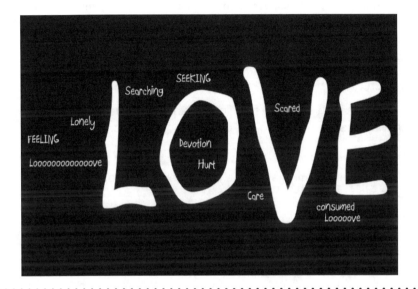

· ·

Ways of accommodating students at different levels of English proficiency

Preproduction and Early Production: Give students an abbreviated form of the poem, and have them go through and pick ten words that they know. Introduce the idea of using size, line quality, and other features to highlight some words over others in a word cloud. Have them make a word cloud with the words they have selected. Have them show the poem to a partner, and then have the partners work together to learn the words they have selected.

Speech Emergence and Intermediate Fluency: Give students a copy of the poem, and have them go through and pick twenty words that they know. Introduce the idea of using size, line quality, and other features to highlight some words over others in a word cloud. Have students make a word cloud with the words they have selected, and then work in pairs to learn the words they have selected. They will then be asked to present their word cloud to the rest of the class.

In small groups, have students discuss the perceived tone of the poem and the descriptive words that were elicited. As discussion progresses on the consideration of tone, ask students to further consider where these ideas stem from. Bring the discussion back to the whole group by examining the poem's topic of love as having some universal understandings, and yet, very individually understood through distinct narratives of experience. Have students imagine the underlying narrative that led to this slam poem on love. To do so, students should each develop sentences to write in-between each phrase of the slam poem, thus exploring the potential issues, considerations, and emotions that might be at play. Following completion of this writing exercise, students work in pairs with one student reading the slam poem aloud phrase by phase and the other student interjecting a line of narrative contextualizing the slam poem. Encourage students to experiment with roles and use of narrative texts. Set a tight time frame for experimentation, and then have students present their version of the poem with accompanying narrative to all class members. In drama journals, have students record ways in which understandings of the poem may have been enlarged through the perceptions and responses of others.

Journal Entry

Chronicle your growing understandings of the poem using a diagram, chart, sketch, written statement, or combination of approaches.

· ·

Ways of accommodating students at different levels of English proficiency

Preproduction and Early Production: Ask the students what they think the poet is saying. Model the use of a diagram, chart, sketch, and written statement to depict their understanding of what the poet is saying, and have students produce a diagram, chart, sketch, or written statement as well. The use of graphic organizers might also be very helpful here. It is also important to reinforce the value of pre-reading, during-reading, and post-reading strategies as methods to help students to consolidate language.

Speech Emergence and Intermediate Fluency: Ask the students what they think the poet is saying. Model the use of a diagram, chart, sketch, and written statement to depict their understanding of what the poet is saying, and have students produce a diagram, chart, sketch, or written statement as well. Have students show their work to a small group of classmates, and have them offer comments to their classmates, indicating what they liked about the work.

Teaching Tip

Imagery, diagrams, maps, and charts can be very useful for making visible ELLs' thinking. Incorporate these teaching materials in your classroom as useful devices for talking with students about their thinking. Encourage students to use them and create their own.

Teaching Tip

Encourage ELL students to share knowledge of customs and traditions about love and courtship in diverse ethnic communities. Prior to the oral discussion, have students jot down initial ideas to support their participation in the discussion, and then to take notes as they share the ideas with their peers, in the form of notes made in the margins of their pages. Have students address some of the questions asked by their peers to further develop their writing, and then compile the final written texts into a booklet for display in the classroom. This idea may be used for many topics and themes, to encourage participation in oral activities and as encouragement to work toward a more polished piece to share with classmates and visitors to the classroom.

Explore the intents of slam poetry by asking how many students have participated and/or performed as a slam poet. Evolve this discussion to include some of the history and traditions of performance that slam poetry embraces and the relations to drama. Ask students to watch the slam poet perform his love poem, looking for the perceiving and responding features that contribute to the completed performance. Have students relay the features that enable the poet to discover the rhythmic aspects that form and articulate, providing dynamics and phrasing within the spoken words. Students should purposefully connect their personal experience of performing the poem, seeking similarities and differences. Ask students to consider what role the background imagery serves as Lucas performs the slam poem. Discuss Lucas's performance in relation to the students' earlier interpretations of his poem.

Generate a collective word cloud using each student's previously created wordle describing the slam love poem. Examine the resulting text as a class to determine primary themes that characterize students' understandings. Have students divide into groups according to the themes. Assign each group the task of re-presenting the theme back to the other members of the class using any dramatic exploration that fits their group and theme. These could include letter exchanges, poems, personal narratives, news reports, silent interpretations, social commentary on matchmaking services, humorous tales, and so on. The emphasis should be on giving expression to the theme with minimal props, and setting considerations.

Teaching Tip

Redirect students who want to spend extensive time on set design, props, or costuming, toward concentrating on re-presenting the theme through performative means. Setting a time allowance and specific constraints will maximize the lesson possibilities for students.

Finalized performances should be no longer than five minutes in length. Students should sit in a circle creating the stage space. Have students perform these scenes in succession, drawing on a cross-section of performative means. The themes should be identified and used as transitions between each group. Encourage students to engage the whole performative experience as a collective expression rather than each separate part. To do so, insist that students move from one presentation to the next with a set transition that introduces the theme similarly for each group with time to only move between center stage and the outside circle. At the completion of all performances, discuss the overall impact. Have students consider connections to the structure of slam poetry, stand-up comedy, and performance art, in the ways they move away from a linear narrative and position with the audience, to one in which the audience engages alongside the performer, seeking meaning. Have students revisit their dramatic explorations and alter one element using one of the ideas from Table 3.8. A list of potential ways to gain a different perspective

TABLE 3.8. Imaginative ways to alter and transform perspectives

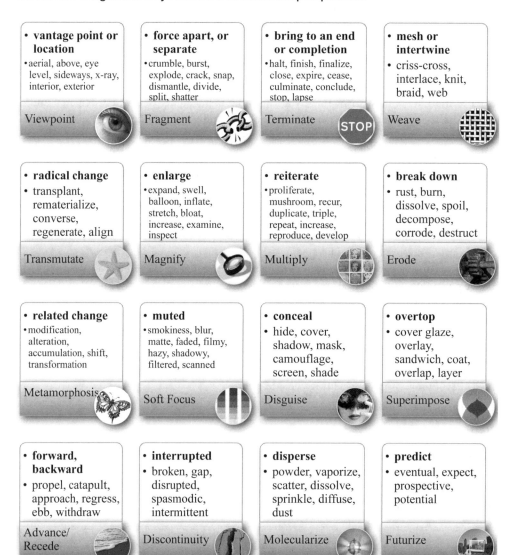

• **vantage point or location** • aerial, above, eye level, sideways, x-ray, interior, exterior Viewpoint	• **force apart, or separate** • crumble, burst, explode, crack, snap, dismantle, divide, split, shatter Fragment	• **bring to an end or completion** • halt, finish, finalize, close, expire, cease, culminate, conclude, stop, lapse Terminate	• **mesh or intertwine** • criss-cross, interlace, knit, braid, web Weave
• **radical change** • transplant, rematerialize, converse, regenerate, align Transmutate	• **enlarge** • expand, swell, balloon, inflate, stretch, bloat, increase, examine, inspect Magnify	• **reiterate** • proliferate, mushroom, recur, duplicate, triple, repeat, increase, reproduce, develop Multiply	• **break down** • rust, burn, dissolve, spoil, decompose, corrode, destruct Erode
• **related change** • modification, alteration, accumulation, shift, transformation Metamorphosis	• **muted** • smokiness, blur, matte, faded, filmy, hazy, shadowy, filtered, scanned Soft Focus	• **conceal** • hide, cover, shadow, mask, camouflage, screen, shade Disguise	• **overtop** • cover glaze, overlay, sandwich, coat, overlap, layer Superimpose
• **forward, backward** • propel, catapult, approach, regress, ebb, withdraw Advance/ Recede	• **interrupted** • broken, gap, disrupted, spasmodic, intermittent Discontinuity	• **disperse** • powder, vaporize, scatter, dissolve, sprinkle, diffuse, dust Molecularize	• **predict** • eventual, expect, prospective, potential Futurize

Source: This table is adapted from the work of Dr. Bill Zuk at the University of Victoria, B.C. Canada. For further reading that embeds imaginative ways to alter and transform perspectives see Zuk, B. & Dalton, R. (2005) First nations art and culture: tradition and innovation. In K. Grauer & R.L. Irwin (Eds.), *Starting with…* (pp. 81-87). Toronto: Canadian Society for Education through Art.

with synonyms is provided. Students may need to access a dictionary for greater understanding of specific terms.

Teaching Tip

Create the conditions and offer ongoing support for students to concretely navigate the lived consequences of changing an element through the dramatic explorations. Watch and work closely with small groups to ensure everyone's involvement, facilitating connections.

Teaching Tip

Some ELL students who are at the pre-production level of English language development and have difficulty participating in spoken roles in some of the activities may find it helpful (and less intimidating) to take part in non-speaking roles. Alternatively, they may assume roles where they are able to participate along with their peers as a group rather than individually. At the same time, it is important to recognize that some students may be open to the challenge of roles requiring longer speaking parts, especially if they are provided support in learning their lines and encouragement from their peers.

Ask students to attend to how one element can change the dramatic atmosphere. Record the consequences of the one change in their dramatic journals.

Journal Entry

Element changed:
Lived consequences:

• •

Ways of accommodating students at different levels of English proficiency

Divide the class into four or five groups, and identify two students in each group to lead a discussion about courtship practices in diverse ethnic communities. Have students decide on one of the practices to act out for the rest of the class, in the form of a skit. Engage all of the students in some way in the performance of the skits. Have students write the skits on a white board (or on printouts) so that all members of the group are able to refer to the words if needed as they present the skit. Provide a short amount of time to practice, encouraging the students to focus on the words rather than props or costumes. Present the skits.

Have students work together to assess how they think their presentations went, and to identify two aspects to change in order to improve upon the skit.

> Have students identify one element to change in the skit. Perform the skits, and then ask the students how they think the changed element contributed to a change in the overall skit.

Have students again share these dramatic explorations as a unit, but alter the order of presentation to create the conditions for students to see/feel physically how structure in dramatic form relates to perception and response. Collectively unpack the perceived differences and the types of responses elicited. Reference Table 3.8 for change element synonyms, and to enable all students to expand and strengthen their understandings of these terms. The list is intended to prompt ways to alter an element in their drama with some students needing to turn to other reference sources for terminology meanings.

Summation

In the drama case example # 2, students are asked to reinterpret aspects of a slam poem on love, exploring how drama can reflect the ideas of individuals, communities, and societies. Students are asked to consider how drama explores current events alongside personal and social issues. They are further asked to evaluate and to synthesize contextual, cultural, historical, and political information to support their artistic choices. Ongoing review and critique of dramatic interpretations will require students to use appropriate terminology, analyze feedback to refine their own and others' works, and evaluate multiple means for re-presenting. ELL students will gain opportunities to value, and to attend closely to social interaction, bringing their own experiences to bear as they re-present and explore issues common and distinct across human interactions. Cognitive flexibility will be gained as they seek personal resonance.

Additional Selected Resources

Slam Poetry

Algarin, M., & Holman, B. (1994). *Aloud: Voices from the Nuyorican Poet's Café*. New York: Henry Holt.
Delvin, P. (2004). *SlamNation—New educational edition*. Slammin' Entertainment. New York: New York Video Group.
Eleveld, M. (2003). *The spoken word revolution: Slam, HipHop, and the poetry of a new generation*. Bel Air, CA: Sourcebooks MediaFusion.
Glazner, G. M. (2000). *Poetry slam*. San Francisco: Manic D Press.
Levin, M. (1998). *Slam*. Vancouver, BC: Lion's gate. Rated: R.
Simmons, R. (2009). *Brave new voices*. Home Box Office, Time Warner Entertainment Company.

Internet Sites

A brief guide to slam poetry (http://www.poets.org/viewmedia.php/prmMID/5672).
Contexts, poets, background information on Brave New Voices (http://www.hbo.com/bravenewvoices/crew/index.html).
Living word project (http://livingwordproject.org/lwp_description.html).
Poetry Slam Incorporated (http://www.poetryslam.com/).
Saul Williams (http://www.poets.org/viewmedia.php/prmMID/5813).

The Nuyorican Poet's Café (http://www.nuyorican.org/).

Youth Speaks (http://youthspeaks.org/word/).

Perspectives of Aboriginal people in Canada (http://www3.nfb.ca/enclasse/doclens/visau/index.php?language=english).

Dramatic poems for the theater (http://www.blackcatpoems.com/d/dramatic_poems.html).

Love poems (http://www.blackcatpoems.com/l/love_poems.html).

Dramatic poetry (http://www.poetry-portal.com/styles11.html).

Dixon, R. (Ed.). (2001). The Living Playbook (http://www.unexpectedproductions.org/living_playbook.htm).

Readers Theater links (http://www.webenglishteacher.com/rt.html).

Readers Theater—It's all in the delivery (http://www.nytimes.com/learning/teachers/lessons/20070427friday.html).

Drama warm-ups (http://www.creativedrama.com/theatre.htm).

Books

Anderson, M., Hughes, J., & Manuel, J. (Eds.). (2008). *Drama and English teaching: Imagination, action, and engagement.* Oxford: Oxford University Press.

Johnstone, K. (1999). *Improv for storytellers.* New York: RoutledgeTheatre Arts Book.

Lundy, K. G. (2008). *Teaching fairly in an unfair world.* Portland, ME: Stenhouse.

Napier, M. (2004). *Improvise: Scene from the inside out.* Portsmouth, NH: Heinemann Drama.

Neelands, J., & Goode, T. (2000). *Structuring drama work: A handbook of available forms in theatre and drama.* Cambridge: Cambridge University Press.

Prendergast, M., & Saxton, J. (Eds.). (2009). *Applied theatre: International case studies and challenges for practice.* Bristol, UK: Intellect.

Prendiville, F., & Toye, N. (2007). *Speaking and listening through drama, 7—11.* London: Paul Chapman.

Spolin, V. (1999). *Improvisation for the theater 3E: A handbook of teaching and directing techniques.* Evanston, IL: Northwestern University.

Drama, Theme III: "Examined Lives in Relation—A Fusion Dinner Party"

Generative Text

Filmmaker Astra Taylor converses with some of today's most influential thinkers within selected contexts, fitting to each one. The thinking each shares is chronicled in her film, *Examined Life* (Taylor, 2008). The film reveals the multiple perspectives from which the world can be seen and lived. In this way, the film becomes the text to re-imagine the perspectives gained and to stage a fusion dinner party. A fusion dinner party intentionally invites meetings across differences. Envisioning, creating, and enacting a fusion dinner party serves as a further generative vehicle for a drama experience enlarging historical and contextual understandings.

About the Text

Viewing the entire DVD of the film *Examined Life* (Taylor, 2008) gives the fullest access to Astra Taylor's intent to invite and to foster conversation on what it means to live right. Alternatively, or in addition, short overviews of the film can be accessed at: http://www.nfb.ca/film/examined-life-trailer/ and http://www3.nfb.ca/webextension/examined-life/.

The persistent questions throughout the film are: how does one live the examined life and why should we invest in doing so? The film reveals that the ways we answer these questions are shaped by our various worldviews. Thus, the film confronts and asks viewers to challenge their values, assumptions, and beliefs connected to one's worldview. The cross-section of contemporary philosophers, including Cornel West, Avital Ronell, Peter Singer, Kwarne Anthony Appiah, Martha Nussbaum, Michael Hardt, Slavoj Zizek, Judith Butler, and Sunaura Taylor, provide intersecting and opposing ideas that engage viewers and invite them to join the conversation. In doing so, viewers will find themselves interacting and deliberating about the film's surfacing issues of courage, responsibility, ethics, power, privilege, indifference, social justice, gender, ableism, and politics, and what this might entail for notions of citizenry and democracy in an increasingly globalized world.

A fusion dinner party is purposefully designed and enacted to embrace differences in perspectives (Lorraine Cockle[4], teacher in Calgary, Alberta, Canada offers the idea of the dinner party, which we adapted). The film *Examined Life* (Taylor, 2008) serves as a generative text providing the "food for thought" from multiple perspectives for the fusion dinner table guests and conversation. Akin to a fusion menu at a restaurant that brings the table ware, cooking, and traditions of several cultures together, the fusion dinner conversation is intended to surface differences, seek insights from one another, and prompt new connections and possibilities. Students are asked to examine their own lives in relation to selected historical and contemporary musicians. In doing so, the relations across the dramatic arts and society will be fore-grounded for all to connect and grow understandings.

Drama Case Example # 3: Embodying Worldviews in Action and Word

Initiate the drama experience with two questions: (a) Who was Walt Whitman? and (b) What historical events marked and characterized the time period and contexts Whitman lived within America, 1819–1892? Some students will have information to contribute, so start this experience with what students know. Connect this information with a brief introduction of Whitman as the American Poet identifying with common people and everyday issues and concerns. Have students watch the Public Broadcasting System (PBS) program *The American Experience* (accessible at: http://www.pbs.org/wgbh/amex/whitman/program/), which tells Whitman's story. A transcript of the program can also be downloaded from the website and a timeline is available on the website, situating the entire account through key events in history and the significances to be found through attention to place. Ask students to attend to the PBS program for historical and personal information that might enable each of them to translate aspects of their understandings of Whitman to others. In their drama journals, have students record their impressions of Whitman in poem, narrative, descriptive words, drawings, or a combination of renderings, sketching their developing insights of the American poet. Sarah Thomas[5], an English teacher at East High School in Lincoln Nebraska contributes specific ideas here, that she includes in her teaching experiences and that we adapt for arts learning experiences.

Teaching Tip

Provide ELL students with a copy of the transcript, and read through the text in a small group with other students who may need extra support in order to better understand the content. This allows the students the opportunity to read through the text at a pace appropriate to their level, and provides them with opportunities to ask questions to clarify their understanding of the issues raised. Encourage them to make notes that will help them to participate in the class activities when the material is used with the rest of the class.

Journal Entry

Sketches of Walt Whitman (poem, narrative, descriptive words, drawings, or combination of forms)

What do you see and feel through Whitman's life experiences?
How does the time period and specifics of places contribute to his identity?

. . . .

Ways of accommodating students at different levels of English proficiency

Preproduction and Early Production: Provide students with a summary about Walt Whitman. Read the summary together, highlighting critical events. Have students do a drawing based on what you have read.

Speech Emergence: Provide students with a summary about Walt Whitman. Read the summary together, highlighting critical events. Watch the PBS program together, and have students work in groups to produce a narrative or a poem. Share their work with the rest of the class.

Intermediate Fluency: Provide a timeline of historical events as well as a summary about Walt Whitman. Have students work together to place details of Walt Whitman's life on the timeline of historical events. Discuss together ways in which historical events of the time period might have contributed to shaping his identity.

Using the historical timeline available on the PBS website *The American Experience* (http://www.pbs.org/wgbh/amex/whitman/program/), have students work in small groups to indicate their associations regarding Whitman's identity through his encounters with, and responses to, place and time, returning to ideas generated through personal journal sketches. Attend to these small groups to ensure focus and redirect as necessary. Listen for insights that will benefit the entire class, and share these in a collective discussion following small group work. Compile information generated across all groups onto a timeline for all to see and revisit.

Talk with students about the materials embedded within history and the important work of the dramatist as historian and researcher. Have students consider the role of empathy in gaining insights into Whitman's life and times. Engage students in accessing Whitman's poem *Song of Myself*, and reading through it to select a stanza that draws their interest. This is accessible at http://rpo.library.utoronto.ca/poem/2288.html.

Have students practice reading the selected stanza aiming for language tone and qualities conveying personality traits, empathizing with the situation, and internalizing the felt experience. Additional background information can be found on the Walt Whitman archive accessible at: http://www.whitmanarchive.org/.

Students should share these interpretations in pairs working together to develop the strongest expressions possible. Work alongside students to foster these efforts. Consider with students how stanzas mark moments and heighten cognizance of their involvement in choosing and expressing a moment of focus, finding form for personal responses and thinking, giving expression to reflection and analysis with sensitive awareness. Select one or two students to share their interpretations with the class as a whole to bring synthesis to this discussion.

Introduce contemporary actor, playwright, and social critic Anna Deavere Smith. Her work reflects careful attention to others and the particulars of situations, constructing and enacting portraitures of people. In doing so, she explores issues of race, identity, and community in America inspired by Walt Whitman's idea "to absorb America." She has interviewed over 2,000 people across the country in a 20-year period and translates these encounters into solo performances, "inhabiting" the persons she meets. Students can access a performance at: http://www.ted.com/speakers /anna_deavere_smith.html.

Teachers should be aware that Deavere Smith's performance demands mature student audiences as there is adult content and some explicit language. A transcript of the entire oral text of the performance can be downloaded from the website to enable teachers' and students' readings. This particular performance gives expression to four Americans: Studs Terkel, a prize-winning author and radio broadcast personality from 1912–2008; Paulette Jenkins, an inmate; Young Soon Han, a Korean-American woman; and Brent Williams, a bull rider. Following a viewing of the performance, have students record responses in their drama journals.

Journal Entry

How does history inform the portrait of each character?
How does place inform the portrait of each character?
How do oral and body language help to convey the characters?
How do class, race, and personal intersect with these portraitures?

• •

Ways of accommodating students at different levels of English proficiency

Preproduction and Early Production: Focus on one of the characters, and work with the students to explore ways in which history and place contribute to shaping the character. To begin with, provide students with a summary of the character, and read the text together. Have students identify historical events, and explore how they might contribute to shaping the character. Examine place next, and discuss ways in which place might contribute to shaping the character.

Speech Emergence and Intermediate Fluency: Begin by focusing on one of the characters. Work with the students to explore ways in which history, place, and class, race, and personal factors intersect to shape the character. Provide students with a summary of the character, and read the text together. Have students identify historical events, and explore how they might contribute to shaping the character. Examine place next, and discuss ways in which place might contribute to shaping the character. Explore the intersection of class, race, and personal, and discuss how these factors might have contributed to the character. Have students work in groups of three to do the same exercise with another character.

Build on the ideas formulated by students in their drama journals, as students examine some of the work of Toni Morrison, an author akin to Deavere Smith who does not shy away from issues of racism and exploitation. Students may have some familiarity with her writings, and this information should be used as the ground to further connect students' thinking. Have students access the oral history archive on Morrison to find out about her biography. Video clips of representative works are accessible on the archive site as well. See: http://www.visionaryproject.com/morrisontoni/.

Assign students in small groups to access one of the video clips and use it to formulate a scenario that re-presents the underlying issues conveyed in the clip particular to: *Beloved, Segregation and Racism in Lorain, Ohio, Motivation for Writing, Challenges as a Female Writer, Nobel Prize Winner, Song of Solomon, Skin Color, Classism in the Community, The Future of African American Literature,* and *Young People and Possibilities.* Student groups should first identify the issues and then collectively develop a scenario foregrounding these issues, purposefully positioning an audience to delve into possible outcomes. The scenarios should depict a problematic event or unresolved dilemma that invites audience engagement. As student groups work on the development of these, assist as needed. Keep the time allowed to develop these scenarios tight to ensure focus, and emphasize the significance of audience interactions and contributions that form the next phase that moves into forum-theater.

In this phase of the experience, groups share their scenarios while others observe. In forum-theater, both actors and audience members can stop the action, redirect, or take over roles toward revealing the many ways the scenario might unfold and the potential considerations at play. Aim for a high intensity of involvement as ideas are re-shaped and multiple perspectives are opened and engaged. As students work through this process let them know the context for forum-theater as derived from Augusto Boal's (1993) *Theater of the Oppressed.*

Teaching Tip

For additional information and resources regarding *Theater of the Oppressed* and its derivatives, see: http://www.wwcd.org/action/Boal.html and http://performance-art.suite101.com/article.cfm/theatre_of_the_oppressed_and_its_derivatives

---

Teaching Tip

Consider putting students into smaller groups such that they are not required to work with and to present in front of so many people. Incorporate repetition of performances to allow students the opportunity to draw upon knowledge and language gained in a previous presentation of the performance. Students might also benefit from the opportunity to watch others practice and perform first before participating themselves, to give them an idea as to expectations for this activity.

The aim to unmask oppression is the work students will be embracing throughout this drama experience and is, of course, at the heart of the works by Walt Whitman, Anna Deavere Smith, and Toni Morrison.

As a means to consider relations and connections across all student scenarios based on Morrison's works, ask students to consider how worldviews are created, adapted, and transformed. The worldview student questionnaire may be useful (see Table 3.5). Keeping considerations generated by students regarding what constitutes one's worldview in mind, have students attend to the generative text of the film *Examined Life*. Astra Taylor, the filmmaker, purposefully selects particular thinkers to engage them in conversation about their worldviews. View the 88-minute film *Examined Life* as a class. Identify each thinker and have students contribute findings so that a composite description is recorded and visible for each thinker. Have students select their favorite thinker from the film and identify and discuss this decision and the particular worldview in their drama journals.

Journal Entry

Favorite Thinker from *Examined Life*

Why this thinker?
How would you describe her/his worldview?

· ·

Ways of accommodating students at different levels of English proficiency

Preproduction and Early Production: Introduce the idea of a worldview, and explore what the term means using well-known political, sports, and media figures (with potentially extreme ideas) as examples. Introduce the idea of a worldview by sharing and elaborating upon your own. Ask students about their idea of a worldview. Encourage students to elaborate of this idea of a worldview by describing and/or providing specific examples to share with their peers.

Speech Emergence and Intermediate Fluency: Introduce the idea of a worldview, and explore what the term means using well-known political, sports, and media figures as examples. Discuss with the students their own worldviews, and share your own. Talk about how they will be watching a film, *Examined*

Life, where the worldviews of a few people will be expressed. Describe the worldviews of a couple of the philosophers and have students listen and watch carefully to identify who they are.

Involve students in small group conversations with each participant noting their favorite thinker from the film and why, comparing the various worldviews. The journal responses should enable these conversations. Bring synthesis to the conversations thus far by reiterating how philosophy generates worldview conversations and how the film generates worldview conversations and then consider how drama generates such conversations. Compile a visible listing of common themes surfacing across all texts such as justice, liberation, respect, and care.

To act on how drama might generate worldview conversations, invite students to a fusion dinner party where they each bring the examined life of a real or fictional civil wartime character to life at the table. Reading excerpts from some of Walt Whitman's writings during the civil war should prompt students' ideas as well as additional historical background films and readings. Provide each student with a formal invitation (Table 3.9). Support the development of student ideas toward realizing the dinner party, setting conference times individually to monitor and prompt the formation of students' selection of a particular character and means to embody the persona. Figure 3.1 (see p. 93) provides an image to discuss with students the nature of genuine conversation.

Plan for a dinner party as simple as providing pizza and salad to more complex meals, asking students to prepare an authentic dish they envision as being appropriate to the selected character. The day of the fusion dinner party arrange a large table with table settings and a chair for each participant. Cover the table with butcher paper to create a unified surface. Invite everyone to sit down to share food, enjoying and celebrating the efforts of the entire class. Each student should stay in character for the entire dinner, conversing and improvising as the dinner party conversation unfolds. Following the dinner, have students relay the common pervading themes and important differences, distinguish concerns and influences, and ascertain the roles of others in

TABLE 3.9. Sample drama invitation, fusion dinner party

YOU ARE INVITED to a FUSION DINNER PARTY

Who— [NAME OF SCHOOL] DRAMA CLASS is hosting the dinner and all students in the class are invited.

Where— Drama room

Why— To foster conversation embodying the complexity of issues contributing to, and impacting, civil wartime America.

When— [The date and the time of the dinner.]

What— At the dinner table represent one created character through:
- Dressing and acting as you imagine the character to be, derived from careful attention to biographical and contextual information and research.

How— Materials and resources to best develop and embody a civil wartime character, giving expression to the influences present in her/his life, expanding everyone's understandings.

the lives of these characters and the potential connecting power within drama for sharing understandings, gaining insights, and transforming lives.

Teaching Tip

Allow students whose language skills may be at beginning stages to refer to the notes they have made about their characters as they take part in the activity, if it would help them to be able to focus their attention on the conversation. Encourage all students to be patient so that they do not feel like they need to rush through the dialogue, allowing extra time in which to respond to verbal input contributes to a higher level of student participation overall.

Summation

In the drama case example # 3, students are asked to consider the role of worldviews as embodied within actions and words. A documentary with contemporary philosophers engaged in conversation about their personal worldviews serves as a generative text. Students conduct research into the lives and assume the identities of a cross-section of Americans during civil war times. They then meet in conversation over dinner. Students synthesize and evaluate cultural, historical, and political information to support artistic choices as they form their selected identity. Students demonstrate that drama can be a reflection of life in particular times, places, and cultures. Collectively, students consider the role of drama as a record of human experience that connects to their own lives, and analyze, understand, and value the influence of drama in creating and reflecting culture. ELL students have important negotiating opportunities to reason, to interpret, and to embody communication, analyzing and organizing this information in order to articulate personal understandings. They contribute to collective understandings alongside fostering artistic sensibilities and appreciation.

Additional Selected Resources

Films

PBS. (n.d.). History Detectives, Civil War Stories (http://www.pbs.org/opb/historydetectives/investigations/era_civilwar.html).

Taylor, A. (2008) *Examined Life*. Toronto: Zeitgeist Films (http://www.zeitgeistfilms.com/film.php?directoryname=examinedlife&mode=downloads).

Books—Drama Related

Anderson, M., Hughes, J., & Manuel, J. (Eds.). (2008). *Drama and English teaching: Imagination, action, and engagement*. Oxford: Oxford University Press.

Boal, A. (1993). *Theatre of the oppressed*. New York: Theatre Communications Group.

Boal, A. (1995). *The rainbow of desire: The Boal method of theatre and therapy*. New York: Routledge.

Boal, A. (2002). *Games for actors and non-actors* (2nd ed.). New York: Routledge.

Goldstein, T. (2003). *Teaching and learning in a multilingual school: Choices, risks, and dilemmas*. Mahwah, NJ: Lawrence Erlbaum.

Johnstone, K. (1999). *Improv for storytellers*. New York: Routledge Theatre Arts Book.

Lundy, K. G. (2008). *Teaching fairly in an unfair world*. Portland, ME: Stenhouse.

McCormick, J. (2004). *Writing in the asylum: Student poets in city schools.* New York: Teachers College Press.

Napier, M. (2004). *Improvise: Scene from the inside out.* Portsmouth, NH: Heinemann Drama.

Neelands, J., & Goode, T. (2000). *Structuring drama work: A handbook of available forms in theatre and drama.* Cambridge: Cambridge University Press.

Prendergast, M., & Saxton, J. (Eds.). (2009). *Applied theatre: International case studies and challenges for practice.* Bristol, UK: Intellect.

Prendiville, F., & Toye, N. (2007). *Speaking and listening through drama, 7–11.* London: Paul Chapman.

Spolin, V. (1999). *Improvisation for the theater 3E: A handbook of teaching and directing techniques.* Evanston, IL: Northwestern University Press.

Supplementary Books/CD/Audio

Coviello, P. (Ed.). (2006). *Walt Whitman's memoranda during the war.* Oxford: Oxford University Press.

Freire, P. (2000). *Pedagogy of the oppressed.* New York: Continuum.

Genoways, T. (2009). *Walt Whitman and the Civil War: America's poet during the lost years of 1860–1862.* Berkeley: University of California Press.

Loving, J. (2000). *Walt Whitman: The song of himself.* Berkeley: University of California Press.

Lowenfels, W. (1989). *Walt Whitman's Civil War.* New York: Da Capo Press.

Morrison, T. (1997). *Sula Audio Book.* New York: Random House Audio.

Roper, R. (2009). *Now the drum of war: Walt Whitman and his brothers in the Civil War.* New York: Walker.

Rossetti, W. M. (Ed.). (2008). *Poems by Walt Whitman.* Bel Air, CA: Biblio Bazaar.

Watts, I. N. (1990). *Just a minute: Ten short plays and activities for your classroom.* Markham, Ontario: Pembroke.

Whitman, W. (Read by Begley, E.). (2008). *Essential Walt Whitman CD.* New York: Caedmon.

Internet Sites

Black history teaching resources at Smithsonian Museum (http://www.smithsonianeducation.org/educators/resource_library/african_american_resources.html).

Hispanic heritage teaching resources at Smithsonian Museum (http://www.smithsonianeducation.org/educators/resource_library/hispanic_resources.html).

National Museum of American History (http://americanhistory.si.edu/).

Sarah Jones as a one-woman global village, TED ideas worth sharing (http://www.ted.com/talks/sarah_jones_as_a_one_woman_global_village.html).

Smithsonian National Museum of African American History and Culture (Future Museum) (http://nmaahc.si.edu/).

Women's history teaching resources at Smithsonian Museum (http://www.smithsonianeducation.org/educators/resource_library/women_resources.html).

3.5
Dance Experiences to Engage ELLs Alongside All Learners

Dance experiences that are focused on making and relating, perceiving and responding, and connecting and understanding, emphasize body–mind connectivity. Active involvement, giving moving expression through dance fosters embodied understandings of notions and experiences. The responsive attunement sought across body and mind increases cognizance and sensitivity to situations, other(s), and self. Dance as a moving form of expression reveals human beings' interdependency with the world. Dance as a community, celebratory, and ritualistic practice across cultures and times reveals itself as a powerful medium for exploring and accessing personal sense making alongside the experiences of others. As a nonverbal form of communication, dance occasions contextual opportunities for ELLs to actively navigate across non-verbal and verbal communicative practices and foster concrete meanings. The kinesthetic and interactive experiences enable the receptivity of ELLs, with time to work through ideas. As students physically move, they are thinking about and making sense of new terms and notions. Interrogating dance movements builds and strengthens understandings across all learners.

Dance, Theme I: "Total Control Can Be the Death of a Work"

Generative Text

Rivers and Tides is a film documenting the elemental sculptural forms in the making by Scottish artist Andy Goldsworthy (2004). The imagery of the film gives physical and material expression to his statement, "Total control can be the death of a work" (Scene 4), providing a vivid and tangible portrayal of artistic thinking in process.

About the Text

The DVD of *Rivers and Tides* (Goldsworthy, 2004) can be viewed in its entirety or teachers may choose to introduce Goldsworthy's elemental sculptures though specific scenes that are accessible on the DVD in short segments. It is 90 minutes in length but the scenes offer a way for students to watch one or more excerpts of about 15 minutes each. Alternatively (or in addition), images of Goldsworthy's sculptural forms are available from Abram Books (http://www.abramsbooks.com/#) and on the web, see (http://www.morning-earth.org/ARTISTNATURALISTS/AN_Goldsworthy.html), (http://www.flickr.com/groups/andygoldsworthy/pool/), and google images (http://images.google.com/imghp?hl=en&tab=wi).

Scene 4 of the DVD *Rivers and Tides, Feelings of Uncertainty* depicts the artist seeking his artistic materials as he negotiates his way about the landscape. Viewers come to see how his sculptural forms are site-specific. Viewers increasingly see how Goldsworthy's knowings of the site and the particulars of the land are a necessity. The scene depicts Goldsworthy watching, listening, touching, and attending to colors, textures, shapes, patterns, weather conditions, and existing features of the terrain, gaining knowledge of the land. Control is never imposed. Goldsworthy meets and works with tensions, resistance, and discord as inherent within the process, expected along the way, and as being productive to his art making.

Dance Case Example # 1: Moving Sensitively Within Given Contexts

Have students sitting on the floor with enough space around each one of them to move their arms and legs without touching anyone. Insist on no talking for these exercises, explaining that dance requires an attunement to one's body only possible through focused, lived inquiry. Participate alongside students in the opening exercises to model and cultivate a supportive learning context. Background music is a catalyst for greater attunement to one's body. Begin with some stretching and breathing exercises with the lights dimmed. Ask everyone to remain on the floor in a seated or prone position, finding ways to twist, stretch, bend, collapse, and swing, their hands, legs, feet, arms, and/or their entire bodies to the accompanying music. The selected music excerpts should elicit very different movement explorations and be loud enough to envelop the context and foster student attention. Encourage students to close their eyes and attend as closely as possible to the music only, letting their bodies respond accordingly. With time, students will become more comfortable on this exercise, so let it continue until you see students beginning to tire. Turn up the lights, and with students remaining seated on their own floor space, talk about the nature of process-oriented dance composition. Encourage students to demonstrate or gesture as they take part in the discussion.

Teaching Tip

Aim for specificity in word choice and use gestures, images, and objects as examples alongside terms and concepts to reinforce word meanings.

Teaching Tip

Even Level 1 ELL students will likely be able to take part in the dance component of this activity, but they may feel intimidated by the language needed in activities that follow. Encourage them to focus on and to fully engage in the dance activity by watching to see what is expected of them, making the most of the language that they understand and are able to use, and then to express their ideas in the best way they are able to using movement, gestures, and language that they have. Highlight that these strategies may be used across a wide range of situations when they are uncertain as to what is expected of them, and whether their language skills are sufficient.

Given that the language used in the questions listed below may be challenging to some ELL students, participation in the discussion may be supported in a number of ways. For example, some of the language used in the questions could be simplified (alternatives are provided in brackets following each set of questions); the teacher could guide or model the discussion by focusing on one question at a time; students could be provided the questions in advance, and offered support in looking up and learning the language used in the questions; or students could work in small groups with others with stronger language skills. The teacher could also videotape previously given lessons or the same lesson in other classes, and have ELLs watch the edited lesson. Alternatively, the teacher could have groups of students edit raw footage with comments, and then give the video to ELLs to re-watch and to learn key language. An activity generator, such as quia.com, could be used.

Guiding questions to prompt discussion include:

1. How did students find themselves searching for appropriate responsive movements? How did the movements unfold into further movements? Did they experience some fluidity and/or pulsing of movement? How did they engage different parts of their body? (How did students get ideas for movements by watching the dance? Repeat one movement from the dance and show how this movement develops into other movements. Do students have other ideas for different movements from the same place in the dance? How could students use different parts of the body for the dance?)

2. How was space a factor throughout? (How did space influence the movements?)
3. What about the energy their bodies expressed throughout? Did energy vary, and if so, why did it? (How did energy from their bodies influence the movements? Did the energy level change sometimes? If so, why do you think it changed?)
4. How would they describe time as an ongoing element that they worked with? Were there moments that were accented, movements that were repeated, tempos that changed and adapted? (How do you think time influenced the movements? Were some moments emphasized? Was there more focus on some moments than others? Were some movements repeated? How about the tempo—did it change at some points?)
5. Were there relationships they became aware of across their own body parts, to others, to space, to music, to lighting, to mood, etc? (Ask students if they see connections between different parts of their bodies and movements in the dance, the movements of others, the space, music, lighting, mood, etc.)

Name the dance elements of body, space, time, energy, and relationship that comprise dance movements and synthesize the learning thus far. McCutchen's (2006) text provides an excellent general reference book. Have these dance elements prominently noted on the classroom walls for everyone to see. Pass out large sheets of paper (2ft x 3ft approximately) and a drawing tool with no erasers (so that drawing time is maximized rather than time spent erasing drawing efforts) to each student and ask them to listen to and to attend to the music again, but this time to draw to it. Create a similar context with the lights low, encouraging students to be immersed in process. As students begin to draw, ask them to consciously attend to the role of the dance elements as they navigate their drawings. At the conclusion of the drawing exercise, have students form small groups to look at each other's drawings and discuss each of the body elements as they experienced them in the drawing exercise. Additionally, ask students to make connections to their first movement explorations to music. To enable this discussion, the following questions offer starting points to examine the recorded movement visible in the drawings. Give students one element to consider at a time and prompt connections within and across groups as necessary:

- Body: How did your arm move throughout? Point to line movements that record specific arm movements. Look for similarities and differences in each other's drawings. How do the lines represent the movements you made in the first exercise?
- Space: How did the size of your paper influence your line movements? Are there any interesting shapes and pathways that emerged? Did you find yourself extending the space at all? And, if so, in what ways did this occur? How do spatial considerations translate into the movements of your body through space?
- Energy: Did your exertion level change affecting the line quality at all? If so, how and why did it change? Explore others' drawings for evidence. What kinds of lines represent the actual movements that you made in the first exercise?
- Time: Did your line movement ever become broken, disjointed, or still? What marks on your drawing indicate these moments? Are there parts of your drawing that are emphasized in any way? If so, what calls your attention? Examine others' drawings to see various ways. The movements you made through time engaged time in various ways. What lines or marks might represent these ways?
- Relationship: How did the music and the context become a part of your drawing? How does the line record your journey? How would you characterize dance to others using the language of the elements of body, space, energy, time, and relationship?

> **Teaching Tip**
>
> Plan for related activities that layer into each other, allowing for multiple avenues for students to grow their understandings of the topic at hand. Continuously enable students to seek learning connections across activities and to be open to the unexpected.

Following small group discussions, facilitated by the teacher as necessary, have students arrange their drawings in their groups so that there are relationships playing across the drawings as a whole. Rearrange the drawings on the floor until groups are pleased with the connections, forming one large drawing. The relationships might be directionally based, oppositional patterns, continuing patterns, etc. The drawings can be rearranged vertically, horizontally, diagonally, and/or overlapped. Display all finalized arrangements of their drawings on the walls of the room.

> **Teaching Tip**
>
> Provide opportunities for ELL students to work with non-ELL students as well as with other ELL students in a wide range of situations. Interaction with non-ELL students pushes ELL students to advance their language development through exposure to language beyond what they are able to produce themselves, and offers opportunities for students from different ethnic backgrounds to learn about the home cultures and perspectives of their peers. Interaction with other ELL students offers different learning opportunities; namely, ELL students are able to gain support for language development from a peer who understands the challenges of English language acquisition, and gain a sense of camaraderie with a peer who is in a similar situation.

Discuss dance as a moving form of expression revealing our interdependence with the world. To convey this interdependence, the dancer must embody features and relations found in a particular context. Identify the features and relations of the context for the movement exercises. Emphasize these by having students demonstrate movements to embody some of the highlighted features and relations as the discussion progresses, and refer to aspects of the drawings that fit with the discussion. Introduce the site-specific sculptures of Scottish artist Andy Goldsworthy that embody the features and relations he finds in places. Have students watch Scene 4 from the DVD *Rivers and Tides*, paying particular attention to what Goldsworthy might mean by his statement, "Control can be the death of a work" (Scene 4). After watching Scene 4 have students address the following questions in their dance journals and then in small groups relay what they saw and heard.

Journal Entry

- What do you think site-specific art forms refer to?
- How do the artistic materials speak to Goldsworthy? How does this translate to dance? Think about the movement exercises.
- What is the role of context?
- Why is place of importance?
- How does Goldsworthy treat the materials and respond as the work is created? Are there some parallels with your experience with dance movements?
- What words describe Goldsworthy's engagement? How does a dancer engage movement?

. . . .

Ways of accommodating students at different levels of English proficiency

Preproduction and Early Production: Ask students what they like to do when they have free time. Use pictures of young people engaged in different sports and recreational activities to help students to generate ideas. As students generate responses, write them down on a whiteboard for them to copy on to index cards for their personal dictionary. Have them ask one another what they like to do in their free time. Model appropriate answers to get the conversations going, but encourage students to elaborate upon their responses as much as possible. Discuss how people often ask about one's interest in sports and recreational activities as a means of initiating further conversation.

Speech Emergence and Intermediate Fluency: Have students work in groups to prepare a dance move to present to classmates. Encourage them to use items in the classroom as props. Engage students in discussion about their reasons for including the selected items as props—what kind of message or impact did they want the items to contribute to the dance? Move into a discussion about the importance and the role of site, and ways in which works of art may be site-specific. Refer to Scene 4 from *Rivers and Tides* for examples and support. Have students change their dance move by incorporating another item and discuss ways in which the item might reveal or express ideas related to the site.

Facilitate small group discussions as necessary. Attend to important insights that groups generate. Bring these insights to a large group discussion that synthesizes the reverence Goldsworthy demonstrates for what is found and encountered in the environment, the integral role of play and his acknowledgment that something is already at play, and his responsive thinking movement that is animated by the spirit of place. Discuss the translation to site-specific dance as using the properties, qualities, and meanings found on site to reveal the complexity of relationships of self and others in the world. Have students state in a written sentence or two in their dance journals what they believe Goldsworthy means by his insistence that control can be the death of a work and how this might be akin to site-specific dance.

Journal Entry

Control can be the death of a dance project by…

∙ ∙

Ways of accommodating students at different levels of English proficiency

Preproduction and Early Production: Have students follow you to take part in a simple dance sequence. End the sequence abruptly and have students work together to add to the sequence. The students will then lead others in the class to participate in their unique dance sequence.

Speech Emergence: Introduce Goldsworthy's notion that too much control can ruin a project, such as a dance. Engage students in talking about what this might mean.

Intermediate Fluency: Introduce Goldsworthy's notion that too much control can ruin a project, such as a dance. Engage students in talking about examples in their own lives when this might have been the case as well.

Direct students to a website describing the dance company *Human Landscape Dance,* located in Washington, DC (see: http://www.hldance.org/). Have students study this site for the intents of the dance company and assign students to look closely at particular descriptions of their choreography. The site lists their site-specific dance projects with associated detailed choreographic statements. Have students note in their dance journals descriptive phrases and words that the choreographer uses to relay the explorations of site-specific dance forms.

Journal Entry

Title of dance project:
What words or phrases from the choreographer's statement seem central to the dance project?

∙ ∙

Ways of accommodating students at different levels of English proficiency

Preproduction: Describe some words or phrases, and have students indicate whether they could be used to describe the dance project. 'True' and 'False' cards that students raise to indicate their agreement or disagreement with the words and phrases could be used.

Early Production: List possibilities of words or phrases from the choreographer's statement, and have students choose from a short list of words or phrases which might be used to describe the dance project.

Speech Emergence: Ask students to describe the dance project in their own words.

> Intermediate Fluency: Write the choreographer's statement down and identify from this statement the words that seem central to the dance project. Work in pairs to develop this response, and then share it with another pair.

Make a collective list of these words and phrases that is visible to all, and then ask the students to play with movements that convey these impressions. Allow students time to explore movements. Discuss how artistic control is talked about or inferred by the *Human Landscape* choreographers. Relate this discussion to Goldsworthy's sculpture and his talk of control. Talk about the authenticity that might be gained and how audiences might be engaged in the *Human Landscape* dance performances.

Brainstorm some local sites such as a skate park, architecturally prominent buildings' exteriors and interiors, parkland, etc. that students suggest would be interesting to create a site-specific dance. Establish the parameters for site visits and have students each pick a site. Every student will then visit their site and complete an observation record of the particular site in their dance journals. These records are dependent on spending time attending closely to the site.

Journal Entry

- Words and sketches that characterize the site:
- Features present:
- Inhabitants observed:
- Relationships involved such as weather conditions, lighting, crowds, that affect the site:

. . . .

Ways of accommodating students at different levels of English proficiency

Preproduction: Show students photos of the sites, and have them match up the names of the sites.

Early Production: Have some photos and some descriptions of sites, and have students complete the missing information, or draw the missing picture. Introduce the sites beforehand, in case some students are not familiar with some of the sites.

Speech Emergence: Have students describe a site using descriptive vocabulary and short sentences so that their classmates are able to guess which site they are referring to.

Intermediate Fluency: Complete the above activity with a classmate, and discuss the responses with another pair of classmates.

Once an observation record has been made, each student should then take 5–10 digital images that best relay the characteristics, topographies, and relations of a site. These images will then be converted into a PowerPoint slide show to be utilized as a medium for suggesting dance movements that are responsive to site.

> **Teaching Tip**
>
> Signs of creative student engagement include: absorption in observing, animation, and physical involvement, with reluctance to quit.

Students return to their dance journal observation records alongside the images to create a three-minute dance movement sequence that amplifies the site selected. Prompt students to think of the site as an active dance partner in this process, returning to the questions explored through Goldsworthy's elemental sculptural forms, as ways to think about embodying the site through physical movement. Keep the time to develop these movements confined to one or two classes, with students given freedom within this time constraint to play with possibilities as they work across the PowerPoint images and the accompanied movements. Whether complete or not, have all students share their work in process at the conclusion of the time allocated. Following each performance of movements alongside images, involve students in a brief discussion of their impression of the site and the contributing features that elicited the movements created. Have students write descriptive words or phrases in their dance journals following each performance, conveying what each found through attending to the site-specific dance movements, alerting them to look at the site in ways not done so before, and seeing more than first envisioned.

> **Journal Entry**
>
> - Site-Specific Dance #1:
> - Site-Specific Dance #2:
> - Site-Specific Dance #3:
>
> •
>
> **Ways of accommodating students at different levels of English proficiency**
>
> Preproduction: Have students identify from a list of adjectives which ones could be used to describe the dance.
> Early Production: Have students generate a list of adjectives to describe the dance.
> Speech Emergence: Have students write a description of the dance and read it to a small group of their classmates.
> Intermediate Fluency: Have students write descriptive words or phrases to convey what they found through attending to the site-specific dance movements. Encourage them to identify features of the site differently in subsequent viewings, focusing on what they may not have seen in previous viewings.

Synthesize the ideas generated across all performances regarding site-specific dance, and conclude by involving students in taking a close look at the website article documenting a site-specific dance, *The Dream Life of Bricks*, performed at the *Massachusetts Museum of Contemporary Art* using some buildings and courtyards no longer regularly used. Amy L. Slingerland writes the article on the *LiveDesign* website (Oct. 1, 2002) titled, *Site-Specific Dance #3: If These Walls Could Talk*. See: http://livedesignonline.com/mag/lighting_sitespecific_dance_walls/.

The historical lineage of the site as a manufacturing and later an electric company extending into the mid 1980s, when its closure caused economic devastation in the community, weaves into the dance choreography. Through images and maps, students will be able to retrace the experience of creating and performing this site-specific dance. This will provide plenty of ways to return to some key ideas of site-specific dance such as:

- moments you cannot plan for in advance;
- commitment to place;
- performances that could not take place anywhere else; and
- experiencing the work as it happens for both dancers and audience.

Summation

In the dance case example # 1, students use elements of body, space, time, and energy awareness, alongside qualities and relationships across dance movement patterns, as they translate features found within the site-specific artistic practices of sculptor Andy Goldsworthy, seeking expression in dance. Goldsworthy's site-specific sculpture is a generative text for students to extend to site-specific dance. Opportunities to explore and to perform follow-up dance movement sequences that build from the ideas and contributions of site-specific dance artists extend and refine students' understandings. ELL students have opportunities to explore the power of nonverbal communication through physical movement, translation of gestures, postures, appearances, and emotions as they move sensitively through environments, and exploring the relationship of dance to space. Embodied understandings are instilled that prompt encoding/decoding opportunities, language acquisition, and enhanced understandings.

Additional Selected Resources

Film/DVD

Goldsworthy, A. (2004). *Rivers and tides: Working with time*, DVD. Directed by Thomas Riedelsheimer. Mediopolis Films.

Journal Article

Hunter, V. (2005). Embodying the site: The here and now in site-specific dance performance. *New Theatre Quarterly, 21*(4), 367–381.

Books

Banes, S., & Lepecki, A. (Ed.). (2006). *The senses in performance*. New York: Routledge.

Carter, A. (Ed.). (1998). *The Routledge dance studies reader*. New York: Routledge.

Desmond, J. C. (1997). *Meaning in motion: New cultural studies of dance*. Durham, NC: Duke University Press.

Dils, A. (2001). *Moving history/dancing cultures: A dance history reader*. Indianapolis, IN: Wesleyan.

Foster, S. (1995). *Corporealities: Body, knowledge, culture, and power*. New York: Routledge.

Jones, C. A. (2006). *Sensorium: Embodied experience, technology, and contemporary art.* Cambridge: MIT Press.

Kozol, S. (2008). *Closer: Performance, technologies, phenomenology.* Cambridge: MIT Press.

Lepecki, A. (2006). *Exhausting dance: Performance and the politics of movement.* New York: Routledge.

McCutchen, B. P. (2006). *Teaching dance as an art in education.* Champaign, IL: Human Kinetics.

Schechner, R. (2006). *Performance studies 2E: An introduction.* New York: Routledge.

Internet Sites

Parsons Dance study guide (http://www.parsonsdance.org/cms/Download_our_New_Study_Guide_.php).

Pearson Widrig Dance Theater (http://www.pearsonwidrig.org/repertory/intro_site-specific-adap.php).

Pilobolus perform "Symbiosis," TED ideas worth sharing (Mature Audience Advisory) (http://www.ted.com/index.php/talks/lang/eng/pilobolus_perform_symbiosis.html).

Sens Production (http://www.sensproduction.org/).

Third Rail Projects (http://www.thirdrailprojects.com/about.html#trp).

Vimeo-time and space, motion and physics—augmenting the dance (http://www.vimeo.com/5323198).

Dance, Theme II: "Responsive Matters of Perception"

Generative Text

A slam poem, *Love*, is authored and performed by Lucas Hines[1], a high school student giving expression to the young man's ongoing perceiving and responding considerations about what it means to be in love. Access the performance of the slam poem at: http://cehs.unl.edu/mlatta/poem.htm.

About the Text

The student's poem on love is situated within a quickly evolving movement of slam poetry occurring over the last 25 years. Poetry found this new venue in 1984 through Marc Smith, a Chicago construction worker experimenting in front of an audience with forms for poetry readings. Slam has since moved from the margins to mainstream, and from a local to global phenomena, revitalizing poetry. A slam is a poetry competition where poets perform original work alone or in teams with audience engagement as judges. These poems represent diverse topics and purposes including comedic, dramatic, personal, and political. A slam poet aims for audience connection. And, with this emphasis on performance, slam poets share their identity, their convictions, and their embedded understandings through spoken word, body language, and stage presence. Poetry slams are now found everywhere in the United States and have expanded to other countries including Australia, Austria, Bosnia-Herzegovina, Canada, the Czech Republic, Denmark, France, Germany, Macedonia, Nepal, the Netherlands, New Zealand, Singapore, South Korea, Sweden, Switzerland, and the United Kingdom.

Dance Case Example # 2: Moving Accordingly, Multi-sensory Engagement

Turn the lights down and begin the experience with background music conducive to breathing and stretching exercises with students each finding their own space on the floor. Have computer-generated imagery and music ready to be experienced on a large screen in the room. For example, a moving kaleidoscope accompanied by Didgeridoo drum music provides rhythmic music that continually reforms motifs. Introduce this experience (or a similar computer-generated one) by having students recall what a kaleidoscope is and how it works. Kaleidoscope artist Emin Arpaci (see: http://kaleidoscopemuseum.tripod.com/arpaci.html) combines imagery with music. Have some kaleidoscopes available for students to pass around and use. Explain that the music is based on an Aboriginal culture in Northern Australia that used a wind instrument with a low drone sound to tell their stories. Further explain that while drums rather than the wind instruments are used in the experience ahead, the music is rooted in the Didgeridoo culture. Access computer-generated imagery of kaleidoscope and music at:

> http://www.youtube.com/watch?v=qvIC2U-ijA8
> http://www.youtube.com/watch?v=Cuu6FQ3mb6A
> http://www.youtube.com/watch?v=1IeVlsSFuyQ
> http://www.youtube.com/watch?v=1O_vz3Dovms

Teaching Tip

As students may be coming to dance class from more traditional learning contexts that are often pace oriented, setting a learning tone that invites students to slow down and genuinely seek attunement within themselves and move accordingly is key.

Engage students in a few more breathing exercises to focus attention and instruct them to attend as fully as possible to the computer-generated imagery of the kaleidoscope with the drum music, feeling the motifs and rhythms created and recreated, keeping visible movement to a minimum for now. This attending experience should be about eight to ten minutes in length to engage the senses and absorb students in perceiving and responding. Following this, introduce the notion "body thinking," referring to the exercise just completed. Explain that a dancer and dance educator, Brenda Pugh McCutchen (2006), uses this notion to refer to the multi-sensory engagement necessary to communicate an idea or concept through motion. Instruct students that thinking with their bodies is their task as a dancer. Have students embrace this task as they move to the imagery/music of the moving kaleidoscope. Allow students time to immerse themselves in this undertaking, finding movements and patterns that are responsive to the imagery and music. Participate with students to cultivate a non-threatening context, and model the responsive attunement being sought.

Teaching Tip

Present dance as an example of ways in which different cultures may be expressed and enjoyed. Encourage students to participate similarly by setting the expectation for all students to participate through the entire process of learning about dances rather than having students perform pieces at a polished level only.

Talk with students about particular movement patterns that they each found to be good choices for responses to the imagery and music. Encourage students to demonstrate their dance movements as they share their findings.

Teaching Tip

Students' demonstrations of their dance movements will occasion language opportunities. Be sure to build upon these.

Teaching Tip

Be sensitive to the fact that in some cultures, the viewing of dance performances and participation in dancing are not considered socially appropriate activities. Teachers may explain to students that dance activities done in school are for educational purposes that contribute to and support their learning experiences, and are not seen as socially inappropriate in the United States and Canada. That said, depending on the families and communities from which students are coming, teachers may need to accommodate for this difference by allowing students to participate in different ways that do not involve performance (e.g., research to develop choreography for dances, direction for practices, identification and exploration of reasons for some movements over others, etc.).

Then, have students work in pairs to study and refine specific movement patterns that each student found to be fitting. Attend closely to student groups offering technique instruction and insights, encouraging students to articulate the joints involved, fostering the precision and alert bodily cognizance required of students. Once again, allow enough time for students to seriously pursue these efforts. Following this exercise, regroup students into a large group to talk about another notion, "body speaking," related to "body thinking," used by McCutchen (2006). Ask students to consider how the body thinking experienced as they studied particular movements became body speaking. McCutchen uses body speaking to refer to nonverbal expression through movement. Clarity and intention are prime considerations. Have students demonstrate their refined movements and engage students in considering the clarity and intention achieved in each demonstration. Have students work again in pairs, taking each refined movement and altering some element of it. See Table 3.8 for potential ideas. The table lists potential ways to alter or gain a different perspective. Synonyms are provided for these ways and may involve students in seeking definitions as necessary. Have students refine these altered movements by critiquing in pairs for increased clarity and intention. Work one-on-one to prompt students to concretely play with movements seeking greater clarity and intention, directly experienced and conveyed through the altered movement. Ask for a few students to volunteer to demonstrate their altered movements for the entire class. Consider together the nature of the change and the consequences for audience perceiving and responding. Ask particular students to convey the felt differences they encountered. Further, ask students to reflect in their dance journals about the specifics of their body thinking and body speaking exercises.

Journal Entry

Body thinking while moving asked me to…
Body speaking was experienced as …

· ·

Ways of accommodating students at different levels of English proficiency

Preproduction and Early Production: Introduce words for different body parts, and have students identify them on a diagram. Adapt this activity to include vocabulary that reflects the age and abilities of the students.

Speech Emergence and Intermediate Fluency: Introduce the idea of 'body speaking' as it relates to 'body thinking.' Play with dance movements together to engage students in talking about how movements can translate ideas and express feelings.

Watch the short film *Pas de Deux* (1968), a cinematic study of choreographic thinking, by master film maker Peter McLaren (accessible at: http://www.nfb.ca/film/pas_de_deux_en/) to further emphasize the roles of body thinking and body speaking with selecting, editing, refining, and choreographing dance works.

Introduce the generative text of the slam poem by asking how many students have participated and/or performed as a slam poet. Evolve this discussion to include some of the history and traditions of performance that slam poetry embraces and the relations to dance performance. Ask students to watch the slam poet perform his love poem, looking for the perceiving and responding features that contribute to the completed performance. Have students relay the features revealing the body thinking attunement and body speaking articulation that characterizes slam poetry. Note these features for everyone to see. Have students individually reflect on connections to be made across the slam poem performance with dance performance, specifically aimed at clarity and intention.

Journal Entry

How do you think the poet selects and organizes his poem? How is he feeling and why?

How is the topic and form of the poem able to inform and engage the audience?

• •

Ways of accommodating students at different levels of English proficiency

Preproduction: Give the students an abbreviated version of the poem, and have them identify a few words that they know. Ask them to identify words that convey feelings, and make a list of these words as they are identified. Have students write out the words for their index cards.

Early Production and Speech Emergence: Select a few of the lines of the poem, and read them together with the students, addressing difficulties that the students may have with some of the words. Ask the students how the poet is feeling, and ask students to identify the words in the poem where this feeling might be expressed.

Intermediate Fluency: Select a few of the lines of the poem, and read them together with the students, addressing difficulties that the students may have with some of the words. Ask the students how the poet is feeling, and have them identify where in the poem this feeling might be expressed. Introduce the question, 'How is the topic and form of the poem able to inform and engage the audience?' and explore this question as a group.

In small groups, have students discuss their journal responses and why love is a topic that is very common to the arts such as in love stories, love songs, love poems, and the drama of love relayed in theater and dance forms. Foster small group discussions and seek student thinking to bring to the attention of the large group.

Teaching Tip

Specifically look for ways to include and value the voices of marginalized and/or quiet students within small groups to grow confidence and promote participatory thinking. Establish practices that encourage students to share their work with one or two classmates. Work with students to develop language structures needed to praise the work of classmates and to encourage their classmates to elaborate upon specific details of their writing. Have students write out possible phrases they could use, and provide opportunities for them to learn and to use them in small group contexts. Provide many different mediums that could be used to support language development; if the teacher notes that some students do not seem engaged in writing activities, try to draw upon other skills to engage the students.

Collectively list some possible poet motivations and intentions for the slam poem on love. Ascertain how the form of the slam poem enables clarity of expression. As the discussion develops, introduce motifs as returning elements in a dance piece that function as part of the larger theme. Have students identify the returning elements in the slam poem and consider how such elements provide unity. Relate motifs to the earlier kaleidoscope imagery and music exercise with the returning elements always surfacing in new ways throughout the piece.

To develop motif in a dance experience, have each student build a one or two minute solo dance around the theme of love using a motif that states and restates the theme in different ways. Incorporate the kaleidoscope imagery and music again. It can play continuously in the background to act as a responsive medium enabling individual efforts. Work one-on-one with students to refine these efforts. As short compositions near completion, encourage students to offer critique in pairs.

Have students stand in the outline of a heart to initiate the dance. Video-record the dance that will unfold. Instruct students that when the music starts they are to perform their compositions, repeating the movement sequence until the music ends. Of course, the heart shape will quickly get lost, but some unexpected relations across movements will arise. Collectively view and celebrate the video performance of the dance. Relate students' dance experience to dance as celebration, ritual, and community across cultures and time. Have each student contribute a term to create a word cloud conveying the vitality and community of their dance. Display the wordle created for everyone to see and recall the dance of love. To create a wordle, see: http://www.wordle.net/.

Summation

In the dance case # 2, students translate a slam poem serving as a generative text into movement sequences that are sensitive and responsive to issues, culture, environment, and communication aspects. Students are asked to convey understandings of how dance celebrates, comments on, and influences issues and events in local and global contexts, both historical and present day. In the process, students critically examine their own dance works and that of others to determine relationships across initial intent and the creative product. ELL students will have multiple opportunities to observe and to practice moving with specific intents, gaining greater cognitive flexibility for interpreting, drawing inferences, and solving problems, addressing English language ambiguities. The personal search for resonance between observed and embodied action will facilitate communication as they describe the source of ideas and reasons for movement decisions that are made.

Additional Selected Resources

Slam Poetry

Algarin, M., & Holman, B. (1994). *Aloud: Voices from the Nuyorican Poet's Café*. New York: Henry Holt.

Delvin, P. (2004). *SlamNation—New educational edition*. Slammin' Entertainment. New York: New York Video Group.

Eleveld, M. (2003). *The spoken word revolution: Slam, HipHop, and the poetry of a new generation*. Bel Air, CA: Sourcebooks MediaFusion.

Glazner, G. M. (2000). *Poetry slam*. San Francisco: Manic D Press.

Levin, M. (1998). *Slam*. Vancouver: Lion's gate. Rated: R.

Simmons, R. (2009). *Brave new voices*. Home Box Office, Time Warner Entertainment Company.

Internet Sites

A brief guide to slam poetry (http://www.poets.org/viewmedia.php/prmMID/5672).

Contexts, poets, background information on Brave New Voices (http://www.hbo.com/bravenewvoices/crew/index.html).

Living Word project (http://livingwordproject.org/lwp_description.html).

Poetry Slam Incorporated (http://www.poetryslam.com/).
Saul Williams (http://www.poets.org/viewmedia.php/prmMID/5813).
The Nuyorican Poet's Café (http://www.nuyorican.org/).
Youth Speaks (http://youthspeaks.org/word/).

Internet Sites for Dance

Brothers of the Knight, Read, Choreographed, and Performed by Debbie Allen (http://www.
  kennedy-center.org/multimedia/storytimeonline/brothers.html).
DanceTeacher magazine (http://www.dance-teacher.com/).
Kinesthetic empathy (http://www.watchingdance.org/index.php).
Parsons Dance, East Village Opera Company, *Remember Me*, a re-telling of a classic story of tragic
  love (http://www.parsonsdance.org/cms/NY_Voices_featuring_Abby_Silva.php).
PBS Free to dance (http://www.pbs.org/wnet/freetodance/).
PBS Great performances (http://www.pbs.org/wnet/gperf/genre/dance.html).
PBS Who is dancing now? (http://www.pbs.org/wnet/dancin/).
Screen dance: *Loose in Flight*, performed and choreographed by Akram Khan and directed by
  Rachel Davies (http://www.watchingdance.org/discussion/discussion_2.php).

Books

Brehm, M. (2007). *Creative dance for learning: The kinesthetic link.* New York: McGraw-Hill.
Cohen, S. J., & Matheson, K. (Eds.). (1992). *Dance as a theatre art: Source readings in dance history
  from 1851 to the present.* Hightstown, NJ: Princeton Book Company.
Gibbons, E. (2007). *Teaching dance: The spectrum of styles.* Bloomington, IN: AuthorHouse.

Dance, Theme III: "Examined Lives in Relation—A Fusion Dinner Party"

Generative Text

Filmmaker Astra Taylor converses with some of today's most influential thinkers within selected contexts, fitting to each one. The thinking each shares is chronicled in her film, *Examined Life* (Taylor, 2008). The film reveals the multiple perspectives from which the world can be seen and lived. In this way, the film becomes the text to re-imagine the perspectives gained and to stage a fusion dinner party. A fusion dinner party intentionally invites meetings across differences. Envisioning, creating, and enacting a fusion dinner party serves as a further generative vehicle for dance experiences invested in giving lived expression to making and relating, perceiving and responding, and connecting and understanding with self and others.

About the Text

Viewing the entire DVD of the film *Examined Life* (Taylor, 2008) gives the fullest access to Astra Taylor's intent to invite and to foster conversation on what it means to live right. Alternatively, or in addition, short overviews of the film can be accessed at: http://www.nfb.ca/film/examined-life-trailer/ and http://www3.nfb.ca/webextension/examined-life/.

The persistent questions throughout the film are: how does one live the examined life and why should we invest in doing so? The film reveals that the ways we answer these questions are shaped by our various worldviews. Thus, the film confronts and asks viewers to challenge their values, assumptions, and beliefs connected to one's worldview. The cross-section of contemporary philosophers, including Cornel West, Avital Ronell, Peter Singer, Kwarne Anthony Appiah, Martha Nussbaum, Michael Hardt, Slavoj Zizek, Judith Butler, and Sunaura Taylor, provide intersecting and opposing ideas that engage viewers and invite them to join the conversation. In doing so, viewers will find themselves interacting and deliberating about the film's surfacing issues of courage, responsibility, ethics, power, privilege, indifference, social justice, gender, ableism, and politics, and what this might entail for notions of citizenry and democracy in an increasingly globalized world. A fusion dinner party serves as a participatory forum exposing differences regarding worldviews and the complex interdependent considerations at play. Students are asked to examine their own lives in relation to selected historical and contemporary artists, musicians, thespians, and dancers. In doing so, the relations across the arts and society will be fore-grounded for all to connect and grow understandings.

Teaching Tip

Assigning students to specific discussion roles can promote individual and collective learning, growth, and confidence in talking with others. These roles might include: detective, synthesizer, chronologist, social commentator, critic, and historian. Define the tasks for each role prior to beginning, and ensure students can access these descriptions for reference. Select roles and students according to the particular intents of the learning experience and your knowledge of individual students.

Dance Case Example # 3: Dance as Commentary

Explore with students the role of philosophy in our lives. Ask students to consider if they consciously operate within a philosophical framework for living. To do so, involve students in examining and discussing in small groups the statement that everyone has a philosophy even if it is never made explicit. To enable this group task, students can complete the worldview questionnaire (Table 3.5, p. 92) and use it as a platform for discussion. Support these small group discussions as necessary and attend to the efforts of each of the student groups to confront the inescapability of philosophy. Discuss your observations and reflections with students collectively, and have students think aloud about the reasons one might examine their philosophy and what might come of such efforts.

Socrates' statement, "The unexamined life is not worth living," provides a bridge for further contemplation before viewing the film *Examined Life* (Taylor, 2008). Ask students to view the film and to listen for various worldviews represented by a cross-section of contemporary philosophers in conversation with filmmaker Astra Taylor. Have students account for these various worldviews in their dance journals and identify the primary ideas or tenets underneath each philosophical view of being in, or of, the world. Have students also account for Taylor's deliberate attention to locations/spaces for each of the interviews.

Journal Entry

Philosopher's name:
Worldview descriptors:
Tenets:
Interview locale/relation:

· ·

Ways of accommodating students at different levels of English proficiency

Preproduction and Early Production: Continue the discussion about worldviews by introducing the use of place or location to reflect worldviews. Elaborate upon how locations/spaces can sometimes convey messages about the individual's worldviews. Introduce vocabulary for locations/spaces that will be used in the film, and have students watch for them in the film, along with the philosophers about whom they have learned in earlier classes.

Speech Emergence and Intermediate Fluency: Continue the discussion about worldviews by introducing the use of place or location to reflect worldviews. Show the film *Examined Life*, and have students identify each of the philosophers and match them with the locations/spaces. Discuss whether students can make a connection between the worldviews expressed and the locations/spaces featured.

Using the responses in the journals as the basis for small group discussion, ask students to consider dance as a lived philosophy expressing the meaning of life. As dancers, have they ever considered themselves to be philosophers? What might such conscious considerations prompt in dance and dancers? Point out to students that philosophers and theorists have written extensively about mind–body connections and intelligence in the body (e.g., Blumenfeld-Jones, 2009; Bresler, 2004; Dewey, 1910/1978, 1934; Gallagher, 2005; Johnson, 2007; Merleau-Ponty, 1968 ; Snow, 2007; Springgay, 2008), and have them consider these ideas as they relate to their own concrete dance experiences. How does one's body learn and remember dance? Following this group discussion, have students relate their lived understandings in their journals of mind-body connections and intelligence in the body as they have experienced these through dance.

Journal Entry

Mind/Body Connections Through Dance

Feelings encountered:
Judgments made:

Actions informed through inquiry:

• •

Ways of accommodating students at different levels of English proficiency

Preproduction: Introduce the idea of mind/body connections through dance. Show videos of different dances and dancers, and have students identify feelings or messages that the dancing might convey. Write these on to the board so that students can copy them on to their index cards to add to their personal dictionary.

Early Production and Speech Emergence: Introduce the idea of mind/body connections through dance. Show videos of different dances, and engage students in a discussion about the kinds of messages being conveyed by the dances presented. Ask the students to elaborate and to refer to their own dance experiences to inform their responses.

Intermediate Fluency: Introduce the idea of mind/body connections through dance. Show videos of different dances, and engage students in discussion about the kinds of messages being conveyed by the dances presented. Ask students to relate their lived understandings of mind–body connections and intelligence in the body as they have experienced these through dance.

Introduce contemporary dancer Diane Eno and her dance company *Fusion Danceworks*. The notion of fusion seems an important lived aspect of Eno's philosophy for dance. Eno writes a carefully constructed philosophical statement on dance that can be found on the website for her dance company. Students can access it at: http://www.fusiondanceworks.net/philosophy.htm. Eno also explores connections between her philosophy and her personal background that provide further insights at: http://www.fusiondanceworks.net/foundersnotes.htm.

Eno draws on her Native American ancestry and her deep commitment to, and respect for, the sacredness of landscape, honoring all creation through contemporary dance fused with Native American sign language. Have students read and critically examine Eno's written philosophy statement for what she is attempting to fuse and how she envisions this fusion occurring. Students should record these considerations in their dance journals.

Journal Entry

Chart or diagram the fusion of Eno's dance works and label or clarify as needed.

• •

Ways of accommodating students at different levels of English proficiency

Preproduction and Early Production: Introduce the notion of fusion, and explore the idea of Eno's dance works as a fusion of many influences in her life. Focus on the fusion of Native American influences and Native American sign language, and try to identify these influences in the dance works.

Speech Emergence: Introduce the notion of fusion, and explore the idea of Eno's dance works as a fusion of many influences in her life. Share a simplified version of Eno's philosophical statement that elaborates upon the many influences in her work. Try to identify these influences in Eno's work.

Intermediate Fluency: Introduce the notion of fusion, and explore the idea of Eno's dance works as a fusion of many influences in her life. Share a simplified version of Eno's philosophical statement that elaborates upon the many influences in the dance works. Have students make a poster to introduce Eno's work, incorporating into the poster some of the influences. Share the work with others in the class.

Follow up on this task by having students look further at Eno's website to access the video clips of some of the choreographed dances. Students will find a dance, *Restful Place*, created to celebrate the ritual of hiking Mt. Monadnock. Dancers gradually transform into the natural elements and surrounding landscape. Another video clip honors through dance the legendary wolves of Monadnock and the trickster ravens often seen flying at the summit. It is titled, *Immrama ... The Journey of the Spirit* (Celtic). Two more video clips of dances look to the mountain as inspirational and evoking prayer. These can be accessed at:

> http://www.fusiondanceworks.net/MMCD04RestingPlcNST.wmv
> http://www.fusiondanceworks.net/MMCD04ImmramaNST.wmv
> http://www.fusiondanceworks.net/Mountains2002NS.wmv
> http://www.fusiondanceworks.net/MMCD04PrayerNST.wmv

Individually, or in pairs, engage students in analyzing and critiquing the dances, keeping in mind the relations to Eno's philosophy. Drawing on the visual thinking strategies model developed by Abigail Housen (2002), have students document their inquiry into each dance in their dance journals (see http//www.vtshome.org).

Alongside their documentation, students can find additional information from Eno about the unique demands of choreography on a mountain, Eno's self-study of her creative process, and Eno's incorporation of Native American sign language at:

> http://www.fusiondanceworks.net/unique_demands.htm
> http://www.fusiondanceworks.net/creative_process.htm
> http://www.fusiondanceworks.net/sign_language.htm

Journal Entry

Dance Title

Accounting: What do you see and experience? Where is the dance taking place and how would you describe the surroundings? Is there more than one dancer? Other?

Constructing: Do you find yourself a part of an unfolding narrative or theme? If so, in what ways and how does the narrative or theme engage your participation?

How do your perceptions, values, and knowledge intersect with the dance? Other?

Classifying: Identify the choreographed dance in terms of place, time, movement motifs, dance categories and traditions, and organization. Other?

Interpreting: How would you describe the mood or tone created? What are the expressive effects of the movements and ensuing relationships creating the continuity of movement throughout? How do the movements convey intent and meaning? What additional questions/considerations come to your mind?

Re-Creating: What insights do you gain as you consider the dance's form, nuances and intricacies, influences, and questions that arise? How successful was the choreography?

. . . .

Ways of accommodating students at different levels of English proficiency

Preproduction: Watch all of the dances, and pick one to focus on. Select one question of each of the categories, and work together with the students to respond to the questions. Watch the selected dance again afterwards, keeping in mind the questions that have been discussed.

Early Production: Watch all of the dances, and pick one to focus on. Select one question of each of the categories, and have students work in groups of three to respond to the questions. Share their responses with other students.

Speech Emergence: Watch all of the dances, and pick one to focus on. Select one question of each of the categories, and have students work in groups of three to respond to the questions. Share their responses with other students, and encourage students to ask questions to encourage one another to elaborate upon their answers.

Intermediate Fluency: Watch all of the dances, and pick one to focus on. Model the process of responding to each of the questions, as they relate to the dance that was selected. Have students select another dance, and work in pairs to respond to the questions. Have students share their responses with other students, and encourage students to ask questions to encourage one another to elaborate upon their answers.

Encourage students to reflexively engage the information across all texts to more fully inform their analyzing and critiquing processes entailing the interrelated processes of accounting, constructing, classifying, interpreting, and re-creating. Then, bring individual thinking to a collective synthesizing discussion about the elemental connectedness Eno seeks in her choreographed dances and desires to elicit in viewers. Her cognizance of nature's role and example in our lives is manifested in her worldview given expression through dance. Other dancers with a similar worldview include Larry McCullough and Jennifer Monson. McCullough choreographs a dance on endangered species, and Monson follows the migration routes of birds and animals to explore the relationships and tensions to humans through dance. Information about these recent performances can be found at:

http://www.pinetreeinstitute.org/larry-mccullough-dance-bio

> http://www.wirenh.com/stage-mainmenu-15/32-stage-general/3647-saving-nature-with-dance.html
> http://www.birdbraindance.org/
> http://www.greenmuseum.org/c/enterchange/artists/birdbrain/

Teaching Tip

Signs of creative engagement include loss of awareness of time, relaying discoveries to others inside and outside of class, and projecting and speculating about consequences.

All of these dance works inform, offering interpretations and enlarging understandings of underlying issues by inviting viewers to connect their understandings and engage in continued dialogue. Each dance work positions the viewer to consider how we are living in the world with others across cultures and creatures. Relate this discussion back to the film *Examined Life* (Taylor, 2008). Assign students a connected task to that embraced by McCullough and Monson of studying an endangered species, and choreographing a dance that tells its particular story and moves accordingly. Incorporate one environmental song to accompany all of the dance works. Selections can be heard and the lyrics accessed at:

> http://www.grinningplanet.com/6001/environmental-songs.htm

Caution students that research is necessary to gain authentic interpretations that will enable the dancer to embody the particular species as closely as possible. Have students recall Eno's description of the demands of the mountain. Students are to be able to articulate the demands of the species they showcase. Support the research and development of the dances, vigilantly monitoring and prompting student care and attention to the task. As the student-choreographed dances progress, have students interview each other about their dance works. These interview questions could include:

1. What is your favorite part of the dance and why?
2. What was the intent, and in what ways was this realized/or not realized?
3. What aspects of the dance convey particular information and how successful are these toward the overall statement?
4. What do you learn though the dance?

The interviews should hone stronger dance works and students' capacities to articulate their accounting, constructing, classifying, interpreting, and recreating processes of choreographing the dance. Have students self-assess their dance works using the journal entry questions previously addressed in association with Eno's choreographed dances (see p. 176).

Journal Entry

Self-Study Assessment

Accounting…
Constructing…
Classifying…
Interpreting…
Recreating…

• •

Ways of accommodating students at different levels of English proficiency

Preproduction and Early Production: Show students a dance and have them learn it with you. After they have learned the dance, ask them to work with a small group of other students to change parts of the dance to make a new dance. Have students present the dance to their classmates. Ask students to identify parts of the dance they liked, and parts they would like to change.

Speech Emergence: Show students a dance and have them learn it with you. After they have learned the dance, ask them to work with a small group of other students to change parts of the dance to make a new dance. Have students present the dance to their classmates. Ask students to identify parts of the dance they liked, and parts they would like to change. Encourage them to make suggestions on how they would change the dance.

Intermediate Fluency: Show students a dance and have them learn it with you. After they have learned the dance, ask them to work with a small group of other students to change parts of the dance to make a new dance. Have students present the dance to their classmates. Ask students to identify parts of the dance they liked, and parts they would like to change. Encourage them to make suggestions on how they would change the dance. Present students with a shortened version of the self-study assessment, and have them respond to the questions in relation to their work of changing the original dance.

Invite students to a fusion dinner party where they each bring the examined life of an endangered species to share in a dance as they gather around the buffet dinner table. Provide each student with a formal invitation (Table 3.10). Plan for a dinner party as simple as providing pizza and salad to more complex meals asking students to prepare an authentic dish they know to be appropriate to the selected species. The day of the fusion dinner party arrange a large buffet table with needed utensils and plates. As the selected song provides accompaniment, have each student move toward and around the buffet table performing their individual dances together. Have someone video the collective dance that transpires. At the completion of the song, invite everyone to eat, enjoying and celebrating the efforts of the entire class as the video is replayed. Following dinner, engage students in sharing their personal revelations, reflections, and responses fostering connections across disciplines, interests, and each other. Consider together how the lyrics and intentions of the song might position humans as the endangered species, and how the song and dance invest all participants in continuing a much needed conversation.

Summation

In dance case example # 3, students consider how dance can reveal a way of living or being with other(s), a philosophy. A documentary providing an overview of philosophical approaches serves as a generative text intended to incite conversation. Students examine the ways in which dance forms can generate conversation through recording and translating ideas, values, and assumptions, demonstrating an understanding of the relationship between local and global connections. Collectively, students consider the role of dance as a record of human experience that connects to their own lives. They analyze, understand, and respond to the influences of dance in creating and

TABLE 3.10 Sample dance invitation, fusion dinner party

YOU ARE INVITED to a FUSION DINNER PARTY

Who— [NAME OF SCHOOL] DANCE CLASS is hosting the dinner and all students in the class are invited.

Where— Dance room.

Why— To foster a collective dance embodying the complexity of issues and concerns of a cross-section of endangered species.

When— [The date and the time of the dinner.]

What— Dance as you imagine the species to be, derived from careful attention to research and study of the particular creature.

How— Materials and resources to seek the traits and habits of a particular endangered species and the environmental relations, expanding everyone's understandings.

reflecting political, social and cultural issues. Students choreograph a dance revealing the particulars of one endangered species, and collectively participate in bringing a gathering of endangered species to life at a dinner party to deliberately generate conversation. ELL students have important negotiating opportunities to reason and to appreciate, exploring a range of possibilities through movements encountered in their dance work alongside ongoing reflection about these decisions. As ELLs examine how dance can offer commentary on issues, embodied cognition is gained as they seek ways to engender cultural transmission, and organize this information so that it reveals personal understandings and contributes to collective understandings.

Additional Selected Resources

Films

PBS. (n.d.). *Journey to planet earth.* (http://www.pbs.org/journeytoplanetearth/education/programs.html).

Taylor, A. (2008). *Examined life.* Toronto, ON: Zeitgeist Films. (http://www.zeitgeistfilms.com/film.php?directoryname=examinedlife&mode=downloads).

Journal Articles

Blumenfeld-Jones, D. (2009). Bodily-kinesthetic intelligence and dance education: Critique, revision, and potentials for the democratic ideal. *Journal of Aesthetic Education, 43*(1), 59–76.

Hanna, J. L. (2008). A nonverbal language for imagining and learning: Dance education in K-12 curriculum. *Educational Researcher, 37*(8), 491–506.

Books

Bresler, L. (Ed.). (2004). *Knowing bodies, moving minds: Towards embodied teaching and learning.* Boston: Kluwer Academic.

Bresler, L. (Ed.). (2007). *International handbook of research in arts education.* Dordrecht, The Netherlands: Springer.

Internet Sites

American Indian heritage teaching resources (http://www.smithsonianeducation.org/educators/resource_library/american_indian_resources.html).

Dance and movement (http://greentopia.net/Dance4theSpecies/).

Dance ethnographies with folklore (http://www.celat.ulaval.ca/acef/301a.htm).

Dance informs understandings of Antarctica (http://www.antarcticanimation.com/content/thesis/abstract.php).

National Museum of the American Indian (http://www.nmai.si.edu/).

National Museum of the American Indian exhibitions (http://www.nmai.si.edu/subpage.cfm?subpage=exhibitions&second=dc&third=current).

National Museum of the American Indian online exhibitions (http://www.nmai.si.edu/subpage.cfm?subpage=exhibitions&second=online).

National Museum of the American Indian past exhibitions (http://www.nmai.si.edu/subpage.cfm?subpage=exhibitions&second=pastthumb).

National Museum of the American Indian teacher workshops (http://www.nmai.si.edu/subpage.cfm?subpage=education&second=dc&third=teacher).

Native American sign language (http://home.online.no/~kcnyhus/sign.htm).

Native American sign language online dictionary (http://www.inquiry.net/outdoor/native/sign/index.htm).

North American Association for Environmental Education (http://eelink.net/pages/EE+Activities+-+Endangered+Species).

Performing the walrus hunt (http://www.teachersdomain.org/resource/echo07.lan.stories.walrus/).

Smithsonian Education e-newsletter (http://www.smithsonianeducation.org/tools/subscribe.asp).

Smithsonian National Zoological Park online animal photo galleries (http://nationalzoo.si.edu/Animals/PhotoGallery/).

Smithsonian National Zoological Park online habitat education program (http://nationalzoo.si.edu/Education/ConservationCentral/default.cfm).

Smithsonian National Zoological Park online resources (http://nationalzoo.si.edu/Education/OnlineResources/default.cfm).

Part 4

Resources

Internet Resources for Teachers

The following are teaching resources that can be found on the Internet that will help enable teachers to meet the needs of their ELLs and arts students. Some annotations have been provided to assist with selections. The sites have been selected for the potential each holds to support and foster rich curricular practices. They have also been selected for accuracy, credibility, and durability. We have tried to give priority to sites whose sponsors have long-standing reputations for service to the public good (e.g., professional organizations, museums, government organizations, and colleges and universities). Nonetheless, keep in mind that because the Internet is fluid, you will need to review content carefully. Remember, too, to check chapters in Part 3 for listings of content-specific websites and associated resources particular to the study of visual arts, music, drama, and dance.

Professional Organizations

ELL Affiliations

American Association for Applied Linguistics (http://www.aaal.org).

American Council on the Teaching of Foreign Languages (http://www.actfl.org).

American Educational Research Association Special Interest Group: Bilingual Education Research Special Interest Group (http://www.aera.net/Default.aspx?menu_id=154&id=1285).

Computer-Assisted Language Instruction Consortium (https://calico.org).

International Association of Applied Linguistics (http://www.aila.info).

Modern Language Association (http://www.mla.org/).

National Association for Bilingual Education (NABE) (http://www.nabe.org).

National Clearinghouse for English Language Acquisition and Language Instruction Educational Programs (http://www.ncela.gwu.edu).

Teachers of English to Speakers of Other Languages (TESOL) (http://www.tesol.org).

Arts Affiliations

American Educational Research Association Special Interest Groups:

> Arts and Learning Special Interest Group (http://uacoe.arizona.edu/alsig/).

> Arts-Based Educational Research (http://aber-sig.org).

> Music Education (http://www.aera.net/Default.aspx?menu_id=192&id=1079).

American Music Conference (http://www.amc-music.org/).

ArtsConnection (http://artsconnection.org).

ARTSEDGE: The National Arts and Education Network (http://artsedge.kennedy-center.org/).

ArtsEdNet (http://www.getty.edu/education/).

Arts Education Partnership (http://www.aep-arts.org/).

International Drama/Theater and Education (IDEA) (http://www.idea-org.net/).

International Society for Education through Art (INSEA) (http://www.insea.org/).

International Society for Music Education (ISME) (http://www.isme.org/).

Keep Arts in Schools (http://www.keepartsinschools.org/).

National Art Education Association (NAEA) (http://www.naea-reston.org/).

National Dance Association (NDA) (http://www.aahperd.org/nda/template.cfm?template+main.html).

National Dance Education Organization (NDEO) (http://www.ndeo.org/).

Public Broadcasting (http://www.pbs.org/arts/).

The Center for Arts Education (http://www.cae-nyc.org/).

The National Association for Music Education (MENC) (http://www.menc.org/).

The National Association for the Teaching of Drama (NATD) (http://www.natd.net).

World Alliance for Arts Education (http://www.worldcreativitysummit.org/user-guide.htm).

World Dance Alliance (WDA) (http://www.yorku.ca/wda/).

Museums/Galleries

Guggenheim Museum (http://www.guggenheim.org/).

Louvre Museum (http://www.louvre.fr/llv/musee/alaune.jsp?bmLocale=en).

Musee d'Orsay (http://www.musee-orsay.fr/en/home.html).

National Gallery of Art (http://www.nga.gov/collection/index.shtm).

National Museum of African Art (http://africa.si.edu/index2.html).

National Museum of Women in the Arts (http://www.nmwa.org/).

National Museum of the American Indian (http://www.nmai.si.edu/).

The Art Institute of Chicago (http://www.artic.edu/aic/collections/).

The Dali Museum (http://www.salvadordalimuseum.org/).

The International Quilt Studies Center (http://www.quiltstudy.org/).

The J. Paul Getty Museum (http://www.getty.edu/visit/exhibitions/).

The Museum of Modern Art (MoMA) (http://moma.org/learn/index).

Picasso Museum (http://w3.bcn.es/V66/Home/V66XMLHomeLinkPl/
0,4589,417470534_417617303_3,00.html).

Smithsonian American Art Museum (http://americanart.si.edu).

Journals

ELL Oriented

Asian EFL Journal (http://www.asian-efl-journal.com).

Bilingual Research Journal, the official journal of the National Association for Bilingual Education (NABE) (http://www.tandf.co.uk/journals/ubrj).

Canadian Modern Language Review (http://www.utpjournals.com/cmlr/cmlr.html).

ESL Magazine (http://www.eslmag.com).

Essential Teacher (http://www.tesol.org/s_tesol/sec_document.asp?CID=206&DID=1134).

Heritage Language Journal (http://www.heritagelanguages.org/).

International Journal of Bilingual Education and Bilingualism (http://select.ingentaconnect.com/
titles/13670050.htm).

Internet TESL Journal (http://iteslj.org/).

Philippines ESL Journal (http://www.philippine-esl-journal.com/).

Rethinking Schools Online – Special Collection on Bilingual Education (http://www.
rethinkingschools.org/special_reports/bilingual/Bil164.shtml).

Rethinking Schools Online (http://www.rethinkingschools.org).

TESOL Quarterly (http://www.tesol.org/s_tesol/seccss.asp?CID=632&DID=2461).

The Modern Language Review (http://www.ingentaconnect.com/content/mhra/mlr/).

Arts Oriented

Art Education: The Journal of the National Art Education Association (http://www.arteducators.org/olc/pub/NAEA/research/research_page_7.html).

Computer Music Journal (http://www.mitpressjournals.org/loi/comj).

International Journal of Education through Art (http://www.intellectbooks.co.uk/journals/view-Journal,id=121/).

International Journal of Music Education (http://ijm.sagepub.com/).

Journal of Arts & Learning (http://uacoe.arizona.edu/alsig/).

Journal for Drama and Theater in Foreign and Second Language (http://www.ucc.ie/en/scenario/).

Journal for Drama in Education (http://www.natd.net/journal.html).

Journal for Learning through the Arts: A Research Journal on Arts Integration in Schools and Communities (http://repositories.cdlib.org/clta/lta/).

Journal for Music in Education (http://journal.music-in-education.org/).

Journal of Dance Education (http://www.jmichaelryan.com/JODE/jode-ad.html).

Journal of Music Teacher Education (http://www.sagepub.com/journalsProdDesc.nav?prodId=Journal201903).

Journal of Research in Music Education (http://jrm.sagepub.com/).

British Journal for Music Education (http://journals.cambridge.org/action/displayJournal?jid=BME).

Philosophy of Music Education Review (http://muse.jhu.edu/journals/pme/).

Research in Drama Education: The Journal of Applied Theatre and Performance (http://www.tandf.co.uk/journals/titles/13569783.asp).

Research Studies in Music Education (http://rsm.sagepub.com/).

Studies in Art Education (http://www.jstor.org/journals/00393541.html).

The International Journal of Education and the Arts (http://www.ijea.org).

The Journal of Aesthetic Education (http://www.press.uillinois.edu/journals/jae.html).

Visions of Research in Music Education (http://www-usr.rider.edu/~vrme/).

Research Centers and Institutes

ELL Related

An ELT Notebook (http://eltnotebook.blogspot.com).
   This blog for English language teachers of all levels of experience serves as a forum to exchange ideas, opinions, and teaching strategies.

Center for Applied Linguistics (http://www.cal.org/crede).

Center for Multilingual Multicultural Research (http://www.usc.edu/dept/education/CMMR/).

Center for Research on Education, Diversity & Excellence (CREDE).
    Government-funded center designed to conduct research and disseminate knowledge to improve the education of marginalized students. Individual research projects are housed at various universities, for example:
    Dr. Jim Cummins' ESL and Second Language Learning Web (http://www.iteachilearn.com/cummins/)
    This website based on the work of Professor Jim Cummins of the Ontario Institute for Studies in Education at the University of Toronto, Canada, makes available research and publications on second language learning and literacy development.

Educational Policy Information Clearinghouse (http://www.eplc.org/clearinghouse_ell.html).
    Links to information resources, research, and reports are provided on this site. Users can also sign up for a free news service

Language Policy Research Unit (http://www.language-policy.org/blog/).
    This website supports interactions among researchers, policy-makers, and other decision-makers interested in language policy and planning for education and society. Links to census data, professional journals, and book reviews are included.

Let Everyone Participate (http://www.lep.gov/).
    A site promoting fair language access to federal programs and serving as a clearinghouse that provides and links to information, tools, and technical assistance regarding Limited English Proficiency and associated language services.

National Clearinghouse for English Language Acquisition and Language Instruction Education Programs (http://www.ncela.gwu.edu/).
    Funded by the U.S. Department of Education, this clearinghouse collects, analyzes, and disseminates information about language instruction educational programs for English language learners.

National Institute on the Education of At-Risk Students (http://www.ed.gov/offices/OERI/At-Risk/index.html).
    The At-Risk Institute supports a range of research and development activities designed to improve the education of students at risk of educational failure because of limited English proficiency, poverty, race, geographic location, or economic disadvantage.

Office of English Language Acquisition (OELA) (http://www.ed.gov/about/offices/list/oela/index.html?src=mr).
    The two-fold mission of OELA is to ensure academic success for English language learners and immigrant students by attaining English proficiency and to assist in building the nation's capacity in critical foreign languages.

Tapestry at the University of South Florida (http://tapestry.usf.edu/).
    Series of free video lectures by experts in the field of teaching English to Speakers of Other Languages. Topics include Legal Issues and ESOL, Special Education and ESOL, Content Instruction, and Dialect Diversity.

TESOL Resource Center (http://www.tesol.org/s_tesol/trc_genform.asp?CID=1253&DID=7561).

Online platform to find and share resources with peers in the profession. Requires membership.

UC Berkeley (http://crede.berkeley.edu).

Arts Related

A/r/tography at the University of British Columbia, Vancouver, Canada (http://m1.cust.educ. ubc.ca/Artography/).
 An inquiry site for the practicing artist/researcher/teacher invested in the arts in education and embracing inquiry as art making, "not separate or illustrative of each other but inter-connected and woven through each other to create additional and/or enhanced meanings" (Irwin, R.).

Center for Arts-informed Research (CAIR) (http://www.utoronto.ca/CAIR/aircrome3.html).
 Committed to articulating, exploring, and supporting alternative forms of qualitative research and infusing elements, processes, and forms of the arts into scholarly work.

Lincoln Center Institute for the Arts in Education (LCI) (http://www.lcinstitute.org/).
 Registration is required on this site but it is free and very quick. LCI is the educational cor-nerstone of Lincoln Center for the Performing Arts and is a global leader in education and the arts. The Institute is known for its inventive repertory, bringing dance, music, theater, film, visual arts, and architecture into classrooms in the New York City area, across the nation, and around the world. Resources and ideas for developing imagination through professional development programs and suggestions for teaching are available.

Project Zero at Harvard Graduate School of Education (http://www.pz.harvard.edu).
 A site committed to understanding and enhancing learning, thinking, and creativity in the arts, as well as humanistic and scientific disciplines, at the individual and institutional levels.

The Getty Museum (http://www.getty.edu/education/for_teachers/).
 Offering workshops and professional development programs that help educators incorporate the study of art into teaching practices.

The Center for Arts Education Research at Teachers College (http://www.tc.columbia.edu/a&h/ ArtEd/detail.asp?Id=Department+Projects&Info=THE+CENTER+FOR+ARTS+EDUCATION +RESEARCH+AT+TEACHERS+COLLEGE).
 An interdisciplinary arts group founded to stimulate and support basic and applied research in the arts in human development, art education, and the arts in education.

Classroom Teaching Resources

ELL Curricular Materials and Supports

Center for Applied Linguistics (www.cal.org).
 Information and links to sites on language acquisition.

Dave's ESL Café (http://www.eslcafe.com).
 This "Internet Meeting Place" can be accessed by teachers and students alike. The easily navigated site offers resources such as idioms, pronunciation help, a photo gallery, and an "idea cookbook" for teachers.

Differentiated Instruction (http://www.frsd.k12.nj.us/rfmslibrarylab/di/differentiated_ instruction.htm).
>   Links, strategies, and tools for effectively reaching all students in a heterogeneous educational environment.

ELL/ESOL Resource Downloads (http://www.missouri-pirc.org/esol_downloads.html).
>   This bilingual (English/Spanish) site from Missouri offers a range of downloadable resources for parents and educators.

ELL Links for the Linguistically Diverse Educator (http://www.western.edu/faculty/kwieseman/ ELL/LDE_Strategies.htm).
>   This gateway site provides dozens of annotated links to assist those who work with ELL students. In addition to information about helpful organizations and federal mandates, links to print resources, strategies for ELL survival, and ideas for instruction are provided.

English Forum (http://www.englishforum.com/00/teachers/).
>   Links for ESL teachers, dictionaries and reference books, and online exercises and quizzes that can be used with students.

English Language Learning (http://www.isbe.state.il.us/bilingual/htmls/ellparents.htm).
>   Created by the Illinois State Board of Education, this site provides resources (print and video) in several languages.

The ESL Area (http://members.aol.com/adrmoser/esl.html).
>   The Teacher Resources section features links, a forum, and tips and techniques for use in the content classroom.

ESL Connect (http://www.eslconnect.com/links.html).
>   This gateway site offers links to scores of other useful ESL sites. The sites are helpfully organized by topics such as ESL Lessons, Homework Help, Crosswords and Puzzles, and English Teaching Ideas.

ESL Infusion (http://eslinfusion.oise.utoronto.ca/index.asp).
>   Offering a practical guide for content teachers on how to infuse the curriculum to meet the needs of ELLs, visitors can also access resources, post questions, share teaching ideas, test your knowledge, and more.

ESL-Kids (http://www.esl-kids.com).
>   Free printable flashcards, worksheets, and games that can be used with ELL students.

ESL Kidstuff (http://www.eslkidstuff.com).
>   Although geared for elementary students, this site nonetheless provides some adaptable materials such as flashcard images, games, and printables.

ESL Lesson Plans and Resources (http://www.csun.edu/~hcedu013/eslplans.html).
>   Links to dozens of lesson plans, resources, and other learning activities.

ESL Lounge (http://www.esl-lounge.com).
>   Teachers can download free lesson plans, learning activities, and worksheets for ESL classroom teaching. Other resources include board games, flashcards, and song lyrics ready for use.

ESL Printables (http://www.eslprintables.com).
> This website offers teachers an opportunity to exchange resources such as worksheets, lesson plans, and learning activities. For each contribution you send, you can download 10 printables free of charge.

ESL Teacher Resources (Purdue University) (http://owl.english.purdue.edu/owl/resource/586/01).
> Links to professional resources, both theoretical and practical. The list includes links to organizations and journals of interest to language teachers and language policy developers, as well as online teaching and reference materials.

Forum for Discussion of Research on Bilingualism and Bilingual Education (http://lists.asu.edu/archives/biling.html).
> Searchable archive of discussions on related issues and topics.

Gateway to 21st Century Skills (http://www.thegateway.org).
> Free and easy access to thousands of lesson plans and other teaching resources.

González, J., & Darling-Hammond, L. (2000). *Programs that prepare teachers to work effectively with students learning English* (http://www.cal.org/resources/digest/0009programs.html).
> This digest provides a summary describing pre-service and in-service programs that prepare teachers to work effectively with English language learners.

Haynes, J. (2004). *Tips on communicating: Show your school's mainstream teachers and students how to communicate with your newcomers from the very first day. (*http://www.everythingesl.net/inservices/tipsoncommunicating.php).
> Useful ideas and confidence enhancing considerations for teachers and ELLs.

Internet TESL Journal (http://iteslj.org).
> Access to articles, research papers, lesson plans, classroom handouts, teaching ideas and related links.

its-teachers (http://www.its-teachers.com/).
> Quarterly online magazine for English language teachers. In addition to articles and research, you will also find practical classroom applications.

Kathy Schrock's Guide for Educators (http://school.discovery.com/schrockguide/world/worldrw.html).
> Links to a wealth of resources for foreign language instruction and ESL education.

Lanternfish (http://bogglesworldesl.com).
> Printable teaching resources such as worksheets and flashcards are provided, along with real-world language applications.

Learn English through Song (http://www.letslets.com/teach_english.htm).
> Designed as a supportive resource for ELLs, this website teaches English grammar, vocabulary, and pronunciation using specially written English language songs.

Letters From Home: An Exhibit-Building Project for the Advanced ESL Classroom (http://www.postalmuseum.si.edu/educators/4b_curriculum.html).
> Intended for grades 8 and above, these enrichment materials help build language and communication skills. The dynamic power of personal letters is highlighted in this collection while students develop English proficiency.

Linguistic Funland: Resources for Teachers and Students of English (http://www.tesol.net/tesl. html).

   Materials, activities, and links are provided in addition to "fun sites" that can be utilized by teachers in the classroom.

Mainstreaming ELLs: Meeting Individual Needs (http://www.celt.sunysb.edu/ell/tips.php).

   Created by the Center for Excellence in Learning and Teaching at Stony Brook University, the site offers tips on how to accommodate individual ELL needs in the classroom.

Mark's ESL World (http://www.marksesl.com/?source=sft).

   A "gateway" site featuring links for teachers, students, and the international ESL community.

National Clearinghouse for English Language Acquisition and Language Instruction Educational Programs (www.ncela.gwu.edu).

   Practice-based materials on curriculum and instruction for all educators who work with Language Instruction Educational Programs or who are otherwise involved with ELLs.

Northwest Regional Educational Laboratory. (http://www.nwrel.org/request/may01/bilingual. html).

   Information to support bilingual and minority teachers—how administrators, teachers, and policy makers can help new teachers succeed.

Resources for English as a Second Language (http://www.usingenglish.com/).

   The ESL Teacher Resources section provides handouts and printable materials, professional articles, lesson plans, and links to other sites. Tests and quizzes are also available on the site as is a discussion forum for other ESOL educators.

Selected Links for ESL Teachers (http://iteslj.org/ESL3a.html).

   In addition to lesson plan and assessment ideas, this site includes language-appropriate readings for students, articles and research papers, and games and activities for language learning.

Tapping into Multiple Intelligences (http://www.thirteen.org/edonline/concept2class/mi/index. html).

   This online workshop allows visitors to explore how multiple intelligences can be used to accommodate ELLs.

Teaching & Learning English Using Online Tools (http://www2.alliance.brown.edu/dnd/ dnd_links.shtml).

   Created by the New York City Board of Education & Office of English Language Learners as well as the Education Alliance at Brown University, this site offers a gateway compendium to sites that allows teachers to think about how to incorporate and embed language learning for ELLs into their content classes.

Teaching Diverse Learners (TDL) (http://www.lab.brown.edu/tdl/index.shtml).

   TDL is dedicated to enhancing the capacity of teachers to work effectively and equitably with all students. It includes information about teaching and learning strategies; assessment; policy; strategies for working with families; and organizations.

teAchnology (http://teachers.teach-nology.com/web_tools/).

   Games, glossaries, and printable page making tools are some of the resources available to teachers on this site.

TESOL CALL-IS (Computer-Assisted Language Learning Interest Section) (http://www.uoregon.edu/~call/cgi-bin/links/links.cgi).
> Collection of "starter sites" that include K-12 resources, content-rich sites, class activities and techniques, and student-centered sites.

Multicultural Curricular Materials and Supports

Cross Cultural Developmental Education Services (http://www.crosscultured.com/articles.asp) (http://www.crosscultured.com/newsletters.asp).
> The site provides articles on ELL, ESL, bilingual classrooms and language development.

Culture Grams (http://www.culturegrams.com/).
> Although this site requires a registration fee, many school libraries and districts opt to subscribe so that the entire faculty has access to these highly informative profiles purporting to provide "an insider's perspective on daily life and culture, including the history, customs, and lifestyles of the world's people."

Intensive English Institute: Internet English Resources (www.iei.illinois.edu/about/).
> Courses, activities, services using the latest ESL teaching techniques.

Multi-Cultural Books and Videos (www.multiculbv.com).
> A large selection of books, videos, audiocassettes, educational materials, and computer software.

The Multiliteracies Project (www.multiliteracies.ca).
> This site documents a three-year research study about literacy and pedagogy in a pluralistic, technological society. The site includes sample projects (e.g. dual language books written by students).

Arts Curricular Materials and Supports

Appalachian Media Institute (AMI) of Appalshop (http://appalshop.org/).
> A non-profit multi-disciplinary arts and education center in the heart of Appalachia producing original films, video, theater, music and spoken-word recordings, radio, photography, multimedia, and books.

Artful Thinking (http://pzweb.harvard.edu/tc/index.cfm).
> A program to help students develop thinking dispositions that support thoughtful learning—in the arts, and across school subjects.

ARTSEDGE (http://artsedge.kennedy-center.org/teach/les.cfm).
> This site provides over 300 lesson plans on visual art, music, theater, and dance in relation to other subjects such as language art, social studies, math, science, and physical education.

Arts for Learning (http://www.arts4learning.org/).
> This site has various lesson plans in the arts (you can download the lesson plans free if you sign up.)

Artslynx International Arts Resources (http://www.artslynx.org/artsed/index.htm).
> Various arts education resources and links in music, theater, dance, visual arts, film, etc.

ArtsWork (http://artswork.asu.edu/arts/teachers/lesson/index.htm).
> K-12 lesson plans in dance, music, theater, visual arts, and integrated arts.

Incredible Art Education—Comprehensive Arts (http://www.princetonol.com/groups/iad/lessons/middle/comparts.htm).
> This site provides the art teacher with resources for music, dance, drama, interdisciplinary units and comprehensive curriculum.

Making Learning Visible (http://pzweb.harvard.edu/mlv/index.cfm).
> Project Zero, Harvard Education: Documentation of student thinking as a way to see how and what children are learning.

TED: Ideas Worth Sharing (http://www.ted.com/).
> Talks by remarkable people from around the world across all topics.

Visual Thinking Strategies (http://vtshome.org/).
> An educational curriculum and teaching approach enabling students to develop aesthetic and language literacy and critical thinking skills.

Visible Thinking (http://pzweb.harvard.edu/vt/VisibleThinking_html_files/VisibleThinking1.html).
> Project Zero, Harvard Education: Features and practices for teachers, school leaders, and administrators in K–12 schools who want to encourage the development of a culture of thinking in their classrooms and schools.

Visual Arts Curricular Materials and Supports

Artcyclopedia (http://www.artcyclopedia.com/index.html).
> A general reference to artists, art movements, and associated resources.

Art Inspired (http://artinspired.pbworks.com/).
> This site provides visual art ideas and resources to inspire and motivate teachers' lessons, artwork, and art curriculum.

HotChalk: Lesson plans (http://www.lessonplanspage.com/Art.htm).
> Access to lesson plans, ideas, and activities in art.

Incredible Art Education Resources: Junior high and middle school lesson plans (http://www.princetonol.com/groups/iad/lessons/middle/middlelessons.html).
> This site provides lesson plans for junior high and middle school art class. Teachers submit their own creative lesson plans on various themes with examples of their students' artwork.

International Quilt Study Center and Museum (IQSC): Resources for Educators (http://www.quiltstudy.org/education_research/educators/schools.html).
> IQSC is housed at the University of Nebraska-Lincoln, USA, and aims to help students in all grades find connections to their world through quilts and quilt-making through an extensive online collection.

Modern Teachers (at MoMA) (http://moma.org/modernteachers/).
> MOMA provides guides and lessons for teachers and educators.

New Hampshire Public Television_ The Arts_ Visual Arts (http://www.nhptv.org/kn/vs/artlaba.asp).
> A general reference to artists, art movements, and associated resources.

sxzTeacherVision (http://www.teachervision.fen.com/art/teacher-resources/6681.html).

This site provides art lesson plans, printables, activities, quizzes, and references, perfect for art teachers at the elementary, middle, or high school level.

TeacherArtExchange (http://www.getty.edu/education/teacherartexchange/) .
Online community where teachers and learners can discuss issues related to art education and share lesson ideas, teacher resources, and network with other teachers from across the US and the world.

The Getty (http://www.getty.edu/education/).
Multiple links providing access to the J. Paul Getty Museum resources and professional development opportunities. These include:
Building Visual Arts Lessons (http://www.getty.edu/education/for_teachers/building_lessons/)
A guide to help teachers and curriculum developers to create successful arts-focused lessons.
Email Newsletter for Teachers (http://www.getty.edu/subscribe/getty_teacher_update/index.html)
Receive regular updates via email.
ESL Enrichment Curriculum—Beginning Language through Art (http://www.getty.edu/education/for_teachers/curricula/esl2/)
An art curriculum designed to motivate and foster English language learning.
Lesson Plans (http://www.getty.edu/education/search/)
Search for lesson plans posted by other teachers through the Getty Museum teacher education section.
Secondary Teachers Institute (http://www.getty.edu/education/for_teachers/resources.html)
Annual three-and-a-half day program to introduce secondary level teachers of literature, social studies, and other humanities-based subject areas to the art and artists from the Getty Museum collection.
Language through Art: An ESL Enrichment Curriculum (http://www.getty.edu/education/for_teachers/curricula/esl/)
A curriculum designed to enhance language learning through art.
Tips for Teaching about Landscapes (http://www.getty.edu/education/for_teachers/curricula/esl/esl_landscapes.html)
Tips for Teaching about Narrative Art (http://www.getty.edu/education/for_teachers/curricula/esl/esl_narrativeart.html)
Tips for Teaching about Portraits (http://www.getty.edu/education/for_teachers/curricula/esl/esl_portraits.html)

UIC Spiral Art Education (http://www.uic.edu/classes/ad/ad382/).
Innovative ideas for the K–College art classroom.

Music Curricular Materials and Supports

Canadian Music Center (CMC) (http://www.musiccentre.ca/home.cfm).
The Canadian Music Centre holds Canada's largest collection of Canadian concert music. The CMC exists to promote the works of its Associate Composers in Canada and around the world. The Centre makes available on loan over 15,000 scores and/or works of Canadian contemporary music composers through its lending library.

HotChalk: Lesson plans (http://www.lessonplanspage.com/Music.htm).
HotChalk provides lesson plans, ideas, and activities in music.

K-12 Resources for Music Educators (http://www.hickorytech.net/~cshirk/k-12music/).
   Resources for band, choral, orchestra, all music and the general classroom teacher.

Mayday Group, Action for Change in Music Education (http://www.maydaygroup.org/).
   Information and resources for scholars, students, and teachers.

Music in Schools Today Teacher Online Resources (http://mustcreate.org/teacher/teach3_0.
shtml).
   Music in Schools Today provides links to online curriculum, sheet music, teaching aids, etc.

Music Resources Online (http://guides.lib.washington.edu/music).
   Offers music resources and research databases recommended by the University of
      Washington music librarians.

NAXOS: Classical Music (http://www.naxos.com).
   Provides biography and albums of classical music composers and artists.

New York Public Library (http://www.nypl.org/research/lpa/mus/musabout.html).
   The music division provides access to many music-specific online databases, including Grove
      Music Online, RILM Abstracts of Music Literature, and the Index to Printed Music.

Oxford Music Online (http://www.oxfordmusiconline.com/subscriber/page/resources).
   A range of pathways into and through the content of Grove Music Online, as well as use-
      ful supplementary content, such as a full list of abbreviations used throughout Grove,
      editorially-compiled music timelines, topical guides, comprehensive research resources,
      and a guide to musical examples on the site.

TeacherVision (http://www.teachervision.fen.com/music/teacher-resources/6647.html).
   Teacher Vision provides lesson plans with printables; multicultural activities incorporating
      Mexican, Native American, Chinese, and South American music; printable instructions
      for building musical instruments; the history of musical genres like Rock 'n' Roll and Jazz
      with detailed references; and song lyrics.

The Classical Music Pages (http://w3.rz-berlin.mpg.de/cmp/classmus.html).
   This website provides you almost everything you need concerning classical music—its
      history, biographical information about composers (with portraits and short sound
      examples), explanations of the various musical forms, and a dictionary of musical
      terminologies.

The National Association of Music Education (MENC) (http://www.menc.org/resources/).
   MENC provides a vast collection of resources for those interested in music education, from
      their own publications to in-depth information on policies, rules, standards, and laws.

University Musical Society (UMS) (http://www.ums.org/s_education_community/teacher_
resource_guides.asp).
   UMS teacher resource guides provide specific information about the performance, artist, and
      genre, along with resources and lesson plans, making connections between the perfor-
      mance and curriculum.

Worldwide Internet Music Resources (http://library.music.indiana.edu/music_resources/).
   Connections to individual musicians and popular groups, composers and compositions,
      genres and types of music, plus additional sites related to performance, selected by
      William and Gayle Cook Music Library, Indiana University School of Music.

Drama Curricular Materials and Supports

Alive & Aloud (http://www.latw.org/EDU-latw/aliveandaloud/aliveandaloud.html).
  An educational outreach program accessing audio recordings of plays performed by some
    of the country's most prominent actors and providing educators with related classroom
    instructional support materials.

ChildDrama (http://www.childdrama.com/mainframe.html).
  Lesson plans, plays, and monologues plus links to associated resources.

Creative Drama and Theatre Education Resource Site (http://www.creativedrama.com/).
  Classroom ideas and theater games, alongside selected additional resources.

Drama in Education (http://www.michaelcoady.com/drama_education/dramlink.htm).
  A site that provides links to support the development of drama across all forms of learning,
    including stagecraft and community theatre projects.

Drama in Education: Lesson Plans (http://www.kentaylor.co.uk/die/materials/lesson.html).
  Access provided to drama-based lesson plans and materials.

Drama Education (http://members.iinet.net.au/~kimbo2/lessons/index.htm).
  This site provides resources from drama teachers for drama teachers including various lesson
    ideas, programs, and warm-up activities.

Public Broadcasting: ExxonMobile Masterpiece Theater (http://www.pbs.org/wgbh/masterpiece/
learn/guides.html).
  This site focuses on the Masterpiece Theatre Series for PBS TV. Learning resources are
    available for teachers to use in their classroom study. The online teacher's guides include
    discussion questions, activities and investigations, and plenty of writing and other
    exercises.

Foreign language writing skills through drama (http://www.drama-in-education.ch/uce/
uce_module_two_intro.html).
  The results of a case study about an exploration of some drama techniques to enhance
    students' creative writing skills in a foreign language along with concrete examples are
    made available.

High School Theatre (http://home.onemain.com/~highschooltheatre/).
  Listing of high school theatre sites on the web.

Integrated Resources for teaching drama, Grades 8–12 (http://www.awesomelibrary.org/
Classroom/Arts/Performing_Arts/Theatre.html).
  Lessons with adaptable activities and generative ideas.

Learn Improv (http://www.learnimprov.com/).
  This site is devoted to the art of improvisational comedy theatre and contains a detailed col-
    lection of improv comedy structures from games to warm-ups.

Performing Arts (http://www.educationindex.com/theater/).
  Many links to associations and groups supporting the performing arts and associated
    resources.

SchoolPlay Productions Ltd (http://www.schoolplayproductions.co.uk/schoolplay.htm).

This site provides school plays and musicals by age group, cast size, length, subject, and writer(s).

TeacherVision: Drama Resources for Teachers (http://www.teachervision.fen.com/drama/teacher-resources/55277.html).
> Access to printables, lessons, and activities; teacher's guides to Shakespeare's plays; activities to connect drama with reading Harry Potter books; printables to encourage students to keep journals as they read plays; lessons connecting science and social studies to the subject of drama.

TESOL-DRAMA (https://www.msu.edu/~caplan/drama/index.html).
> Access to extensive teacher resources to support language growth through drama.

Web English Teacher (http://www.webenglishteacher.com/drama.html).
> Lesson plans and activities for plays are listed by the name of the playwright.

Dance Curricular Materials and Resources

Dance is B.E.S.T (http://danceisbest.com/lessonplans.htm).
> Lesson plans and resources for developing dance teaching.

Greek Dancing through the Centuries (http://annaswebart.com/culture/dancehistory/index.html).
> An overview of Greek dance traditions and history.

Critical Dance Forum and Ballet-Dance Magazine (http://www.ballet-dance.com/).
> A magazine with articles and resources supporting dance in education.

Dance Education Laboratory (DEL) (http://www.92y.org/shop/category.asp?category=School+of+the+Arts888Harkness+Dance+Center888Dance+Education+Laboratory+%28DEL%29888).
> A professional development program for all educators and artists interested in developing their dance education curricula.

Culturally Responsive Teaching

Educating All Our Students (http://www.ncela.gwu.edu/pubs/ncrcdsll/edall.htm).
> This final report for the National Center for Research on Cultural Diversity and Second Language Learning outlines effective instructional strategies for linguistically diverse students.

Teaching Diverse Learners (The Education Alliance, Brown University) (http://www.lab.brown.edu/tdl/tl-strategies/crt-research.shtml).
> Provides a listing of research-based strategies and links to promote culturally responsive instruction and learning.

Principles for Culturally Responsive Teaching (http://www.alliance.brown.edu/tdl/tl-strategies/crt-principles.shtml).
> A definition and discussion of what is entailed in a culturally responsive pedagogy.

The Heinz Endowments: Culturally Responsive Arts Education Report (http://www.heinz.org/programs_cms.aspx?SectionID=1&ParentID=233).
> The Culturally Responsive Arts Education Initiative aims to bring the power of the arts to bear on the particular educational challenges facing African American children. It is based

on empirical and anecdotal evidence that the arts, positive racial identity, and cultur-ally responsive pedagogy can lead to increased achievement and resilience in African American children.

Clip Art and Image Banks

In addition to all the large search engines (altavista, google, yahoo, etc.), the following are useful sites to access royalty-free clipart and line drawings for educational use.

AMICO (http://www.amico.org/).
   Art Museum Image Consortium.

Clip Art Collection for Foreign/Second Language Instruction (http://tell.fll.purdue.edu/JapanProj//FLClipart).
   A royalty-free collection of clipart and line drawings for educational use. Categories include verbs, adjectives, food, sports, and events.

Classroom Clip Art (http://classroomclipart.com/).
   Multiple categories of clip art available.

Kathy Schrock's Guide for Educators: Clip Art Gallery (http://school.discovery.com/clipart/index.html).
   Graphics available across multiple categories.

My Florida Digital Warehouse (http://myfdw.com).
   A collection of audio, clipart, photographs, maps, movies, and additional visual resources.

Marwen (http://www.marwen.org/site/epage/28440_431.htm).
   Online gallery of students' artwork.

Modern Teachers (at MoMA) (http://moma.org/modernteachers/images.php).
   Access to thematically organized images and lessons.

Exhibitions and the Collection at MoMA (http://moma.org/explore/collection/index).
   Online image bank.

National Portrait Gallery (http://www.npg.si.edu/).
   Shows the most influential characters in United States history portrayed by the finest artists of their generation.

NCRTEC: Using Pictures in Lessons (http://www.ncrtec.org/tl/camp/lessons.htm).
   Lessons created by teachers that demonstrate some ways in which pictures and other graphic resources might be useful in a classroom.

SILS Art Image Browser (http://www.si.umich.edu/Art_History/).
   Art, architectural, and museum object images from four museums' collections.

Multimedia

Art Inspired (http://artinspired.pbworks.com/).
   This site provides visual art ideas and resources to inspire and motivate teachers' lessons, artwork, and art curriculum.

Dance Media.com (http://dancemedia.com/channels).
   On this site, people share various kinds of dance videos including instructional videos and performances of ballet, ballroom dance, tap dance, hip hop, contemporary dance, etc.

Footprints: Environment and the Way We Live (http://www3.nfb.ca/footprints/for-teachers/).
   National Film Board of Canada website for secondary and post-secondary students to support learning about the intersection of society, culture, and the environment. Includes lesson plans, and access to films selected from the NFB collection.

Hyperscore (http://www.hyperscore.com/).
   Music software that lets anyone compose music. The first music software program designed to teach students and adults how to compose music simply by drawing lines on the screen.

Infinity Dance Theater (http://www.infinitydance.com/video.html).
   A non-traditional dance company committed to expanding the boundaries of dance by featuring dancers with and without disabilities provides some videos of wheelchair-incorporated dances.

MoMA Multimedia (http://moma.org/explore/multimedia/videos-all).
   Audio, video, interactive media.

National Film Board of Canada (NFB) (http://www.nfb.ca/).
   This website provides documentaries, animations and arts and cultural films on the web.

Red Studio (at MoMA) (http://redstudio.moma.org/).
   Developed by MoMA in collaboration with high school students, explores issues and questions raised by teens about modern art, today's working artists, and what goes on behind the scenes at a museum.

Print and Associated Resources for Teachers

There is a wealth of resources available to teachers offering practical research findings and advice on teaching ELL students. This section provides a list of some reader-friendly research articles and texts with some annotations for teachers who would like to read more on specific subjects/topics. Also provided is a list of instructional materials that teachers can use in classrooms to help accommodate ELLs.

Culturally Sensitive/Responsive Pedagogy

Brisk, M. E., Horan, D. A., & Macdonald, E. (2007). A scaffolded approach to learning to write. In L. S. Verplaetse & N. Migliacci (Eds.), *Inclusive pedagogy for English language learners: A handbook of research-informed practices* (pp. 15–32). New York: Lawrence Erlbaum.

Gay, G. (2000). *Culturally responsive teaching: Theory, research and practice.* New York: Teachers College Press.

Irvine, J. J., Armento, B. J., Causey, V. E., & Cohen, J. (2000). *Culturally responsive teaching: Lesson planning for elementary and middle grades.* New York: McGraw-Hill.

Nieto, S. (1999). *The light in their eyes: Creating multicultural learning communities.* New York: Teachers College Press.

Robinson, B. J., Kelly, C., & Oberg, M. (1997). *Creating culturally responsive classrooms.* Washington, DC: American Psychological Association.

Cultural and Newcomer Information

Axtell, R. E. (1997). *Gestures: The do's and taboos of body language around the world.* New York: John Wiley.

Dresser, N. (1996). *Multicultural manners: New rules of etiquette for a changing society.* New York: John Wiley.

Levitan, S. (Ed.). (1998). *I'm not in my homeland anymore: Voices of students in a new land.* Toronto, ON: Pippin.

Pipher, M. (2003). *The middle of everywhere: Helping refugees enter the American community.* New York: Harvest Books.

Teaching Through the Arts

Ball, A., & Heath, S. B. (1993). Dances of identity: Finding an ethnic self in the arts. In S. B. Heath & M. W. McLaughlin (Eds.), *Identity and inner-city youth: Beyond ethnicity and gender* (pp. 69–93). New York: Teachers College.

Bleiberg, L. (2002). Dancing around arts education: How can kids learn about art without doing it themselves? *ARTicles, 8,* 88–97.

Burnaford, G., Aprill, A., & Weiss, C. (Eds.). (2001). *Renaissance in the classroom: Arts integration and meaningful learning.* Mahwah, NJ: Lawrence Erlbaum.

Burton, J. M., Horowitz, R., & Abeles, H. (2000). Learning in and through the arts: The question of transfer. *Studies in Art Education, 41*(3), 228–257.

Catterall, J. S. (2002). The arts and the transfer of learning. In R. J. Deasy (Ed.), *Critical links: Learning in the arts and student academic and social development* (pp. 151–157). Washington, DC: Arts Education Partnership.

Chalmers, E. G. (1996). *Celebrating pluralism: Art, education, and cultural diversity.* Los Angeles, CA: The Getty Education Institute for the Arts.

Chalmers, E. G. (2002). Celebrating pluralism six years later. *Studies in Art Education, 43*(4), 293–306.

Chanda, J. (1992). Multicultural education and the visual arts. *Arts Education Policy Review, 94*(1), 12–16.

Cole, J., Muenz, T., Ouchi, B., Kaufman, N., & Kaufman, A. (1997). The impact of pictorial stimulus on written expression output of adolescents and adults. *Psychology in the Schools, 34*(1), 1–9.

Consortium of National Arts Education Associations. (1994). *National standards for arts education: Dance, music, theatre, visual arts—What every young American should know and be able to do in the arts.* Reston, VA: Music Educators National Conference.

Davis, J. H. (2008). *Why our schools need the arts.* New York: Teachers College Press.

Deasy, R. J. (Ed.). (2002). *Critical links: Learning in the arts and student academic and social development.* Washington, DC: Arts Education Partnership.

Dorn, C. M., Madeja, A. S., & Sabol, F. R. (2004). *Assessing expressive learning: A practical guide for teacher-directed authentic assessment in K-12 art education.* Mahwah, NJ: Lawrence Erlbaum.

Efland, A. (2002). *Art and cognition: Integrating the visual arts in the curriculum.* New York: Teachers College Press.

Ehrenworth, M. (2003). Literacy and the aesthetic experience: Engaging children with the visual arts in the teaching of writing. *Language Arts, 81*(1), 43–51.

Eisner, E. W. (2002). *The arts and the creation of mind.* New Haven: Yale University Press.

Erickson, M. (2002). What are artworlds and why are they important? In M. Erickson & B. Young (Eds.), *Multicultural artworlds: Enduring, evolving, and overlapping traditions* (pp. 17–25). Reston, VA: National Art Education Association.

Gee, K. (2000). *Visual arts as a way of knowing.* York, ME: Stenhouse.

Goldberg, M. (2001). *Arts and learning: An integrated approach to teaching and learning in multicultural and multilingual settings* (2nd ed.). New York: Addison Wesley Longman.

Goldberg, M. (Ed.). (2004). *Teaching English language learners through the arts: A SUAVE experience.* Boston, MA: Pearson Education.

Goldberg, M. (Ed.). (2006). *Integrating the arts: An approach to teaching and learning in multicultural and multilingual settings.* Boston, MA: Pearson Education.

Greene, M. (1995). *Releasing the imagination: Essays on education, the arts and social change.* San Francisco: Jossey-Bass.

Hanna, J. L. (1999). *Partnering dance and education: Intelligent moves for changing times.* Champaign, IL: Human Kinetics.

Hanna, J. L. (2000). Learning through dance. *American School Board Journal, 187*(6), 47–54.

Olshansky, B. (1995). Picture this: An arts-based literacy program. *Educational Leadership, 53*(1), 44–47.

O'Toole, J., Stinson, M., & Moore, T. (2009). *Drama and curriculum: A giant at the door.* Dordrecht, The Netherlands: Springer.

Prendergast, M., & Saxton, J. (Eds.). (2009). *Applied theatre: International case studies and challenges for practice.* Bristol, UK: Intellect.

Root-Bernstein, M., & Root-Bernstein, R. (2005). Body thinking beyond dance. In L. Y. Overby & B. Lepczyk (Eds.), *Dance: Current selected research. Vol. 5. Dance education* (pp. 173–201). New York: AMS Press.

Saldana, J. (1995). *Drama of color: Improvisation with multiethnic folklore.* Portsmouth, NH: Heinemann.

Saldana, J. (Ed.). (2005). *Ethnodrama: An anthology of reality theatre.* Lanham, MD: Alta Mira Press.

Smith-Autard, J. (2002). *The art of dance in education* (2nd ed.). London: A & C Black.

Stinson, S. W. (1997). A question of fun: Adolescent engagement in dance education. *Dance Research Journal, 29*(2), 49–69.

Woodson, S. E. (2004). Creating an educational theatre program for the twenty-first century. *Art Education Policy Review, 105*(24), 25–30.

Worthy, J., & Prater, K. (2002). "I thought about it all night:" Readers theatre for reading fluency and motivation. *The Reading Teacher, 56*(3), 294–298.

Wright, L., & Garcia, L. (1992). Dramatic literacy: The place of theatre education in schools. *Arts Education Policy Review, 93*(4), 25–29.

Teaching English Language

Akhavan, N. (2006). *Help! My kids don't all speak English*. Portsmouth, NH: Heinemann.
This book explains how to set up a "language workshop" that helps to expand students' language skills and thinking strategies. Although it has an elementary focus, the sample lesson plans, classroom-tested units of study, and ready-to-use graphic organizers included are nonetheless helpful and can be modified for older students.

Brownlie, F., Feniak, C., & McCarthy, V. (2004). *Instruction and assessment of ESL learners: Promoting success in your classroom*. Winnipeg, MN: Portage & Main.
Provides useful ideas to support and grow the learning of ESLs.

Cary, S. (2000). *Working with second language learners: Answers to teachers' top ten questions*. Portsmouth, NH: Heinemann.
This easy-to-use book explores topics such as students' cultural backgrounds, encouraging reluctant speakers, and teaching grade level content.

deJong, E. J., & Harper, C. A. (2005). Preparing mainstream teachers for English language learners: Is being a good teacher good enough? *Teacher Education Quarterly, 32*(3), 101–124.
Discusses the issues and concerns impacting classrooms today.

Echevarria, J., & Goldenberg, C. (1999). *Teaching secondary language minority students*. Center for Research on Education, Diversity & Excellence, (http://www.cal.org/crede/pubs/ResBrief4.htm).
Access to readings with practical ideas for inclusive classrooms.

Echevarria, J., Vogt, M., & Short, D. (2007). *Making content comprehensible for English learners: The SIOP Model* (3rd ed.). Boston: Pearson, Allyn & Bacon.
Using a sheltered instruction approach, the authors offer guidelines for implementing their program. An accompanying CD features classroom clips, reproducible resources, and interviews with the authors.

Giambo, D., & Szecsi, T. (2005/06). Opening up to the issues: Preparing pre-service teachers to work effectively with English language learners. *Childhood Education, 82*(2), 107–110.
Identifying the issues with suggested teaching ideas for ELL instruction.

Gibbons, P. (2002). *Scaffolding language, scaffolding learning: Teaching second language learners in the mainstream classroom*. Portsmouth, NH: Heinemann.
Concrete ways to teach for second language learner understanding.

Helmer, S. (2003). *Look at me when I talk to you: ESL learners in non-ESL classrooms.* Toronto: Pippin.
Helpful advice and suggestions for the mainstream classroom teacher.

Law, B., & Eckes, M. (1995). *Assessment and ESL: On the yellow big road to the Withered of Oz.* Winnipeg, Manitoba: Peguis.
Access to assessment techniques and examples that can be modified to suit teachers and their students.

Law, B., & Eckes, M. (2000). *The more-than-just-surviving handbook: ESL for every classroom teacher.* Winnipeg, Man: Peguis.
Strategies and practical suggestions for the mainstream classroom teacher.

Lewis-Moreno, B. (2007). Shared responsibility: Achieving success with English language learners. *Phi Delta Kappan, 88*(10), 772–775.
Ways to create meaningful learning contexts for ELLs.

Linquanti, R. (1999). *Fostering academic success for English language learners: What do we know?* (http://www.wested.org/policy/pubs/fostering/index.htm#sect5)
ELL guidelines and considerations to keep in mind.

O'Malley, J. M. (2002). *Authentic assessment for English language learners: Practical approaches for teachers.* Reading, MA: Addison-Wesley.
Assessment practices that support ELLs.

Peitzman, F., & Gadda, G. (Eds). (1994). *With different eyes: Insights into teaching language minority students across the disciplines.* White Plains, NY: Longman.
Provides access to varied perspectives and experiences that can inform teaching practices.

Reiss, J. (2005). *Teaching content to English language learners.* White Plains, NY: Pearson.
This practical book helps content-area teachers to apply second language learning theories in their classrooms. Emphasis is on making content more accessible, strengthening vocabulary, and increasing student participation.

Samway, K. Davies & McKeon, D. (1999). *Myths and realities: Best practices for language minority students.* Portsmouth, NH: Heinemann.
This book dispels common myths related to ELL students by providing basic background information on issues such as second language acquisition, legal requirements for educating linguistically diverse students, assessment and placement.

Short, D. J. (1991). *How to integrate language and content instruction: A training manual.* Washington, DC: Center for Applied Linguistics.
This manual, intended for teachers, administrators, and teacher educators, presents strategies for integrating language and content. Topics include materials adaptations, lesson plan development, and assessment issues.

Tambini, R. F. (1999). Aligning learning activities and assessment strategies in the ESL classroom. *Internet TESL Journal, 5*(9) (http://iteslj.org/Articles/Tambini-Aligning.html)
Provides examples that teachers can adapt to their classrooms.

Walqui, A. (2000). *Strategies for success: Engaging immigrant students in secondary schools.* (http://www.cal.org/resources/digest/0003strategies.html)
Potential ways to enable immigrant youth in school settings.

Walter, T. (2004). *Teaching English language learners: The how to handbook*. White Plains, NY: Longman.

> This user friendly book includes discussions on culture, language acquisition, literacy development, and academic/content area development. A list of resources is also included.

ESOL Textbooks

Gonzalez, V., Yawkey, T., & Minaya-Rowe, L. (2006). *English-as-a-second-language (ESL) teaching and learning*. Boston: Pearson Allyn & Bacon.

> Provides theoretical and practical discussions of best approaches and strategies for increasing the academic achievement of at-risk English language learners. Authors include pertinent case studies, thought-provoking questions, and activities in each chapter. Especially interesting is the history of immigrant ESL students in the U.S.

Zainuddin, H., Yahya, N., Morales-Jones, C. A., & Ariza, E. N. (2002). *Fundamentals of teaching English to speakers of other languages in K–12 mainstream classrooms*. Dubuque, IA: Kendall Hunt.

> This book includes discussions on culture shock, how language influences culture, differences in verbal and nonverbal communication, and teaching and learning styles.

Home–School Collaboration

Ada, A. F. (1988). The Pajaro Valley experience: Working with Spanish-speaking parents to develop children's reading and writing skills in the home through the use of children's literature. In T. Skutnabb-Kangas & J. Cummins (Eds.), *Minority education: From shame to struggle*. Clevedon, England: Multilingual Matters.

Gonzalez, N., Moll, L., Floyd-Tennery, M., Rivera, A., Rendon, P., & Amanti, C. (1993). Funds of knowledge for teaching in Latino households. *Urban Education, 29*(4), 443–470.

Moll, L., Armanti, C., Neff, D., & Gonzalez, N. (1992). Funds of knowledge for teaching: Using a qualitative approach to connect homes and classrooms. *Theory and Practice, 31*(2), 132–141.

Audio-Visual Materials

The second language literacy case: A video ethnography of bilingual students' literacy development. CD-ROM (2003). Annela Teemant, Stefinee Pinnegar, and Ray Graham.

> This allows mainstream teachers to see and hear the second language literacy accounts of nine diverse second language learners, their teachers, and families. The cases explore who second language readers and writers are, their literacy needs, and their experiences in and outside school.

The SIOP model: Sheltered instruction for academic achievement. Video (2002).

> The 77-minute video illustrates the eight components of the SIOP model for sheltered instruction in detail. The video presents extended footage from middle and high school classrooms. It features interviews with six outstanding teachers and SIOP researchers. It is designed especially for use in sustained programs of staff development and teacher education and is to be used in conjunction with using the SIOP model.

Helping English learners succeed: An overview of the SIOP model. Video (2002).
This 26-minute video provides an introduction to a research-based model of sheltered instruction. The video uses classroom footage and researcher narration to concisely present the eight components of the SIOP model. This video will be useful to administrators, policymakers, or teachers. It also serves as a fitting supplement in teacher methodology courses.

Publishers

Alta Books (www.altaesl.com).

Benchmark Education Company (www.benchmarkeducation.com).

Cambridge University Press (www.cambridge.org/us/esl).

Center for Applied Linguistics (www.cal.org).

Delta Publishing Group (www.delta-systems.com/deltslinks.htm).

Heinemann (http://books.heinemann.com/categories/11.aspx).

Oxford University Press (www.oup.com/us/corporate/publishingprograms/esl?view=usa).

Pearson ESL (www.longman.com).

Thomson English Language Teaching (http://elt.thomson.com/namerica/en_us/index.html#).

Resources for Students

In addition to the resources presented here, note that each of the chapters in Part 3 also lists useful resources that may be utilized by students.

Dictionaries

Cambridge learner dictionaries. (http://www.cambridge.org/elt/dictionaries/cld.htm).
　　This collection includes beginners' and advanced learners' dictionaries. Pronouncing dictionaries and grammar resources are supplemented with CDs to aid comprehension. The publication *English grammar in use* is a self-paced study and reference guide for intermediate and above language learners.

Hill, J., & Lewis, M. (Eds.). (1997). *The LTP dictionary of selected collocations.* Sydney: Language Teaching.
　　Designed for intermediate and advanced learners, frequently used collocations are grouped by nouns, adjectives, verbs, and adverbs.

Lea, D. (2002). *Oxford collocations dictionary for learners of English.* New York: Oxford University Press.
　　This unique dictionary provides over 170,000 common word combinations to help students speak and write English more naturally and fluently.

Longman learner dictionaries. (http://www.longman.com/ae/dictionaries).
　　This collection offers dictionaries for beginning, intermediate, and advanced language learners. Basic picture dictionaries, pronunciation dictionaries, and bilingual dictionaries are

all included in this series. Additionally, the *Longman American Idioms Dictionary* helps students understand common American expressions.

Longman Dictionary of American English. (2004). Upper Saddle River, NJ: Pearson Education.
    Intermediate-level dictionary including full-color pictures and interactive CD-Rom.

Agnes, M. E. (Ed). (1998). *Webster's New World Basic Dictionary of American English.* New York:
Wiley, John & Sons.
    Defines the most commonly used words that readers will encounter in their daily lives.

Online Dictionaries

Alpha Dictionary (http://www.alphadictionary.com/index.shtml).

Cambridge Dictionaries Online (http://dictionary.cambridge.org).

Dictionary.com (http://dictionary.reference.com/).

Die.net Online Dictionary (http://dict.die.net/).

Encarta World English Dictionary (http://encarta.msn.com/encnet/features/dictionary/
dictionaryhome.aspx).

Lexicool (http://www.lexicool.com/).

Merriam-Webster Dictionary (http://www.m-w.com/dictionary.htm).

Omniglot (http://www.omniglot.com/links/dictionaries.htm).

One Look Dictionary Search (http://www.onelook.com/).

Oxford Dictionaries (http://www.askoxford.com/dictionaries/?view=uk).

Word2Word (http://www.word2word.com/dictionary.html).

Your Dictionary (http://www.yourdictionary.com/).

Online Translation Services

AltaVista Babel Fish (http://world.altavista.com/).

Applied Language Solutions (http://www.appliedlanguage.com/free_translation.shtml).

Google Language Tools (http://www.google.com/language_tools?hl=en).

Im Translator (http://freetranslation.imtranslator.com/lowres.asp).

Omniglot (http://www.omniglot.com/links/translation.htm).

World Lingo (http://www.worldlingo.com/en/products_services/worldlingo_translator.html).

Internet Sites

English Language Support

DiscoverySchool.com (http://school.discovery.com/students)

Study tools and learning adventures help students with homework and class work.

EFL/ESOL/ESL songs and activities (http://www.songsforteaching.com/esleflesol.htm).
Lyrics and sound clips are offered for a variety of songs that help students learn vocabulary for things such as colors, shapes, and food, among many other topics.

English Forum (http://www.englishforum.com/00/students/).
Online study resources, interactive English language exercises, online dictionaries and other tools. Full texts of popular novels are also included.

ESL Connect (http://www.eslconnect.com/links.html).
Student visitors to this gateway site can access links to Homework Help, Crosswords and Puzzles, and other activities that support English language learning.

ESL: English as a second language (http://www.eslgo.com/quizzes.html).
Tests students' knowledge of subject-verb agreement, prepositions, punctuation, and vocabulary.

ESL Independent Study Lab (http://www.lclark.edu/~krauss/toppicks/toppicks.html).
The ESL Center, housed at Lewis and Clark College in Portland, Oregon, contains speaking and listening exercises and activities that promote learning English as a second language.

ESL Partyland (http://www.eslpartyland.com).
Billed as "the cool way to learn English," this website allows users to enter depending on whether they are a teacher or a student. Students can access interactive quizzes, discussion forums, a chat room, and interactive lessons on a variety of topics.

eViews: English Listening Exercises (http://www.eviews.net).
Although there is a fee associated with this site, there is a free trial available. The listening exercises are designed for intermediate to advanced English students. English is recorded at normal speed and comprehension checks are included.

Grammar Safari (http://www.iei.uiuc.edu/student_grammarsafari.html).
This site provides "grammar safari" activities wherein students "hunt" and "collect" common, specific words as they are used in documents accessible on the Internet.

Grammar and ESL Exercises (http://owl.english.purdue.edu/owl/resource/611/01).
Hosted by Purdue University, this site offers the ELL interactive exercises, printable (offline) exercises, and concise explanations of grammar and punctuation rules.

Intensive English Institute: Internet English Resources (http://www.iei.uiuc.edu/student_internet_res.html).
Listening resources, oral communication resources, and a movie guide for English language learners are just a few of the helpful links provided on this site.

Interesting Things for ESL Students (http://www.manythings.org).
This website is for people studying English as a Second Language (ESL) or English as a Foreign Language (EFL). There are quizzes, word games, word puzzles, proverbs, slang expressions, anagrams, a random-sentence generator and other study materials.

Internet Treasure Hunts for ESL Students (http://iteslj.org/th/).
Links to scavenger hunts on the Internet that develop language skills.

iTools (http://www.itools.com/).

Language tools, translation services, and researching resources.

Learn English (http://www.learnenglish.de).
  Online games, tests, quizzes, and pronunciation guides assists students learning English.

Longman English Language Teaching (http://www.longman.com).
  In addition to free access to the Longman Dictionary of Contemporary English Online,
  the ELT Teens Resource Library includes online activities, support materials, and free
  resources for teenage learners of English.

OWL (Online Writing Lab) (http://owl.english.purdue.edu/handouts/esl/eslstudent.html).
  Help with idioms, grammar, spelling, and vocabulary. Links to quizzes, tests, and interactive
  sites.

Randall's ESL Cyber Listening Lab (http://www.esl-lab.com).
  Listening lab that allows students to practice listening skills, develop a natural accent, and
  understand slang.

Resources for English as a Second Language (http://www.usingenglish.com/).
  The English Language Reference section provides a glossary of grammar terms, English
  idioms, and irregular verbs.

Self-Study Quizzes for ESL Students (http://a4esl.org/q/h).
  These self-paced quizzes allow ELLs to test their understanding of language features such as
  vocabulary, homonyms, grammar, and idioms.

To Learn English (http://www.tolearnenglish.com/).
  Placement tests, lessons, exercises, clubs, forums, and tools to support ELL.

Print Materials that Support English Language and Cultural Learning

Becijos, J. (1995). *Global views: A multicultural reader with language exercises.* Upper Saddle
River, NJ: Dominie Press.
  Biographies, holidays, folktales, and descriptions of people and places from representative
  areas around the world. Language and content learning are supported through geographic
  questions, grammar exercises, and language information.

Chamot, A. U. (2004). *Keys to learning: Skills and strategies for newcomers.* Upper Saddle River,
NJ: Pearson ESL.
  This guidebook provides middle and high school newcomers with step-by-step tools for
  developing academic skills and literacy. Workbook with consumables is also available.

Claire, E. (2004). *American manners and customs: A guide for newcomers.* McHenry, IL: Delta.
  The most often required manners and customs are discussed and explained, including greet-
  ings, table manners, and body language.

Clark, R. C., & Hawkinson, A. (2006). *Living in the United States.* McHenry, IL: Delta.
  Written in language appropriate for intermediate students, this book has information on food
  and restaurants, communications, and customs and values.

Collis, H., & Kohl, J. (2000). *101 American customs.* Lincolnwood, IL: Passport Books.
  Basic overview of American customs.

Dixson, R. J. (2003). *Essential idioms in English: Phrasal verbs and collocations.* Upper Saddle River, NJ: Pearson Education.
General reference for common English use.

Francis, E. J. (2006). *A year in the life of an ESL student: Idioms and vocabulary you can't live without.* Victoria, BC, Canada: Trafford.
Quick reference for common English use.

Gaines, B. K. (1997). *Idiomatic American English: A workbook of idioms for everyday use.* Tokyo: Kodansha International.
Everyday English reference.

Gilbert, J. (2004). *Clear speech student's book: Pronunciation and listening comprehension in American English.* London: Cambridge University Press.
Assists with English pronunciation and comprehension.

Holleman, J. (2006). *American English idiomatic expressions in 52 weeks: An easy way to understand English expressions and improve speaking.* Hong Kong: Chinese University Press.
The meanings of 3,300 commonly used idioms are explained and contextual examples are provided.

Johnston, D. B. (2000). *Speak American: A survival guide to the language and culture of the U.S.A.* NY: Random House Reference.
General reference.

Lutter, J. G. (1999). *The pronunciation of standard American English.* Granada Hills, CA: Garrett.
English language pronunciation guide.

Orion, G. F. (1997). *Pronouncing American English: Sounds, stress, and intonation.* Belmont, CA: Heinle.
English language pronunciation guide.

Spears, R. A. (2002). *Common American phrases in everyday contexts: A detailed guide to real-life conversation and small talk.* New York: McGraw-Hill.
Conversational English language guide.

Spears, R. A., Birner, B. J., & Kleinedler, S. R. (1995). *NTC's dictionary of everyday American English expressions.* New York: McGraw-Hill.
With more than 7,000 up-to-date phrases, this dictionary covers situations from talking to a doctor to ordering a meal, and helps learners communicate personal feelings, and make small talk.

Swick, E. (2004). *Practice makes perfect: English grammar for ESL learners.* New York: McGraw-Hill.
English language grammar guide.

Yates, J. (1999*). The ins and outs of prepositions: A guidebook for ESL students.* Hauppauge, NY: Barron's Educational Series.
Using prepositions correctly in the English language.

Audio-Visual Materials

Childs, C. (2003). *Improve your American English accent: Overcoming major obstacles to understanding.* NY: McGraw-Hill. Audio CD.

Collis, H. (2007). *101 English idioms and CD.* NY: McGraw-Hill. Book and CD.

Dale, P, & Poms, L. (2004). *English pronunciation made simple.* City, ST: Pearson ESL. Book and two CDs.

Gilbert, J. (2004). *Clear speech from the start: Basic pronunciation and listening comprehension in North American English.* London: Cambridge University Press. Student's book with audio CD.

Gillett, A. (2004). *Speak English like an American.* Ann Arbor, MI: Language Success Press. Book and audio CD set.

Yates, J. (2005). *Pronounce it perfectly in English.* Hauppauge, NY: Barron's. Sound recording (four CDs).

Glossary

Additive bilingualism: Theory that the acquisition of a second language does not interfere in the learning of the native language; second language can be acquired either simultaneously or after native language development.

BICS: Basic interpersonal communication skills; in effect, language skills needed for everyday personal and social communication.

Bilingual education: Although most instruction is in English, concepts are explained in students' primary language and a sheltered English approach is used for academic subjects.

CALP: Cognitive/academic language proficiency; language skills needed for cognitive/academic tasks in the mainstream classroom.

Comprehensible input: Language presented at the student's level of comprehension. Input is made comprehensible through the use of visuals, context, and other cues.

Developmental bilingual education: Instruction is provided in the student's native language for an extended time period while simultaneously learning English, resulting in bilingualism; often used synonymously with "late exit bilingual education."

Dual-language programs: Instruction occurs in both the native language and in English to develop strong skills and proficiency in both. Also known as two-way immersion.

Early exit bilingual education: Transition to English as quickly as possible, often using sheltered instructional strategies; some content instruction in the native language is provided; transition to mainstream in two to three years.

English language learner (ELL): Student whose limited proficiency in English affects his or her academic achievement in school. Also known as limited English proficient student.

English as a new language (ENL): Used by the National Board for Professional Teaching Standards.

English as a second language (ESL): The learning of English by speakers of other languages; often used synonymously with ESOL (see below).

English to speakers of other languages (ESOL): The learning of English by speakers of other languages; often used synonymously with ESL (see above).

Heritage learners: Student who is exposed to a language other than English at home. Heritage learners usually have varying degrees of knowledge of the home language.

Immersion: Instructional approach wherein 100 percent of the instructional time is spent communicating through the target language; in contrast to submersion, the class is composed mostly of speakers of the target language with only a few non-native speakers.

Immersion language instruction: Instruction—including academic content—in the student's *non-native* language. Students are mainstreamed into regular, English-only classrooms with no special support.

Language minority (LM) student: A student whose primary home language is not English. LM students may have limited English proficiency or may be fluent in English.

Late exit bilingual education: In contrast to early exit bilingual education, transition to mainstream occurs in four to six years; significant amount of instruction in native language while gradually increasing instruction in English.

Limited English proficiency students: Students whose limited proficiency in English affects their academic achievement in school. Also known as English language learners.

Mainstreaming: Practice of integrating ELLs into regular classrooms.

Maintenance bilingual education: Instruction is delivered in both native language and target language; often used synonymously with "late-exit bilingual education."

Pull-out: Students are pulled out of their regular, English-only classrooms for special instruction to develop English language skills.

Self-contained: ELL classrooms located in "regular" schools but separate from regular education classrooms; ELLs are provided special instruction apart from their peers.

Sheltered English instruction: Using comprehensible content and strategies to teach grade-level subject matter in English while simultaneously also developing English language skills. Also known as specially designed academic instruction in English.

Sheltered immersion: Instructional approach that promotes English language development while providing comprehensible grade-level content.

Silent period: Common, varying period of time during which a new language learner listens to, but does not speak in, the new language.

Specially designed academic instruction in English (SDAIE): Using comprehensible content and strategies to teach grade-level subject matter in English while simultaneously developing English language skills.

Structured immersion: Students' proficiency levels in English are taken into account so subject matter is comprehensible.

Submersion: Instructional approach wherein the class is composed entirely of students learning a target language; 100 percent of the instructional time is spent communicating through the target language.

Subtractive bilingualism: When the acquisition of a second language interferes with the maintenance of the native language, effectively replacing the first language.

Total physical response: Instructional approach integrating both verbal and physical communication (and often movement) so that students can internalize and eventually "code break" a new language; especially effective with beginning language students, vocabulary instruction, and with students who are primarily kinesthetic learners.

Transitional bilingual education: Language acquisition theory emphasizing fluency in learner's native language first, before acquiring fluency in second language.

Two-way immersion: Instruction occurs in both the native language and in English to develop strong skills and proficiency in both. Also known as dual-language programs.

Notes

Introduction

1 Chris Maly's narrative of teaching experience is shared with his permission and with the permission of Lincoln Public Schools, Lincoln, NE.

1.1 Orientation

1 Proposition 227 was part of a referendum in California to abolish bilingual education for ELLs in favor of more instruction in English. The No Child Left Behind legislation is a federal initiative to oversee teacher performance and student improvement in literacy and numeracy through such accountability measures as standardized testing in schools.

1.7 Not All Parents are the Same: Home-School Communication

1 Two research studies from the Center for Research on Education, Diversity & Excellence (CREDE) have recently been published through the Center for Applied Linguistics. The two books arising out of a four-year and a three-year study respectively, center on the solidification of home-school ELL communication. The first, entitled *Creating Access: Language and Academic Programs for Secondary School Newcomers,* describes the ins and outs of an effective education model—newcomer programs for immigrant students—and is designed to help district personnel create a newcomer program or enhance an existing program. The second book, *Family Literacy Nights: Building the Circle of Supporters Within and Beyond School for Middle School English Language Learners,* discusses a project to improve students' education through a home-school collaboration called "Family Literacy Nights." The program brought parents of linguistically and culturally diverse students together with teachers and students, resulting in greater parental involvement and improved student learning. This report offers practitioners strategies for implementing similar programs.

2.2 Qualities Instilling Artistic Thinking

1 Teacher, Jen Deets, and Lincoln Public Schools, Lincoln, NE, both granted permission for us to include a narrative account based on Jen Deets' classroom context.

3.1 Introduction

1 Teacher, Jodi Heiser, and Ralston Public Schools, Ralston, NE, both granted permission for us to include a narrative account based on Jodi Heiser's classroom context.

3.2 Visual Arts Experiences to Engage ELLs alongside All Learners

1 The text and performance of the slam poem is made accessible with the permission of the poet, Lucas Hines, and the knowledge of Lincoln Public Schools, Lincoln, NE.
2 This learning experience is based on some of the teaching ideas and practices of Chris Maly, and is used and modified with his permission and the knowledge of Lincoln Public Schools, Lincoln, NE.
3 This learning experience is based on some of the teaching ideas and practices of Lorraine Cockle, a community arts educator in Calgary, Alberta, Canada, and is used and modified with her permission.
4 Table 3.5, Alberta Education, Copyright © 2007, *Personal Worldview Questionnaire*, http://www.learnalberta.ca/content/sssm/html/exploringworldview_sm.html. Reproduced with permission.

3.3 Music Experiences to Engage ELLs alongside All Learners

1 The text and performance of the slam poem is made accessible with the permission of the poet, Lucas Hines, and the knowledge of Lincoln Public Schools, Lincoln, NE.
2 This learning experience is based on some of the teaching ideas and practices of Lorraine Cockle, a community arts educator in Calgary, Alberta, Canada, and is used and modified with her permission.

3.4 Drama Experiences to Engage ELLs alongside All Learners

1 This learning experience is based on some of the teaching ideas and practices of Chris Maly, and is used and modified with his permission and the knowledge of Lincoln Public Schools, Lincoln, NE.
2 The text and performance of the slam poem is made accessible with the permission of the poet, Lucas Hines, and the knowledge of Lincoln Public Schools, Lincoln, NE.
3 Table 3.8, Imaginative Ways to Alter and Transform Perspectives is adapted with permission from the work of Dr. Bill Zuk at the University of Victoria, B.C., Canada.
4 This learning experience is based on some of the teaching ideas and practices of Lorraine Cockle, a community arts educator in Calgary, Alberta, Canada, and is used and modified with her permission.
5 This learning experience is based on some of the teaching ideas and practices of Sarah Thomas, and is used and modified with her permission and the knowledge of Lincoln Public Schools, Lincoln, NE.

3.5 Dance Experiences to Engage ELLs alongside All Learners

1 The text and performance of the slam poem is made accessible with the permission of the poet, Lucas Hines, and the knowledge of Lincoln Public Schools, Lincoln, NE.

References

Series Introduction

Ladson-Billings, G. (2001). *Crossing over to Canaan: The journey of new teachers in diverse classrooms*. San Francisco: Jossey-Bass.

Introduction

Banks, J. A. (2008). *An introduction to multicultural education* (4th ed.). New York: Pearson Education.

Bresler, L. (Ed.). (2007). *International handbook of research in arts education*. Dordrecht, The Netherlands: Springer.

Chan, E. (2009). Teacher experiences of culture in the curriculum. In D. J. Flinders & S. J. Thornton (Eds.), *The curriculum studies reader* (3rd ed., pp. 348–361). New York: Routledge.

Clair, N. (1995). Mainstream classroom teachers and ESL students. *TESOL Quarterly, 29,* 19–196.

Cochran-Smith, M. (2004). *Walking the road: Race, diversity, and social justice in teacher education*. New York: Teachers College Press.

Dewey, J. (1926). Art in education—and education in art. *The New Republic: A Journal of Opinion, 586*(XLVI), 12–14.

Doll, W. (2009). The four R's—An alternative to the Tyler rationale. In D. J. Flinders & S. J. Thornton (Eds.), *The curriculum studies reader* (3rd ed., pp. 267–274). New York: Routledge.

Eisner, E. W. (2002). *The arts and the creation of mind*. London: Yale University Press.

Kindler, A. (2002). *Survey of the states' limited English proficient students and available educational programs and services, 2000–2001 summary report*. Washington, DC: NCELA. Available at: http://www.ncela.gwu.edu/policy/states/reports/seareports/001.pdf

Ladson-Billings, G. (2001). *Crossing over to Canaan: The journey of new teachers in diverse classrooms*. San Francisco, CA: Jossey-Bass.

Menken, K., & Antunez, B. (2001). *An overview of the preparation and certification of teachers working with limited English proficient (LEP) students.* U.S. Department of Education Office of Bilingual Education and Minority Languages Affairs in cooperation with the ERIC Clearinghouse on Teaching and Teacher Education and Center for the Study of Language and Education Institute for Education Policy Studies, Graduate School of Education and Human Development, The George Washington University.

National Center for Education Statistics. (2002). *School and staffing survey 1999–2000: Overview of the data for public, private, public charter and Bureau of Indian Affairs elementary and secondary schools.* Washington, DC: U.S. Department of Education.

Nieto, S., Bode, P., Kang, E., & Raible, J. (2007). Chapter 9—Identity, community, and diversity: Retheorizing multicultural curriculum for the postmodern era. In F. M. Connelly, M. F. He, & J. Phillion (Eds.), *Handbook of curriculum and instruction* (pp. 176–197). Thousand Oaks, CA: Sage.

Seidel, S., Tishman, S., Winner, E., Hetland, L., & Palmer, P. (2009). *The qualities of quality: Understanding excellence in arts education.* A report commissioned by The Wallace Foundation and with additional support from the Arts Education Partnership. Cambridge, MA: Project Zero, Harvard Graduate School of Education.

Thornton, S. J. (2005). *Teaching social studies that matters: Curriculum for active learning.* New York: Teachers College Press.

Uhrmacher, P. B., & Matthews, J. (2005). *Intricate palette: Working the ideas of Elliot Eisner.* Upper Saddle River, NJ: Pearson.

U.S. Census (2002). *United States Census 2000 Supplementary Survey.* Washington, DC: U.S. Bureau of the Census. Retrieved September 24, 2002, from http://www.census.gov/main/www/cen2000.html

Part 1

Baca, L., & Cervantes, H. (2004). *The bilingual special education interface.* Columbus, OH: Merrill.

Bailey, A. L., Butler, F. A., Borrego, M., LaFramenta, C., & Ong, C. (2002). Towards a characterization of academic language. *Language Testing Update, 31*, 45–52.

Baker, C. (2001). *Foundations of bilingual education and bilingualism* (3rd ed.). Clevedon, UK: Multilingual Matters.

Bassoff, T. C. (2004). Three steps toward a strong home-school connection. *Essential Teacher, 1*(4). Retrieved July 17, 2007, from www.tesol.org/s_tesol/sec_document.asp?CID=659&DID=2586.

Boscolo, P., & Mason, L. (2001). Writing to learn, writing to transfer. In P. Tynjälä, L. Mason, & K. Lonka (Eds.), *Writing as a learning tool: Integrating theory and practice* (pp. 83–104). Dordrecht, The Netherlands: Kluwer Academic.

Brinton, D. (2003). Content-based instruction. In D. Nunan (Ed.), *Practical English language teaching* (pp. 199–224). New York: McGraw-Hill.

Carrasquillo, A. L., & Rodriguez, V. (2002). *Language minority students in the mainstream classroom* (2nd ed.). Boston: Multilingual Matters.

Clark, D. (1999). *Learning domains or Bloom's taxonomy.* Retrieved August 3, 2007, from www.nwlink.com/~donclark/hrd/bloom.html

Coady, M., Hamann, E. T., Harrington, M., Pacheco, M., Pho, S., & Yedlin, J. (2003). *Claiming opportunities: A handbook for improving education for English language learners through comprehensive school reform.* Providence, RI: The Education Alliance at Brown University.

Collier, V. P. (1995, Fall). *Acquiring a second language for school: Directions in language and education, 1*(4). Washington, DC: National Clearinghouse for Bilingual Education.

Collier, V., & Thomas, W. (1997). *School effectiveness for language minority students.* Washington, DC: National Clearinghouse for Bilingual Education. Retrieved February 21, 2007, from www.ncela.gwu.edu/pubs/resource/effectiveness/

Consent Decree. (1990). Retrieved January 17, 2007, from http://www.firn.edu/doe/aala/lulac.htm

Crawford, J. (2004). *Educating English learners: Language diversity in the classroom* (5th ed.). Los Angeles: Bilingual Educational Services.

Cummins, J. (1979). Cognitive/academic language proficiency, linguistic interdependence, the optimum age question and some other matters. *Working papers on Bilingualism, 19*, 121–129.

Cummins, J. (1980). The cross-lingual dimensions of language proficiency: Implications for bilingual education and the optimal age issue. *TESOL Quarterly, 14*(2), 175–187.

Cummins, J. (1981). The role of primary language development in promoting educational success for language minority students. In C. F. Leyka (Ed.), Schooling and Language Minority Students: A theoretical framework. Los Angeles: California State University, Evaluation, Dissemination and Assessment Center.

Cummins, J. (1986). Empowering minority students: A framework for intervention. *Harvard Educational Review, 56*(1), 18–36.

Cummins, J. (1992). Bilingual education and English immersion: The Ramírez report in theoretical perspective. *Bilingual Research Journal, 16*, 91–104.

Cummins, J. (2001). *Negotiating identities: Education for empowerment in a diverse society* (2nd ed.). Los Angeles: California Association for Bilingual Education.

Dalton, J., & Smith, D. (1986). *Extending children's special abilities: Strategies for primary classrooms.* Retrieved February 19, 2007, from www.teachers.ash.org.au/researchskills/dalton.htm.

de Valenzuela, J. S., & Niccolai, S. L. (2004). Language development in culturally and linguistically diverse students with special education needs. In L. Baca & H. Cervantes (Eds.), *The bilingual special education interface* (4th ed., pp. 125–161). Upper Saddle River, NJ: Merrill.

Diaz-Rico, L., & Weed, K. Z. (2006). *The crosscultural language and academic development handbook* (3rd ed.). Boston: Pearson Education.

Echevarria, J., & McDonough, R. (1993). *Instructional conversations in special education settings: Issues and accommodations. Educational Practice Report 7.* National Center for Research on Cultural Diversity and Second Language Learning. Retrieved May 10, 2007, from http://www.ncela.gwu.edu/pubs/ncrcdsll/epr7.htm.

Ellis, R. (2005) *Instructed second language acquisition: A literature review.* Report to the Ministry of Education, New Zealand. Retrieved January 18, 2007, from http://www.educationcounts.edcentre.govt.nz/publications/downloads/instructed-second-language.pdf.

Gay, G. (2000). *Culturally responsive teaching: Theory, research, and practice.* New York: Teachers College Press.

Genesee, F. (Ed.). (1999). *Program alternatives for linguistically diverse students.* Santa Cruz, CA: Center for Research on Education, Diversity and Excellence. Retrieved January 8, 2007, from www.cal.org/crede/pubs/edpractice/Epr1.pdf.

Gold, N. (2006). *Successful bilingual schools: Six effective programs in California.* San Diego: San Diego County Office of Education.

Gollnick, D. M., & Chinn, P. C. (2002). *Multicultural education in a pluralistic society* (6th ed.). New York: Merrill.

Hakuta, K., Butler, Y. G., & Witt, D. (2000). *How long does it take English learners to attain proficiency?* Santa Barbara: University of California Linguistic Research Institute Policy Report (2000–2001).

Hoover, J. J., & Collier, C. (1989). Methods and materials for bilingual education. In M. Baca & H. T. Cervantes (Eds.), *The bilingual special interface* (pp. 231–255). Columbus, OH: Merrill.

Kern, R. (2000). *Literacy and language teaching.* Oxford, UK: Oxford University Press.

Kindler, A. (2002). *Survey of the states' limited English proficient students and available educational programs and services: 2000–2001 summary report.* Washington, DC: National Clearinghouse for English Language Acquisition.

Krashen, S. D. (1981) *Principles and practice in second language acquisition.* English Language Teaching Series. London: Prentice-Hall International.

Krashen, S.D., & Terrell, T. D. (1983). *The natural language approach: Language acquisition in the classroom.* London: Prentice Hall Europe.

Long, M. (1996). The role of the linguistic environment in second language acquisition. In W. Ritchie & T. Bhatia (Eds.), *Handbook of second language acquisition* (pp. 413–468). San Diego: Academic.

Long, M. H. (2006) *Problems in SLA.* Mahwah, NJ: Lawrence Erlbaum.

Lyster, R. (1998). Recasts, repetition and ambiguity in L2 classroom discourse. *Studies in Second Language Acquisition, 20,* 51–81.

Lyster, R. (2001). Negotiation of form, recasts, and explicit correction in relation to error types and learner repair in immersion classrooms. *Language Learning, 51*(Suppl. 1), 265–301.

Lyster, R. (2004). Differential effects of prompts and recasts in form-focused instruction. *Studies in Second Language Acquisition, 26*, 399–432.

Lyster, R. (2007). *Learning and teaching languages through content: A counterbalanced approach.* Amsterdam/Philadelphia: John Benjamins.

Lyster, R., & Mori, H. (2006). Interactional feedback and instructional counterbalance. *Studies in Second Language Acquisition, 28*, 321–341.

Lyster, R., & Ranta, L. (1997). Corrective feedback and learner uptake: Negotiation of form in communicative classrooms. *Studies in Second Language Acquisition, 19*, 37–66.

Meltzer, J. (2001). *The adolescent literacy support framework.* Providence, RI: Northeast and Islands Regional Educational Laboratory at Brown University. Retrieved August 11, 2004, from http://knowledgeloom.org/adlit.

Meltzer, J., & Hamann, E. T. (2005). *Meeting the literacy development needs of adolescent English language learners through content-area learning. Part Two: Focus on classroom teaching strategies.* Providence, RI: Education Alliance. Brown University.

Oberg, K. (1954). *The social economy of the Tlingit Indians of Alaska.* Unpublished doctoral dissertation, University of Chicago.

Ortiz, A. (1984). Language and curriculum development for exceptional bilingual children. In C. P. Chinn (Ed.), *Education of culturally and linguistically different exceptional children* (pp. 77–100). Reston, VA: The Council for Exceptional Children–ERIC Clearinghouse on Handicapped and Gifted Children.

Ovando, C., & Collier, V. (1998). *Bilingual and ESL classrooms: Teaching in multicultural contexts.* Boston: McGraw-Hill.

Pienemann, M. (1988). Determining the influence of instruction on L2 speech processing. *AILA Review, 5*, 40–72.

Pienemann, M. (1989) Is language teachable? Psycholinguistic experiments and hypotheses. *Applied Linguistics, 10*(1), 52–79.

Pienemann, M. (2007). Processability theory. In B. van Patten & J. Williams (Eds.), *Theories in second language acquisition: An introduction* (pp. 137–154). Mahwah, NJ: Lawrence Erlbaum.

Ragan, A. (2005). Teaching the academic language of textbooks: A preliminary framework for performing a textual analysis. *The ELL Outlook.* Retrieved August 13, 2007, from http://www.coursecrafters.com/ELL-Outlook/2005/nov_dec/ELLOutlookITIArticle1.htm.

Richards, H. V., Brown, A. F., & Forde, T. B. (2004). *Addressing diversity in schools: Culturally responsive pedagogy.* National Center for Culturally Responsive Educational Systems. Retrieved July 27, 2007, from http://www.nccrest.org/Briefs/Diversity_Brief.pdf.

Ruiz, N. T. (1989). An optimal learning environment for Rosemary. *Exceptional Children, 56*(2), 130–144.

Ruiz, N. T. (1995a). The social construction of ability and disability: I. Profile types of Latino children identified as language learning disabled. *Journal of Learning Disabilities, 28*(8), 476–490.

Ruiz, N. T. (1995b). The social construction of ability and disability: II. Optimal and at-risk lessons in a bilingual special education classroom. *Journal of Learning Disabilities, 28*(8), 491–502.

Scarcella, R. (2003). *Academic English: A conceptual framework. Technical Report 2003–1.* The University of California Linguistic Minority Research Institute. Retrieved July 2, 2007 from http://www.ncela.gwu.edu/resabout/literacy/2_academic.htm.

Skehan, P. (1998). *A cognitive approach to language learning.* Oxford: Oxford University Press.

Swain, M. (1995). Three functions of output in second language learning. In G. Cook & B. Seidlhofer (Eds.), *Principle and practice in applied linguistics* (pp. 125–144). Oxford: Oxford University Press.

Thomas, W., & Collier, V. (1997) *School effectiveness for language minority students.* Retrieved December 2, 2006, from http://www.ncela.gwu/pubs/resource/effectiveness/index.htm.

U.S. Census Bureau. (2005) *Statistical abstract of the United States.* Retrieved February 24, 2008, from www.census.gov/prod/www/statistical-abstract.html.

Valdéz, G. (2000, Winter). Nonnative English speakers: Language bigotry in English mainstream classes. *The Associations of Departments of English Bulletin, 124*, 12–17.

Zamel, V., & Spack, R. (1998). *Negotiating academic literacies: Teaching and learning across language and cultures.* Mawah, NJ: Lawrence Erlbaum.

Zehler, A. (1994). *Working with English Language Learners: Strategies for elementary and middle school teachers*. NCBE Program Information Guide, No. 19. Retrieved May 25, 2007, from www.ncela.gwu.edu/pubs/pigs/pig19.htm.

Part 2

Abbs, P. (2007). The art of creativity. In L. Bresler (Ed.), *International handbook of research in arts education* (pp. 1247–1252). Dordrecht, The Netherlands: Springer.

Abrahams, D. (2006). Differentiating instruction in the choral rehearsal: Strategies for choral conductors in urban schools. In C. Frierson-Campbell (Ed.), *Teaching music in the urban classroom: A guide to survival, success, and reform* (pp. 109-116). Toronto, ON: Rowman & Littlefield Education.

Ada, A. F. (1988). The Pajaro Valley experience: Working with Spanish-speaking parents to develop children's reading and writing skills in the home through the use of children's literature. In T. Skutnabb-Kangas & J. Cummins (Eds.), *Minority education: From shame to struggle*. Clevedon, England: Multilingual Matters.

Andrzejczak, N., Trainin, G., & Poldberg, M. (2005). From image to text: Using images in the writing process. *International Journal of Education and the Arts*, 6(12). Retrieved October 2, 2008 from http://www.ijea.org/v6n12/.

Anttila, E. (2007). Children as agents in dance: Implications of the notion of child culture for research and practice in dance education. In L. Bresler (Ed.), *International handbook of research in arts education* (pp. 865–879). Dordrecht, The Netherlands: Springer.

Assessment Reform Group. (1999). *Assessment for learning: Beyond the black box*. Cambridge: University of Cambridge School of Education.

Banks, J. A. (1995). Multicultural education: Its effects on students' racial and gender role attitudes. In J. A. Banks & C. A. McGee Banks (Eds.), *Handbook of research on multicultural education* (pp. 617–627). New York: Simon & Schuster Macmillan.

Barrett, J. R. (2007). Currents of change in the music curriculum. In L. Bresler (Ed.), *International handbook of research in arts education* (pp. 147–162). Dordrecht, The Netherlands: Springer.

Barrett, M. (2007). Music Appreciation: Exploring similarity and difference. In L. Bresler (Ed.), *International handbook of research in arts education* (pp. 605–619). Dordrecht, The Netherlands: Springer.

Benedict, C. (2006). Defining ourselves as Other: Envisioning transformative possibilities. In C. Frierson-Campbell (Ed.), *Teaching music in the urban classroom: A guide to survival, success, and reform* (pp. 3–14). Toronto, ON: Rowman & Littlefield Education.

Biesta, G. (2004). Mind the gap! Communication and the educational relation. In C. Bingham & A. Sidorkin (Eds.), *No education without relation* (pp.11–22). New York: Peter Lang.

Bingham, C., & Sidorkin, A. (Eds.). (2004). *No education without relation*. New York: Peter Lang.

Black, P., & William, D. (1998a). Assessment and classroom learning. *Assessment in Education: Principles, Policy, and Practice*, 5(1), 7–74.

Black, P., & William, D. (1998b). *Inside the black box: Raising standards through classroom assessment*. London: School of Education, King's College.

Blair, D. (2009). Learner agency: To understand and to be understood. *British Journal of Music Education*, 26(2), 173–187.

Blocker, H. G. (2004). Varieties of multicultural art education: Some policy issues. In E. W. Eisner & M. D. Day (Eds.), *Handbook of research and policy in art education* (pp. 187–199). New Jersey and London: Lawrence Erlbaum.

Blumenfeld-Jones, D. (1995). Curriculum, control, and creativity. *Journal of Curriculum Theorizing*, 11(1), 73–96.

Boughton, D. (2004). Assessing art learning in changing contexts: High-stakes accountability, international standards, and changing conceptions of artistic development. In E. Eisner & M. Day (Eds.), *Handbook of research and policy in art education* (pp. 585–605). New Jersey and London: Lawrence Erlbaum.

Bowman, W. (2005). Music education in nihilistic times. In D. K. Lines (Ed.), *Music education for the new millennium* (pp. 29–45). Oxford: Blackwell.

Bresler, L. (Ed.). (2004). *Knowing bodies, moving minds: Towards embodied teaching and learning*. Boston: Kluwer Academic.

Bresler, L. (Ed.). (2007). *International handbook of research in arts education*. Dordrecht, The Netherlands: Springer.

Bruner, J. (1990). *Acts of meaning*. Cambridge, MA: Harvard University Press.

Cantor, J. S. (2006). Fearless innovation—Songwriting for our lives: Inspiring learners with arts-based practices that support creativity. *Multicultural Education, 14*(2), 57–64.

Chalmers, F. G. (2002). Celebrating pluralism six years later: Visual transculture/s, education, and critical multiculturalism. *Studies in Art Education, 43*(4), 293–306.

Chen, J. (2005). Weaving art education into the texture of a community. In M. Stokrocki (Ed.), *Interdisciplinary art education: Building bridges to connect disciplines and cultures* (pp. 90–106). Reston, VA: National Art Education Association.

Chicago, J. (2006). *Through the flower: My struggle as a woman artist*. Mustang, OK: Authors Choice.

Cohen, V. (2002). Musical creativity: A teacher training perspective. In T. Sullivan & L. Willingham (Eds.), *Creativity and music education* (pp. 218–237). Edmonton, Alberta: Canadian Music Educators' Association.

Conrad, D. (2008). Exploring risky youth experiences. In P. Leavy (Ed.), *Method meets art* (pp. 162–178). New York: Guilford.

Costantino, T. (2007) Articulating aesthetic understanding through art making. *International Journal of Education and the Arts, 8*(1). Retrieved November 10, 2008 from http://www.ijea.org/v8n1/.

Csikszentmihalyi, M. (1997). *Finding flow: The psychology of engagement with everyday life*. New York: Basic Books.

Cummins, J. (1996). *Negotiating identities: Education for empowerment in a diverse society*. Ontario, CA: California Association for Bilingual Education (CABE).

Cummins, J. (2001). *Negotiating identities: Education for empowerment in a diverse society* (2nd ed.). Los Angeles, CA: California Association for Bilingual Education.

Cummins, J., Bismilla, V., Chow, P., Cohen, S., Giampapa, F., Leoni, L., Sandhu, P., & Sastri, P. (2005). Affirming identity in multilingual classrooms. *Educational Leadership, 63*(1), 38–43.

Custodero, L. A. (2005). Being with: The resonant legacy of childhood's creative aesthetic. *Journal of Aesthetic Education, 39*(2), 36–57.

Delandshire, G. (2002). Assessment as inquiry. *Teachers College Record, 104*(7), 1461–1484.

Dewey, J. (1910/1978). How we think. In J. A. Boydston (Ed.), *John Dewey: The middle works, 1889–1924* (Vol. 6, 1910–1911, pp. 177–356). Carbondale, IL: Southern Illinois University Press.

Dewey, J. (1934). *Art as experience*. New York: Perigee.

Dils, A. (2007). Moving into dance: Dance appreciation as dance literacy. In L. Bresler (Ed.), *International handbook of research in arts education* (pp. 569–580). Dordrecht, The Netherlands: Springer.

Dolamore, J. P. (2006). The string chorale concept. In C. Frierson-Campbell (Ed.), *Teaching music in the urban classroom: A guide to survival, success, and reform* (pp. 125–138). Toronto, ON: Rowman & Littlefield Education.

Donmoyer, R., & Yennie-Donmoyer, J. (1995). Data as drama: Reflections on the use of Readers' Theatre as a mode of qualitative data display. *Qualitative Inquiry, 1*(4), 402–428.

Dorn, C. M. (1999). *Mind in art: Cognitive foundations in art education*. Mahwah, NJ: Lawrence Erlbaum.

Dorn, C. M., Madeja, A. S., & Sabol, F. R. (2004). *Assessing expressive learning: A practical guide for teacher-directed authentic assessment in K–12 art education*. Mahwah, NJ: Lawrence Erlbaum.

Dowdy, J. K., & Campbell, D. (2008). The dance of diversity: White male teachers and arts based instruction for classrooms. *The High School Journal, 91*(4), 1–11.

Duncum, P. (2005). Popular visual culture and ten kinds of integration. In M. Stokrocki (Ed.), *Interdisciplinary art education: Building bridges to connect disciplines and cultures* (pp. 107–120). Reston, VA: National Art Education Association.

Echevarria, J., Vogt, M. E., & Short, D. J. (2000). *Making content comprehensible for English language learners: The SIOP model*. Needham Heights, MA: Allyn & Bacon.

Efland, A. D. (2002). *Art and cognition: Integrating the visual arts in the curriculum*. New York: Teachers College Press.

Efland, A. D. (2004). The arts and the creation of mind: Eisner's contributions to the arts in education. *The Journal of Aesthetic Education, 38*(4), 71–80.

Eisner, E. W. (1972). *Educating artistic vision*. New York: Macmillan.

Eisner, E. W. (2002). *The arts and the creation of mind.* London: Yale University Press.

Eisner, E. W. (2004). What can education learn from the arts about the practice of education? *International Journal of Education and the Arts, 5*(4), 1–12.

Eisner, E. W. (2005). *Reimagining schools.* New York: Routledge.

Eisner, E. W., & Day, M. (2004). *Handbook of research and policy in art education.* London: Lawrence Erlbaum.

Elliot, D. J. (Ed.). (2005). *Praxial music education: Reflections and dialogues.* Oxford: Oxford University Press.

Eubanks, P. (2002). Students who don't speak English: How arts specialists adapt curriculum for ESOL students. *Art Education, 55*(2), 40–45.

Feuerverger, G. (1994). A multicultural literacy intervention for minority language students. *Language and education, 8*(3), 123–146.

Frierson-Campbell, C. (Ed.). (2006). *Teaching music in the urban classroom: A guide to survival, success, and reform.* Toronto, ON: Rowman & Littlefield Education.

Gadamer, H. G. (1960/1992). *Truth and method* (J. Weinsheimer & D. Marshall, Trans.). New York: Continuum. (Original work published 1960.)

Gallagher, K., & Lortie, P. (2007). Building theories of their lives: Youth engaged in drama research. In D. Thiessen & A. Cook-Sather (Eds.), *International handbook of student experience in elementary and secondary school* (pp. 405–438). Dordrecht, The Netherlands: Springer.

Garcia, E. (2002). *Student cultural diversity: Understanding and meeting the challenge* (3rd ed.). Boston, MA: Houghton Mifflin.

Gardner, H. (2006). *Multiple intelligences: New horizons in theory and practice.* New York: Basic Books.

Gay, G. (2000). *Culturally responsive teaching: Theory, research and practice.* New York: Teachers College Press.

Goble, S. (2010). *What's so important about music education?* New York: Routledge.

Goldberg, M. (Ed.). (2004). *Teaching English language learners through the arts: A SUAVE experience.* Boston, MA: Pearson Education.

Goldberg, M. (Ed.). (2006). *Integrating the arts: An approach to teaching and learning in multicultural and multilingual settings.* Boston, MA: Pearson Education.

Goldstein, T. (2003). *Teaching and learning in a multilingual school: Choices, risks, and dilemmas.* Mahwah, NJ: Lawrence Erlbaum.

Grauer, K. (2005). Starting with art: Relating children's visual and written expression. In K. Grauer & R. L. Irwin (Eds.), *Starting with…* (pp. 111–117). Toronto: Canadian Society for Education through Art.

Grauer, K., & Irwin, R. L. (Eds.). (2005). *Starting with…* Toronto: Canadian Society for Education through Art.

Green, E., & Shapiro, A. (2006). Music of every culture has something in common and can teach us about ourselves: Using the aesthetic realism teaching method. In C. Frierson-Campbell (Ed.), *Teaching music in the urban classroom: A guide to survival, success, and reform* (pp.165–176). Toronto, ON: Rowman & Littlefield Education.

Greene, M. (2000). *Releasing the imagination: Essays on education, the arts, and social change.* San Francisco, CA: Jossey-Bass.

Gustafson, R. (2000). Give us a taste of your quality! A report from the heartland on the role of the arts in multicultural settings. *Multicultural Education, 8*(1), 20–25.

Hamann, E. T. (2008). Meeting the needs of ELLs: Acknowledging the schism between ESL/bilingual and mainstream teachers and illustrating that problem's remedy. In L. S. Verplaetse & N. Migliacci (Eds.), *Inclusive pedagogy for English language learners* (pp. 305–316). New York and London: Lawrence Erlbaum.

Hanna, J. L. (2008). A nonverbal language for imagining and learning: Dance education in K–12 curriculum. *Educational Researcher, 37*(8), 491–506.

Hegel, G. W. F. (1964/1886). The philosophy of fine art. In A. Hofstadter & R. Kuhns (Eds.), *Philosophies of art and beauty* (pp. 382–445). Chicago: University of Chicago Press. (Original work published 1886.)

Henry, C. (1999). *Standards for art teacher preparation.* Reston, VA: National Art Education Association.

Henry, C. (2007). Teaching in another culture: Preparing art educators for teaching English language learners. *Art Education, 60*(6), 33–38.

Henry, M., & Costantino, T. (2006). *Visual art as cultural mediator.* Paper presented at the 4th International Conference on Imagination and Education, Vancouver, BC, Canada.

Hostetler, K., Macintyre Latta, M., & Sarroub, L. (2007). Retrieving meaning in teacher education: The question of meaning. *Journal of Teacher Education, 58,* 231–244.

Igoa, C. (1995). *The inner world of the immigrant child.* New York: St. Martin's Press.

Iken, K. (2006). The small, big city in music education: The impacts of instrumental music education for urban students. In C. Frierson-Campbell (Ed.), *Teaching music in the urban classroom: A guide to survival, success, and reform* (pp. 139–149). Toronto, ON: Rowman & Littlefield Education.

Irwin, R. L., & de Cosson, A. (Eds.). (2004). *a/r/tography: Rendering self through arts-based living inquiry.* Vancouver: Pacific Educational Press.

Irwin, R. L., Rogers, T., & Wan, Y. (1999). Making connections through cultural memory, cultural performance, and cultural translation. *Studies in art education, 40*(3), 198–212.

Janzen, J. (2008). Teaching English language learners in the content areas. *Review of Educational Research, 78*(4), 1010–1038.

Johnson, L. (2002). Art-centered approach to diversity education in teaching and learning. *Multicultural Education, 9*(4), 18–21.

Jorgensen, E. R. (2008). *The art of teaching music.* Bloomington: Indiana University Press.

Joshua, M. (2007). The effects of pictures and prompts on the writing of students in primary grades: Action research by graduate students at California State University, Northridge. *Action in Teacher Education, 29*(2), 80–93.

Kant, I. (1952/1790). *The critique of judgment.* Oxford, England: Clarendon Press. (Original work published 1790.)

Kuster, D. (2006). Back to the Basics: Multicultural theories revisited and put into practice. *Art Education, 59*(5), 33–39.

Ladson-Billings, G. (2001). *Crossing over to Canaan: The journey of new teachers in diverse classrooms.* San Francisco, CA: Jossey-Bass.

Macintyre Latta, M. (2001). *The possibilities of play in the classroom: On the power of aesthetic experience in teaching, learning, and researching.* New York: Peter Lang.

Macintyre Latta, M. (2005). The necessity of seeing relational accountability in teaching and learning. *Journal of Teacher Education, 56*(4), 399–403.

Macintyre Latta, M., Buck, G., & Beckenhauer, A. (2007). Formative assessment requires artistic vision. *International Journal of Education and the Arts, 8*(4). Retrieved October 2, 2008 from http://www.ijea.org/v6n12/.

Macintyre Latta, M., & Buck, G. (2008). Enfleshing embodiment: Falling into trust with the body's role in teaching and learning. *Educational Philosophy and Theory, 40*(2), 315–329.

Macintyre Latta, M., Buck, G., Leslie-Pelecky, D., & Carpenter, L. (2007). Terms of inquiry. *Teachers and Teaching: Theory and Practice, 13*(1), 21–41.

Mayday Group, Action for Change in Music Education. (n.d.). Retrieved December 2, 2009, from http://www.maydaygroup.org/.

McAnally, E. A. (2006). Motivating urban music students. In C. Frierson-Campbell (Ed.), *Teaching music in the urban classroom: A guide to survival, success, and reform* (pp. 99–108). Toronto, ON: Rowman & Littlefield Education.

McCutchen, B. P. (2006). *Teaching dance as art in education.* Champaign, IL: Human Kinetics.

Meskill, C. (2005). Infusing English language learner issues throughout professional educator curricula: The Training All Teachers Project. *Teachers College Record, 107*(4), 739–756.

Mienczakowski, J. (2009). *Pretending to know: Ethnography, artistry and audience.* New York: Routledge.

Milbrandt, M. K. (2006). A collaborative model for art education teacher preparation. *Arts Education Policy Review, 107*(5), 13–21.

Mixon, K. (2006). Building an instrumental music program in an urban school. In C. Frierson-Campbell (Ed.), *Teaching music in the urban classroom: A guide to survival, success, and reform* (pp. 117–124). Toronto, ON: Rowman & Littlefield Education.

National Center for Education Statistics. (2002). *School and staffing survey 1999–2000: Overview of the data for public, private, public charter and Bureau of Indian Affairs elementary and secondary schools.* Washington, DC: U.S. Department of Education.

Neelands, J., & Goode, T. (2008). *Structuring drama work: A handbook of available forms in theatre and drama.* Cambridge: Cambridge University Press.

Nieto, S., & Bode, P. (2008). *Affirming diversity: The sociopolitical context of multicultural education* (5th ed.). New York: Longman.

Noddings, N. (2003). Is teaching a practice? *Journal of Philosophy of Education, 37*(2), 241–251.

Noddings, N. (2005).*The challenge to care in schools* (2nd ed.). New York: Teachers College Press.

Norris, J. (2000). Drama as research: Realizing the potential of drama in education as a research methodology. *Youth Theatre Journal, 14*, 40–51.

O'Donoghue, D. (2007). "James always hangs out here": Making space for place in studying masculinities at school. *Visual Studies, 22*(1), 62–73. Special Issue, The Visible Curriculum.

O'Toole, J., & O'Mara, J. (2007). Proteus, the giant at the door: Drama and theater in the curriculum. In L. Bresler (Ed.) *International handbook of research in arts education* (pp. 203–218). Dordrecht, The Netherlands: Springer.

Parsons, M. (1998). Integrated curriculum and our paradigm of cognition in the arts. *Studies in Art Education: A Journal of Issues and Research, 39*(2), 103–116.

Pinar, W. F. (2008). The primacy of the particular. In E. C. Short & L. J. Waks (Eds.), *Leaders in curriculum studies: Intellectual self-portraits* (pp. 143–156). The Netherlands: Sense.

Pinar, W., Reynolds, W. M., Slattery, P., & Taubman, P. M. (1995). *Understanding curriculum.* New York: Peter Lang.

Reeves, J. (2004). "Like everybody else:" Equalizing educational opportunity for English Language Learners. *TESOL Quarterly, 38*(1), 43–66.

Reeves, J. R. (2006). Secondary teacher attitudes toward including English-Language Learners in mainstream classrooms. *The Journal of Education Research, 99*(3), 131–142.

Reimer, B. (2005). Eisner's thinking from a music educator's perspective. In P. B. Uhrmacher & J. Matthews (Eds.), *Intricate palette: Working the ideas of Elliot Eisner* (pp. 103–114). Upper Saddle River, NJ: Pearson Education.

Risner, D. (2009). *Stigma and perseverance in the lives of boys who dance.* Lewiston. NY: Edwin Mellen.

Robinson, K. (1982). *The arts in schools: Principles, practice and provision.* London, England: Calouste Gulbenkian Foundation.

Robinson, K. (2001). *Out of our minds: Learning to be creative.* Mankato, MN: Capstone.

Robinson, K. (2006). White teacher, students of color: Culturally responsive pedagogy for elementary general music in communities of color. In C. Frierson-Campbell (Ed.), *Teaching music in the urban classroom* Vol. 1: A guide to survival, success, and reform. Lanham, MD: Rowman & Littlefield.

Ruthmann, A. (2008). Whose agency matters? Negotiating pedagogical and creative intent during composing experiences. *Research Studies in Music Education, 30*(1), 43–58.

Saldana, J. (1999). Playwriting with data: Ethnographic performance texts. *Youth Theatre Journal, 13*, 60–71.

Schiller, F. (1954/1795). *On the aesthetic education of man in a series of letters.* New York: Frederick Unger. (Original work published 1795.)

Schon, D. (1983). *The reflective practitioner.* London: Jossey-Bass Limited.

Seidel, S., Tishman, S., Winner, E., Hetland, L., & Palmer, P. (2009). *The qualities of quality: Understanding excellence in arts education.* A report commissioned by The Wallace Foundation and with additional support from the Arts Education Partnership. Cambridge, MA: Project Zero, Harvard Graduate School of Education.

Shepard, L. A. (2000). The role of assessment in a learning culture. *Educational Researcher, 29*(7), 4–14.

Shively, J. (2002). Constructing musical understandings. In B. Hanley & T. Goolsby (Eds.), *Musical Understanding* (pp. 201–214). Toronto: Canadian Music Educators Association.

Snow, C. N. (2007). The soul moves: Dance and spirituality in educative practice. In L. Bresler (Ed.), *International handbook of research in arts education* (pp. 1449–1456). Dordrecht, The Netherlands: Springer.

Soto, L. D. (1997). *Language, culture, and power: Bilingual families and the struggle for quality education.* Albany, NY: State University of New York Press.

Spina, S. U. (2006). Worlds together ... words apart: An assessment of the effectiveness of Arts-based curriculum for second language learners. *Journal of Latinos and Education, 5*(2), 99–122.

Springgay, S. (2008). *Body knowledge and curriculum.* New York: Peter Lang.

Stake, R. E. (2004). *Standards-based and responsive evaluation.* Urbana-Champaign: University of Illinois.

Stinson, S. W. (1997). A question of fun: Adolescent engagement in dance education. *Dance Research Journal, 29*(2), 49–69.

Stokrocki, M. (2005). *Interdisciplinary art education: Building bridges to connect disciplines and cultures.* Reston, VA: National Art Education Association.

Tavin, K. (2005). An unbecoming child: A (per)verse growth chart. *The Journal of Social Theory in Art Education, 25,* 14–15.

Valdés, G. (2001). The world outside and inside schools: Language and immigrant children. *Educational Researcher, 27*(6), 4–18.

Verplaetse, L. S. (1998). How content teachers interact with English language learners. *TESOL Journal, 7,* 24–28.

Villegas, A. M. (1991). *Culturally responsive pedagogy for the 1990's and beyond.* Princeton, NJ: Educational Testing Service.

Webster, P. R. (2002). Creative thinking in music: Advancing a model. In T. Sullivan & L. Willingham (Eds.), *Creativity and music education* (pp. 18–34). Edmonton, Alberta: Canadian Music Educators' Association.

Wiggins, J. (2002). Creative process as meaningful musical thinking. In T. Sullivan & L. Willingham (Eds.), *Creativity and music education* (pp. 78–88). Edmonton, Alberta: Canadian Music Educators' Association.

Wiggins, J. (2009). *Teaching for musical understanding.* Rochester, MI: Oakland University.

Wilson, B. (2004). Child art after modernism: Visual culture and new narratives. In E. W. Eisner & M. D. Day (Eds.), *Handbook of research and policy in art education* (pp. 299–328). New Jersey and London: Lawrence Erlbaum Associates.

Part 3

Blumenfeld-Jones, D. (2009). Bodily-kinesthetic intelligence and dance education: Critique, revision, and potentials for the democratic ideal. *Journal of Aesthetic Education, 43*(1), 59–76.

Boal, A. (1993). *Theatre of the oppressed.* New York: Theatre Communications Group.

Bresler, L. (Ed.). (2004). *Knowing bodies, moving minds: Towards embodied teaching and learning.* Boston: Kluwer Academic.

Brown, V., & Pleydell, S. (2005). A visit to the rainforest: How the creative arts promote language and literacy. *Head Start Bulletin, 78,* 78.

Cantor, J. S. (2006). Fearless innovation—Songwriting for our lives: Inspiring learners with arts-based practices that support creativity. *Multicultural Education, 14*(2), 57–64.

Cowen, R. (1998). George Gershwin: He Got Rhythm, *The Washington Post.* Retrieved June 29, 2010 from http://www.washingtonpost.com/wp-srv/national/horizon/nov98/gershwin.htm.

Cruz, B. C., Nutta, J. W., O'Brien, J., Feyton, C. M., & Govoni, J. M. (2003). *Passport to learning: Teaching social studies to ESL students.* Silver Spring, MD: National Council for the Social Studies.

Cruz, B. C., & Thornton, S. J. (2009). Teaching social studies to English language learners. In T. Erben, B. C. Cruz, & S. J. Thornton (Eds.), *Teaching English language learners across the curriculum series.* New York: Routledge.

Dewey, J. (1910/1978). How we think. In J. A. Boydston (Ed.), *John Dewey: The middle works, 1889–1924* (Vol. 6, 1910–1911, pp. 177–356). Carbondale, IL: Southern Illinois University Press.

Dewey, J. (1934). *Art as experience.* New York: Perigee.

Doll, W. (2009). The four R's—An alternative to the Tyler rationale. In D. J. Flinders & S. J. Thornton (Eds.), *The curriculum studies reader* (3rd ed., pp. 267–274). New York: Routledge.

Eisner, E. W. (2002). *The arts and the creation of mind.* London: Yale University Press.

Gallagher, S. (2005). *How the body shapes the mind.* Oxford: Oxford University Press.

Gee, J. P. (2000). New people in new worlds: Networks, capitalism and school. In B. Cope & M. Kalantzis (Eds.), *Multiliteracies: Literacy learning and the design of social futures* (pp. 43–68). London: Routledge.

Goldberg, M. (Ed.). (2004). *Teaching English language learners through the arts—A SUAVE experience.* Boston, MA: Pearson Education.

Goldsworthy, A. (2004). *Rivers and tides: Working with time,* DVD. Directed by Thomas Riedelsheimer. Mediopolis Films.

Greene, M. (1995). *Releasing the imagination: Essays on education, the arts, and social change.* San Francisco: Jossey-Bass.

Hanna, J. L. (2008). A nonverbal language for imagining and learning: Dance education in K–12 curriculum. *Educational Researcher, 37*(8), 491–506.

Housen, A. (2002), Aesthetic thought, critical thinking and transfer. *Arts and Learning Journal, 18*(1), 99–132.

Jensen, A. P. (2008). Multimodal literacy and theater education. *Arts Education Policy Review, 109*(5), 19–26.

Johnson, L. (2002). Art-centered approach to diversity education in teaching and learning. *Multicultural Education, 9*(4), 18–21.

Johnson, M. (2007). *The meaning of the body: Aesthetics of human understanding.* Chicago, IL: University of Chicago Press.

Kuster, D. (2006). Back to the basics: Multicultural theories revisited and put into practice. *Art Education, 59*(5), 33–39.

McCutchen, B. P. (2006). *Teaching dance as art in education.* Champaign, IL: Human Kinetics.

Merleau-Ponty, M. (1968). *The visible and the invisible.* Evanston, IL: Northwestern University Press.

Noddings, N. (2006). *Critical lessons: What our schools should teach.* New York: Cambridge University Press.

Sarroub, L. K. (2008). Living "glocally" with literary success in the Midwest. *Theory into Practice, 41*(1), 59–66.

Seidel, S., Tishman, S., Winner, E., Hetland, L., & Palmer, P. (2009). *The qualities of quality: Understanding excellence in arts education. A report commissioned by the Wallace Foundation and with additional support from the Arts Education Partnership.* Cambridge, MA: Project Zero, Harvard Graduate School of Education.

Snow, C. N. (2007). The soul moves: Dance and spirituality in educative practice. In L. Bresler (Ed.), *International handbook of research in arts education* (pp. 1449–1456). Dordrecht, The Netherlands: Springer.

Springgay, S. (2008). *Body knowledge and curriculum.* New York: Peter Lang.

Taylor, A. (2008). *Examined life.* Toronto, ON: Zeitgeist Films.

Taylor, C. C. W. (Ed.). (2003). *From the beginning to Plato: Routledge history of philosophy* (Vol. 1). New York: Routledge.

Thornton, S. J. (2005). *Teaching social studies that matters: Curriculum for active learning.* New York: Teachers College Press.

Zuk, B., & Dalton, R. (2005). First Nations art and culture: Tradition and innovation. In K. Grauer & R. L. Irwin (Eds.), *Starting with …* (pp. 81–87). Toronto: Canadian Society for Education through Art.

Index